CASTLE ADAMANT IN HAMPSTEAD

by Janet Sondheimer

CASTLE ADAMANT
IN HAMPSTEAD

A history of Westfield College
1882 - 1982

by

Janet Sondheimer

WESTFIELD COLLEGE

UNIVERSITY OF LONDON

1983

Most of the illustrations are drawn from material preserved
at Westfield College, whether in the Archives or by the
Westfield College Union of Students. Individual members
of the College who kindly made specific photographs
available were: Dr WA (Minnie) Courtney (Zoology Department), Miss EM James, Miss SM Weston and Mr A Whyte.

As well as photographs, the College possesses a
number of original portraits. Four are reproduced here:
Miss Dorothy Chapman by Harold Speed (p110);
Dr Kathleen Chesney by Patrick Phillips (p131); Professor
Caroline Skeel and Miss Lilian Whitby (104) both by
F Amicia de Biden Footner, an artist who specialised in
drawings of academic subjects.

We are most grateful to the Worshipful Company of
Goldsmiths for permission to publish a reproduction of their
portrait of Lord Alverstone (p71); to the BBC Hulton
Picture Library for the pictures of Sir Thomas Inskip
(later Lord Caldecote), p99 and of Baronness Stocks (p130);
to the Master and Fellows of St Peter's College, Oxford, for
the photograph of St Peter's (p120), by Vernon Brooke
Photography Ltd, Oxford; to the family of the late
Professor EM Carus Wilson for permission to publish
photographs of her mother, Mary LG Petrie, and grandfather,
Martin Petrie, and to quote from Mary Petrie's diaries; to
Dr Mary Bradburn, Royal Holloway College and sometime
member of Westfield College Council, for the loan of Hilda
Green's letters, which she has since very kindly donated to
the Westfield College Archives.

Published by Westfield College
University of London
Kidderpore Avenue
Hampstead
London NW3 7ST

ISBN 0 904188 05 1

Book design and production by Jennie Smith
Cover design by Jennie Smith; photograph by Yogish Sahota
Typesetting by Bryony Dalefield.
Manufactured in Great Britain by Acies Print Ltd, Leicester.

CONTENTS

FOREWORD

Westfield College, one of four Colleges established for women in the second half of the nineteenth century and later admitted to membership of the University of London, celebrated its centenary, which fell on the second of October 1982, with a varied programme of events lasting from June to December. To mark the occasion in tangible form, the College's Honorary Archivist, Dr Janet Sondheimer, was asked to produce a full length history of Westfield from the wealth of material available at the College and elsewhere.

Westfield owes its existence to the vision of two women, Constance Maynard and Ann Dudin Brown; their efforts were supported by men and women who belonged, as they did themselves, to a circle in which the desire to enlarge opportunities for the higher education of women was actuated by strongly-held religious convictions. The College's subsequent development reflected the changing moods, opinions and aspirations that emerged as the nineteenth century came to an end and the twentieth century progressed on its way. The history of Westfield therefore exemplifies the movement for the higher education of women as it developed in this country, particularly in London. Janet Sondheimer's penetrating and scholarly account, fully annotated with source material, will delight friends of the College, interest anyone who knows Hampstead (which has been Westfield's home since its foundation) and provide historians with a new window on to education of the period. Her lightness of touch and sympathetic treatment of everyday happenings has produced a highly readable book in which the well-chosen illustrations complement the text.

J E WEBB
Chairman of the Westfield College
Centenary Committee

Ut Prosim, *meaning 'May I do good', was the motto chosen for Westfield in the 1920s by students of the day; the motto it superseded, 'Behold the handmaid of the Lord' (in Greek) appears not to have survived the retirement of the founding Principal, Miss CL Maynard. Although it did not achieve official recognition through incorporation in the College's grant of arms (no request for the inclusion of a motto was submitted), in its heyday* **Ut Prosim** *commanded an allegiance which remains strong among former students who are now among the College's most senior members. It therefore seems fitting to give* **Ut Prosim** *a place of honour at the start of this centenary history.*

Castle Adamant *is the sub-title of Gilbert and Sullivan's* **Princess Ida** *(1884), which was written as 'a respectful operatic per-version of Tennyson's* **Princess** *' (1847). In both the original and in its 'per-version', the story is set in a castle inhabited exclusively by women intent on study, and the presiding figure in both is a 'Princess Ida'. Tennyson, rather than Gilbert and Sullivan, must have provided the title, 'The dream of Princess Ida', given to an article on Westfield which appeared in the* **Girls' Own Paper** *for December 1883; ninety-nine years later the compliment was repeated, albeit at one remove, by the presentation of Gilbert and Sullivan's* **Princess Ida** *at Westfield as part of the centenary celebrations.*

AUTHOR'S
INTRODUCTION

In 1932, the year of Westfield's Golden Jubilee, 'it occurred' to a group of former students 'that it might be of interest to make some record of the first fifty years of Westfield's growth and of its first Principals while it was still possible to do so from first-hand recollections.' The resulting slim volume, Westfield College 1882-1932, was compiled from reminiscences and appraisals contributed by members of Council, staff, former Senior Students and Editors of Hermes, the College magazine, skilfully woven together by Eleanora Carus-Wilson, whose family connection with Westfield was coeval with the College's foundation. Brief though it is, the 'Jubilee History' touches informatively on every side of College and in a series of vivid character sketches brings to life the contrasting personalities of the first four Principals, Miss CL Maynard ('The Mistress'), Miss Agnes de Sélincourt, Dame Bertha Newall (formerly Miss BS Phillpotts) and Miss EC Lodge, not omitting the first Vice-Principal, Miss A W Richardson. Without the guidance of its predecessor, which is of value as much in matters of sentiment as of fact, this centenary history would be much the poorer. But although the ground of the first fifty years has already been worked over by the 'Jubilee historians', it is covered here in greater detail and with help from sources which they did not choose to consult or to which they had no access. Of these the most important are: the official records of the College; correspondence dealing with constitutional and other important matters; and the personal papers of Miss Maynard. These last unfortunately include only a handful of the countless letters on official business which she wrote as Mistress, the vast majority of which she burned on the eve of her retirement (an action she afterwards regretted). Against this loss, however, can be set the extant diaries and intimate journals — two sets running in parallel — kept by Miss Maynard from her sixteenth year until a few days before her death aged 86 in 1935, which thus embrace her time as a student at Girton as well as the long years as Mistress of Westfield. Quite apart from

their interest as a self-revealing personal history, Miss Maynard's diaries and 'Green Books'* (the name she used for her intimate journal) have the great virtue of actuality, which is necessarily lacking from retrospective accounts: indeed there can be few other documents in the history of the movement for the higher education of women which witness so fully and so tellingly to the experiences of the pioneers, whether as students or in positions of authority.

In later life Miss Maynard embarked on an autobiography; begun in 1916 and worked at only intermittently, it was still incomplete when she died. The project of writing Miss Maynard's life happily appealed to Dr Catherine B Firth, who had graduated with First Class honours in History in 1905 and was among the five former students appointed by Miss Maynard to be her literary executors. Dr Firth's biographical study, Constance Louisa Maynard, Mistress of Westfield, which appeared in 1949 to coincide with the centenary of its subject's birth, must be accounted one of the finest examples of its kind and remains indispensable to our understanding of the influences, religious, intellectual and emotional which formed both Constance Maynard herself and the College she guided through the first thirty years of its existence. Dr Firth quotes at length, and to great effect, from Miss Maynard's papers, to which she was first to have access. These have since been deposited at Westfield and are frequently referred to in this present volume where as a rule the contemporary evidence of the 'diaries' is quoted in preference to the version of the same event given by Miss Maynard in her 'autobiography'.

For the second half-century the nearest equivalent in point of immediacy to Miss Maynard's diaries is the Principal's Log Book, a running record of College events begun by Miss Lodge in 1921 and maintained by her successors until it was allowed to lapse in 1952. Two of the Principals

---

*Cited respectively as CLM Diary and CLM Green Book.

who contributed to this often candid comentary on the passing scene subsequently became the authors of memoirs, in which recollections of Westfield are naturally included: EC Lodge, Terms and Vacations *(published postumously 1938) and MD Stocks*, My Commonplace Book *(1970) and* Still More Commonplace *(1973)*.

For the 'student's eye' view of things, the aid of Hermes *has been as much invoked by the present author as it was by the 'Jubilee historians', for whom it was a major source. Although now produced under the sole auspices of the Westfield College Association and addressed to former students (hence the change of the name to* Hermes News-letter*), for most of its history* Hermes *concerned itself chiefly with the doings and opinions of present students and in its decorous way anticipated the more vociferous student publications of recent years. In both its guises* Hermes *has yielded much useful information about the activites in later life*

of Westfield students and its obituary tributes have supplied details of human interest not easily recoverable from other sources.

Reminiscences contributed by individuals have played an important part in the compilation of this history and I should like here to thank most warmly all the people who responded to my request for written recollections; whether quoted directly or not, they have all been of value and will be preserved in the College Archives. Equally deserving of thanks are the donors or lenders of photographic and other mementoes, several of which were included in the Centenary Exhibition mounted at Westfield in October 1982 and again at Burgh House, Hampstead, in May 1983. The officers of the WCA, who were instrumental in making these wants

known, have also provided timely help in other ways and I would like in particular to thank Professor RMT Hill, President of the Association, and Mrs Diana Simons, Editor of the Hermes News-letter.

Members of the present student body whose assistance has been much appreciated include: Christopher Austin, Margaret Davine (postgraduate), David Frusher, Georgina Morley (graduated 1982), Kate Standen and Stephen Webb.

My indebtedness to fellow members of the Senior Common Room, past and present, is manifold. The part of it incurred in respect of specialist contributions in the last chapter is gratefully acknowledged in the appropriate place. Here I must also thank the College Secretary and the Registrar for placing so readily at my disposal official records in their custody, the staff of the Caroline Skeel Library, which houses the Archivist along with a large proportion of the Archives, for their tolerance and willing help, and Miss Sue Lewis, the Principal's Secretary, whose resourcefulness was never called on in vain. Above all I must mention the unflagging support of the Principal, Dr Bryan Thwaites, and of Professor JE Webb, who as chairman of the Westfield Centenary Committee shouldered overall responsibility for the book's production; both read the manuscript in its entirety and by their constructive comments rescued it from many an error and infelicity; any that remain are of my own making.

The Centenary Committee was extremely fortunate to enlist at the outset the professional services of Mrs Jennie Smith, who chose the illustrations, designed and executed the art work and prepared the book for publication. At every stage she has been the most patient and sympathetic of collaborators and it is thanks to her care and skill that Castle Adamant in Hampstead *appears in a dress worthy of its occasion. The Index, a feature too often lacking from publications of this genre, is the work of Mrs Margery M Palmer, by a happy coincidence a former Westfield student.*

Of the many well-wishers who have watched anxiously over the progress of this book, none has had to do so at such close quarters as my husband, Ernst Sondheimer, Professor of Mathematics at Westfield from 1960-1982, whose sustained interest in the project has been the best possible of all encouragments.

JANET SONDHEIMER
Westfield College, 1983

CHAPTER 1 GENESIS
1880~1882

Westfield College, which started life on 2 October 1882, was the first college to open with the specific object of preparing women for the degrees of the University of London, and the first women's college in London to follow the example of the pioneer foundations in Cambridge and Oxford in making residence an essential ingredient of its educational programme.

The foundation was well-timed. Coming into existence only four years after the University of London had become the first university in the United Kingdom to open its degrees to women on equal terms with men, Westfield could be seen to fill an evident need: Bedford College, founded in 1849, although already preparing students for London degrees, was not residential, and the same was true of University College, which had at once followed the University's lead by admitting women students to most of its faculties in 1878[1]. In 1882, moreover, a decade after the first graduates had begun to emerge from the pioneer colleges in Cambridge, academically qualified women, with experience of the collegiate way of life, were not as impossible to find as they had been when Girton and Newnham were launched.

As might be guessed from this chronology, the women appointed to direct the internal life and work of the College at its inception were not elderly. They were not even middle-aged; Constance Maynard*, its Mistress, was thirty-three, her earliest assistants young women in their twenties. When Miss Maynard accepted the office of Mistress, it was with

Constance Louisa Maynard c 1880.

the intention of making the College her life's work, and so it became; when she retired in 1913 she had been Mistress for thirty-one years, and she retained that title, which it was agreed must remain unique to herself, even into retirement. Miss Anne Richardson*, appointed lecturer in 1887 but attached to Westfield as a student from January 1884, was ten years younger than Miss Maynard and served ten years longer, retiring as Vice-principal in 1925. Having between them made and witnessed so much of Westfield's history, Miss Maynard and Miss Richardson were often called on to give an account of the early days. Two unpublished writings, one from each pen and both dating from about 1927, provide a convenient standpoint from which to view the College as seen by two people who had been in at, or close to, the beginning.[2]

It comes as no surprise that both authors declare their solidarity with the general aims of the movement, originating in the second half of the nineteenth century, to secure the intellectual enfranchisement of women. Of this movement, which manifested itself in the seventies and eighties in the spread of women's colleges and girls' high schools and the opening of medical studies to women, Westfield is seen, with undisguised satisfaction, to have been a part. But there is a no less emphatic insistence on the importance of a second motive: the desire on the part of the founders to establish a college which, instead of 'keep-

* Names marked thus figure in the Biographical Index.

ing clear from all religious connections' (the tendency hitherto of 'groups influential in the advance of women's education') would acknowledge the Christian faith as the pivot of its life and work. How these two motives came to be combined is explained by Miss Maynard, who quotes from her experience as an early student at Girton, which she entered in 1872.

'My home was of the Evangelical and even Puritan type, and we lived apart from all the recognized amusements of the world, but with a fine atmosphere of cultivation in many directions. Hearing accidentally of Girton College...I was seized with an overwhelming desire to go there, and though my dear par-

ents to some extent shared in the prejudices of the age in favour of the early Victorian view, I was permitted to enter. The plunge into the currents of the thought of the age was to me bewilderingly interesting and delightful, and with much that I heard I was in eager sympathy, but the distrust of the very foundations of the Christian Faith, and the open rejection of the Bible as a revelation given from God, were painful beyond words. Not many weeks had I lived in these new mental surroundings when one day...a sort of vision came to me of what a College might be, and of the fine influence it might exert for the service of God; a College just like the one whose shelter and direction I was enjoying,

Constance Maynard (seated second on the left) with fellow-students at Girton, which she entered in 1872. Girton, founded 1869, was the first residential college to prepare women for examinations.

just like it in the scope and energy of learning, the freedom of action in the present and the high aims for the future, but where the Name of Christ should be loved and honoured.'

The consolidation of this undergraduate vision is described by Miss Richardson, whose long friendship with the Mistress entitled her to speak with authority: 'To Miss Maynard...it became ever clearer that religion and education could not rightly be dissevered if either was to fulfill its purpose....She never ceased to reverence the self-sacrificing devotion to missions of mercy and charity characteristic of the Evangelical faith of her upbringing, but she was convinced it had another, equally important mission in helping the minds of girls and women to the culture and training without which breadth of outlook and power of achievement must be for the most part lacking.'

While rightly insistent that the idea of the College was Miss Maynard's, both these accounts pay tribute to the woman whose beneficence made the College a reality: Miss Ann Dudin Brown*. As the 'financial foundress' of the College, and as the arbiter for the first few decades of its external (and sometimes of its internal) affairs, Miss Dudin Brown holds a position in Westfield's history equivalent in importance to that of Miss Maynard. Her vision of the College, so far as it can be ascertained, was rather different from Miss Maynards's and they were widely separated in age; but they shared the influence of an Evangelical upbringing and recognised in each other a kindred spirit. They met for the first time in February 1882, having been brought together by a chain of events which extends backwards to 1880. There is a good case for regarding those two years, 1880 to 1882, as the era of Westfield's prehistory. Although punctuated by false starts and disappointments, and peopled in part by figures who quickly faded from the scene, it was also the time when some ideas and associations of lasting importance were formed.

The story starts in the household of Lieutenant Colonel Martin Petrie. In 1880, after an army career spent latterly in administrative duties at the War Office, Martin Petrie was living in semi-retirement with his wife and two young daughters (Mary, born 1861 and Irene, born 1864) in their family home, Hanover Lodge, close to Holland Park. The pocket diaries kept by Mary Petrie tell of a close-knit, unstifling family life, filled with a diversity of intellectual, cultural and religious activities in which the daughters were encouraged to take a full share. Indeed, so far as their education was concerned, the daughters appear to have taken the lead: Mary, in enrolling as a student at University College in 1878, and Irene in pleading, successfully, to be sent to one of the new schools for girls which had opened in the neighbourhood, Notting Hill High School.[3]

Whatever they took up, the Petries went into thoroughly; a case in point was a scheme they learned of, through Miss Caroline Cavendish, a friend of Mrs Petrie's, to promote the Higher Christian Education of Women. It soon became clear that what was envisaged

Mary Petrie (afterwards Mrs Ashley Carus-Wilson).

was a form of education which would fit young women for the pastoral and practical work among the poor and ignorant to which many middle class girls with a strong Christian commitment were attracted, without having adequate preparation for the difficulties they would encounter. This was a problem with which Miss Cavendish was well-acquainted since she was closely involved in the running of a charitable institution requiring many helpers, the Princess Mary Village Homes (for the daughters of women criminals) at Addlestone in Surrey, of which Colonel Petrie was a trustee.[4] In her search for a solution she had found an ally in an ex-army officer, a man of good standing in Evangelical circles as 'the soldier missionary': Major Charles Hamilton Malan.*

While stationed on army service abroad, Malan had engaged in evangelistic work with his men and their families; this had brought him into contact with American women missionaries who had been educated at one of the earliest of the women's colleges, Mount Holyoke, whose founder, Mary Lyon, had instituted a regime in which a forward-looking academic curriculum was combined with daily prayers, frequent Bible readings and the sharing of household tasks. Having gone to see this 'seminary' for himself (and having persuaded Miss Cavendish to do likewise), he published a pamphlet entitled *The Higher Christian Education, Mental and Practical, of the Young Women of Great Britain* (1880) in which he proposed 'the adoption in Great Britain of a system of Christian education for young women, highly mental and most usefully practical, as demonstrated by forty years of success at Mount Holyoke'.

Mary Petrie was present with her father at the drawing room meeting Major Malan held at his house to launch the idea in February 1880. Always eager to share with others the fruits of her experience as a student, over the next few months she busied herself with plans for what she described as 'Miss Cavendish's College'.[5] It seems, however, that neither she nor her father were aware that in May the organisers had started negotiations with a potential head of the 'English Mount Holyoke':

Constance Maynard.[6]

For the past three years Constance Maynard had been teaching in St Andrews having gone there, with a Girton friend, Louisa Lumsden, to assist in the opening of a new girls' school (shortly to become St Leonards). This was by no means the only offer of work which had come her way since completing her course at Girton in 1875. Having emerged with the equivalent of a good honours degree (a second class in the Moral Sciences Tripos),[7] she was in line for several headships,[8] but for one reason or another had turned them down — as she had also turned down the offer of marriage from a persistent suitor. But no one had previously come forward with a proposal so close to the image of her 'ideal college', and the more she read about it, the more she longed to be identified with 'the life and spirit' Mary Lyon had breathed into Mount Holyoke.[9] Yet she hesitated to give assent to a plan which in her eyes had two grave defects. Miss Maynard's first objection, which she thought likely to be shared by the clientele it was hoped to attract,[10] was the emphasis on domestic training. More serious was Malan's insistence, in rigid adherence to his admired American model, on fifteen as the age of admission, which she considered too early for a serious commitment to a life of Christian service; and she was confirmed in her view by the forthright condemnation of 'this running after children and forcing religion on them' voiced by Miss Lumsden.[11] Moreover, she had her doubts about the competence of Major Malan. At their one meeting early in May she found him deplorably impractical: 'Because it was to be the Lord's work there was to be no business, no method, no standard, social or intellectual, I had almost said no sense'. This was a harsh judgement to pass on a man whose precise aim was to bring more order into the conduct of the Lord's work, but it shows that Miss Maynard, unlike Major Malan, was aware of the criteria by which, in a secular world, any Christian undertaking would inevitably be judged. Still in two minds, she departed for a summer vacation in Italy, from which she returned to find her decision was no longer needed. Malan, never an easy man to work with, as his army superiors could testify, had fallen out with Miss Cavendish and withdrawn whatever financial backing the scheme could be said to possess.

The shortlived campaign for an 'English Mount Holyoke' was not without sequel. For one thing it proved to be a turning point in the life of Constance Maynard, who had been sufficiently attracted by the plan to resign from St Andrews. With no other work in view, she enrolled in October 1880 as a part-time student at the Slade School of Art. In this way she was able, while mingling with students, to revive an earlier love of drawing and painting and at the same time keep in touch with Miss Cavendish, whose enthusiasm for advancing the Higher Christian Education of Women had not diminished. Miss Cavendish

Major Malan, commemorated here, was the founder and editor of 'Africa' quarterly.

AFRICA.
A QUARTERLY JOURNAL.
"I will even make a way in the wilderness."

No. 7.]   LONDON, JULY, 1881.   [PRICE TWO PENCE. *By Post* 10d. *per annum.*]

In Memoriam.

MAJOR MALAN. *(From a Photograph taken at Cape Town, 1874).*

MAJOR CHARLES HAMILTON MALAN.
BY THE AUTHOR OF "MEMORIALS OF CAPTAIN HEDLEY VICARS."

Charles Hamilton Malan was born at Brighton, towards the close of the year 1837. His mother was, from her earliest childhood, a singularly devoted Christian, living in constant found that Major Malan's defection had still left her with enough supporters to justify the formation of a more regularly constituted body, the Christian Women's Education Union (CWEU), whose policies, worked out in a series of fortnightly meetings, indicate an intention to advance on a broader front.

By December 1880 the CWEU had amassed about forty members and formulated four objectives: to permeate existing schools with Christian teaching; to promote 'among young ladies in their homes' the cultivation of their intellects for Christ; to establish a college on a Christian basis; and to start a periodical to give news of efforts in support of Christian education in all parts of the world.[12] A start was quickly made with the second of these objectives by the setting up of the self-explanatory 'College by Post': every student followed a systematic course of Bible study, but apart from that was free to choose from a fair range of academic subjects. Mary Petrie, not yet twenty, was placed in charge and among those roped in to help was Constance Maynard, who prepared and marked papers in logic. There was therefore reason for the two to be in frequent correspondence and we know that they met from time to time over a frugal lunch in a teashop close to their respective places of study in Gower Street.[13]

Thought was also being given to ways of achieving the CWEU's other objectives. In January 1881, at the suggestion of Miss Maynard, a selected group of schoolmistresses and medical women was invited to a small conference.[14] Two topics were debated: the problems facing Christian teachers working in non-denominational establishments; and the principles and practice that should guide the founders of a Christian college. In this present context our interest fastens naturally on the second part of the proceedings, from which it is clear that the participants' idea of a college owed more to the prototypes in Cambridge and Oxford than it did to Mount Holyoke.

The chief point of principle considered was the issue of compulsion: was exposure to the religious influence to be compulsory, in the form of obligatory attendance at Bible classes and so on, or was it to be left to the personal

influence of principal and staff to make the desired impression? No conclusion was reached, but the sense of the meeting was fairly clear: it could do nothing but good to 'let it be known that Christians....seek higher and more thorough education' for their daughters; there was everything to be said for framing the prospectus in such a way that it attracted girls from religious homes; but there was a distinct danger, if the element of compulsion was present, of unduly limiting the public to which the College would appeal.

Discussion of the academic side of college management — age of entry, staffing, minimum entrance requirements — was briskly professional, as might be expected from a gathering of experienced schoolteachers. A suggestion from Miss Cavendish for a two tier establishment, part school, part college, with entry to the bottom tier at fifteen — was dismissed with arguments that have a familiar ring today, turning as they do on the disruption such a plan would bring about in the work of secondary schools:

'It would not be good for the girls, and most unwelcome to the mistresses. The High Schools would be loth indeed to lose their best pupils at fifteen, and sink into mere elementary schools, and the warfare of interests thus aroused would be both unfair and endless'.

Recommendations about entrance requirements and staffing assumed that the College would prepare students for London degrees, the case for this having been put by Constance Maynard at the outset:

'You are aware that no distinct college as yet exists for the London degrees — the B A and the B Sc; these are the only degrees...legally open to women in England, and I do not even know of a good boarding house where students can live to work for them. The fairest field in all England lies open and unclaimed before us.'

Accordingly, the London Matriculation was taken as the standard entrance requirement, on the supposition that it, unlike the Senior Cambridge (the examination more commonly taken in girls' schools), provided grounding for the later stages of the course. This led on to a comparison of the London degree courses, which at that date were broadly based, with the more specialised requirements of the Cambridge tripos system: did the latter 'afford the right lines of work to qualify good teachers for the London BA and BSc degrees?' Since the Cambridge colleges were regarded as the most likely source of the 'resident teaching power' this was an issue not to be shirked. It was agreed that the only difficulty would be the teaching of foreign languages (for which Cambridge made no provision); but this could be got round by the appointment of visiting lecturers, whose services would in any case be needed during the early stages when student numbers must inevitably be small. Miss AJS Ker, one of the medical women, ventured to hope that the outsiders would be male, observing that 'in a whole society of women' their visits would be a 'sort of change and refreshment'.

It comes as something of a shock that the 'college' which was the subject of all these confident resolutions was still no more than 'a distant possibility'. Miss Maynard saw no likelihood of it being realized for 'at any rate...two or three years'. Yet in two ways the 'little conference' of January 1881 marks a significant advance. The 'blueprint' it produced is much closer to the eventual Westfield than Major Malan's of the year before, and by engaging the interest of schoolmistresses it brought into play a group whose influence with potential students and their parents could not be neglected. Especially valuable, as it turned out, was the support of one head mistress in particular, Miss Fanny Metcalfe. She was co-proprietor, with her elder sister Anna, of Highfield, a well-regarded boarding school at Hendon; equally important, Miss Fanny Metcalfe had served almost from the outset on the organising committee of Girton.[15]

The 'CWEU College' did not have behind it, as Girton had had, an organising committee with the single-minded drive to thrust it forward. It had to vie for attention with the College by Post,[16] and although there was talk by Miss Cavendish in June 1881 of 'reviving the College Council that Major Malan began', it is only in November, by which time

Colonel Martin Petrie, founder member of Westfield College Council.

a bewildering assortment of proposals had come up for consideration, that we learn from Miss Maynard of the existence of a committee.[16] If co-ordination existed, it was of the loosest kind. There was nevertheless a growing understanding that contact must be established with the sort of people most likely to have the will and the means to turn the 'ideal college' into a reality, in other words with the Evangelical public. The burden of presenting the case to evangelical audiences fell chiefly on Constance Maynard. In May she spoke on 'an ideal college' at the annual rally of Evangelical organisations held at Mildmay Park in north London (and was 'very ably supported by Colonel Petrie'). In October she delivered a more formal address to the Christian Women's Union,[17] meeting in annual conference at Liverpool. Her paper, to which she gave the title *Some thoughts on the Cultivation of the Intellect*,[18] was her first public statement of the theme that was to underlie her work at Westfield: that the training of young women

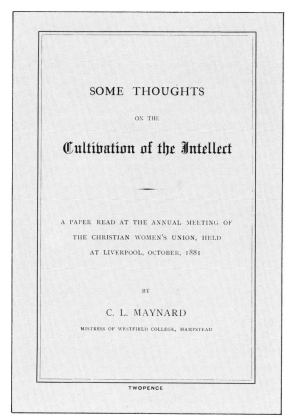

SOME THOUGHTS

ON THE

Cultivation of the Intellect

—

A PAPER READ AT THE ANNUAL MEETING OF

THE CHRISTIAN WOMEN'S UNION, HELD

AT LIVERPOOL, OCTOBER, 1881

BY

C. L. MAYNARD

MISTRESS OF WESTFIELD COLLEGE, HAMPSTEAD

TWOPENCE

Cover of the 1899 issue.

to use their minds in the service of Christ was as valid an apostolate as the more usual works of charity and mercy. She gave no hint however, that plans for a Christian college were actually under consideration, an omission which may explain why one of her hearers, Mrs Grattan Guinness, came forward with the bold suggestion that she should apply for the principalship of the college for women which the wealthy Mr Holloway was in the process of founding at Egham.

To the group around Miss Maynard this appears to have been the first intimation that a potential rival to their 'little attempt' was looming on the horizon; one can understand her reaction, that in the face of something 'so vast, so well backed up, so enormously rich... it would be sheer folly to start up an opposition.' The temptation to avoid competition by seeking to effect what might be described as an ante-natal merger must have been strong. Naturally, this could only be contemplated if the

terms of Mr Holloway's foundation were compatible with the conduct of a Christian college as conceived by Miss Maynard and the CWEU. The Trust Deed, sent for by the ever-resourceful Petries,[19] made it plain that they were not.

Investigation of the Holloway idea occupied most of the autumn of 1881, but it was not the only hare being chased. As Constance Maynard noted in her diary towards the end of November: 'It is useless to write down hopes, plans and ideas about the college which this day month may have every one shifted ground. Suffice it to say that it has cost thought and labour of late and is ever in mind, chiefly now connected with Miss Metcalfe'. This last remark refers to a variant of Miss Cavendish's two tier plan, with the Miss Metcalfes' school at Hendon as the bottom tier: Constance Maynard was shown the field, 'all spotted with cows', on which the college might stand. On the other side of London, however, Miss Cavendish was busy with plans for a missionary training institute to be attached to the Village Homes at Addlestone, which was in effect a reversion to her original idea; offered the headship, Miss Maynard turned it down without a moment's hesitation. What brought this period of cross purposes and unilateral initiatives to an end was the sudden appearance on the scene of an entirely new figure, a lady known to be desirous of starting a college, 'the means and influence being in her hand'[20]: Miss Ann Dudin Brown.

The link was provided by the Petries, in whose circle Miss Dudin Brown first appears at the end of 1879.[21] Miss Dudin Brown, who was without home or family and resided from choice in hotels, may have become acquainted with the Petries through their common interest in the work of the Church Missionary Society (CMS). However it started, the friendship was sufficiently advanced by January 1882 for Miss Dudin Brown to take the Petries into her confidence and to consult them on aspects of her proposed undertaking of which she had no experience: all her previous major benefactions had been in aid of churches to serve the increasingly populous neighbourhood of Penge, the part of

London where she grew up, and she had no nephews or nieces to keep her in touch with current developments in education. It is possible that Miss Dudin Brown's consultations with the Petries (which continued throughout January) steered her thoughts in a direction they had not formerly taken, that is to say towards the foundation of a college of university standing; for there are indications, as we shall see, that she would have been content with something less ambitious. However that may be, a critical point must have been reached when, on 24 January 1882, as she records in her diary, Mary Petrie despatched to Miss Dudin Brown 'the London regulations and my college class book'. By the end of the month Miss Dudin Brown's mind was sufficiently made up for her to agree to the next step: inspection of the 'learned lady' recommended by the Petries as the ideal candidate for principal.

The inspection took place at the Slade School, on a February day so ordinary that Constance Maynard had almost nothing to say of it in her diary: she saw no need to mention the visit, which, as she said afterwards, she rather resented, of an elderly friend of the Petries', asking to see over the School. She did describe it, however, when she came to look back over the year's events in the following December: 'I could see no motive in her coming and the more she tried to bring me forward, the more I stood back till as I closed the door after her I felt relieved yet partly relenting, as if I had been abrupt and rude.' A few days later she learned from Mary Petrie what was afoot and 'with a bold stroke' offered to attend the meeting Miss Dudin Brown had already called for the following Saturday, 11 February.[22]

The record of that meeting stands as the first item in the Minute Book of the Council of Westfield College. Six people were present. Two of them, Martin Petrie and Constance Maynard, were by now seasoned compaigners on behalf of a Christian college and came with their positions prepared. To join them Miss Dudin Brown had invited three Anglican clergymen who by their presence introduced a sectarian element hitherto absent from disc-

ussions about a Christian college. Miss Dudin Brown's respect for their opinions must certainly have played a part in shaping her own views about the College and its objectives. The identity of the chosen three is thus important as a pointer to what she had in mind.[23]

Canon James Fleming,* vicar of St Michael's Chester Square, was one of the most influential clergymen in London. As well as having great drawing power as a preacher he presided over a church which, in the words of his biographer, was equipped 'with all the organisation of a parish maintained at high watermark'.[24] Since his church was also very near to Miss Dudin Brown's current place of residence, the Buckingham Palace Hotel, it seems more than likely that she was a member of his congregation. The other two, Thomas Pownall Boultbee and William Hagger Barlow,* were heads of institutions of still greater significance in the Evangelical world: Dr Boultbee was Principal of a college, St John's Hall, Highbury, which trained candidates for the ministry; Dr Barlow was Principal of an institution set up and run by CMS to prepare clergymen for service in the mission field. The three in fact had a great deal in common: in one way or another they were all concerned, and professionally concerned, with evangelism and the training of evangelists; they were all Anglicans of a determinedly Protestant stamp; they all had influence in spheres most likely to produce students for a Christian college; and they had none of them demonstrated any previous sympathy with the movement for the higher education of women, of which Girton and Newnham were the first fruits.

This last statement applies equally to Miss Dudin Brown, from which it may appear odd that she chose to make a college for women the object of a major benefaction. Her views on female education, as subsequently reported by Miss Maynard, seem in fact to have been conservative: she looked, it is said, 'with regret and dismay on the changes in girls' education, fearing that they would encourage the pursuit of aims wholly unfitted for a woman'.[25] Her idea of the work that was fitting for women, and that she might fittingly patronize, owed nothing to the struggle to

First Meeting. Feb. 11ᵗʰ

At a Meeting held (by kind permission of Miss Dudin Brown) at Buckingham Palace Hotel, on Saturday Feb 11ᵗʰ 1882. Present ;—

Miss Dudin Brown.

Miss Maynard.

Rev. J. P. Boultbee.

Rev. W. H. Barlow.

Colonel Petrie.

Rev. Canon Fleming.

Prayer was offered by Mr. Barlow. Canon Fleming then stated that they were met to confer on the following point ;—

"As to the need of a College for Ladies, with all the high educational advantages of Girton and Newnham and others, but founded on a scriptural basis, and conducted on distinctly religious principles. Was there room for such ? "

Oxford does not confer Degrees on women, and the ground at Cambridge seemed fully occupied. In London there seemed to be room for such a College.

After some discussion in which the relative advantages of Cambridge or London were weighed, the following definite agreement was arrived at ;—

1. That there is need and room for such a College.
2. That its locality should be in the neighbourhood of London,
3. That it would be desirable to commence it in some building already existing,
4. That it should be on the basis of the Church of England.

obtain university degrees, for which she could see little necessity. Having formed the resolution to expend her inherited wealth on 'the extension of the Kingdom of Heaven in this world', she hoped through her college to see that 'one talent' (which she did not greatly prize) multiplied. As the supporter of a wide variety of evangelistic and charitable concerns (over thirty are named as beneficiaries under her will), she would be aware, from reading their publications, of the many fields in which suitably educated young women, with a proven Christian commitment, could be of use. Her objectives were thus not far removed from those envisaged for the 'English Mount Holyoke'. According to Miss Maynard's later testimony this was no accident: Miss Dudin Brown knew, through his writings, of Major Malan's project and took it as her model.[26] A different source points to Dr Barlow as the person chiefly responsible for shaping Miss Dudin Brown's intention to found a college, as the result, it is said, of a conversation between them at some time during 1881.[27] These two accounts do not necessarily conflict. For while Malan's concern was to recruit and prepare women for missionary work in general, with especial emphasis, it would seem, on the home mission field, Dr Barlow, as a representative of the CMS, could be expected to press the claims of missions overseas. In the early 1880s these claims were in fact quite urgent, since the CMS was now giving active consideration to the recruitment of women as missionaries in their own right, rather than as the adjuncts — wife, sister, daughter — of men already in the field. Since the Society's only training institution, of which Dr Barlow was the head, was geared exclusively to men, and to men seeking ordination or already ordained, there was an obvious gap waiting to be filled.[28]

Constance Maynard came to the 'First Meeting' much more sure of herself than in the days when she had first been approached about a college by Miss Cavendish and Major Malan. Her activities with the CWEU, in particular the organisation and writing up of the January conference (1881), the experience she had gained of speaking in public, perhaps too

her liberation from the irksome routines of schoolteaching, had all been beneficial in building up her confidence. With time to spare, she had for the past twelve months contrived to observe the workings of a number of institutions concerned with female education: visits are recorded to the London School of Medicine, to two of the leading day schools for girls, the King Edward VI High School in Birmingham and the North London Collegiate School in Camden Town (where she had an hour's talk with Miss Buss 'about the Holloway affair'), to an industrial school for girls in the Midlands. By a happy coincidence she was elected in 1881 to represent the old students on the Girton Executive Committee and was thus given opportunity, as she was quick to note, of learning about 'external structures'; she was impressed by the 'judgement and promptness' with which the Committee despatched its business, so different from the 'want of method' which marred the proceedings of CWEU.

This was a period, too, when 'Christian work' received a greater share of Constance Maynard's attention than it had during the

Irene Petrie (Mary Petrie's sister) exemplified the woman missionary of the period. Considered the most brilliant and cultured of all the CMS ladies, she worked in Lahore and Kashmir, dying of fever in the summer of 1897, in the Himalayas.

years of teaching in a non-denominational school, where she had felt constrained to keep silent or else to adopt a false position on the matters she cared about most. Spiritually revived, with 'the past rubbed out like a wrong sum', she returned with renewed enthusiasm to the 'genuine Evangelicalism' of her girlhood. Where opportunity offered, she took Bible classes and prayer meetings, joining to some extent in the activities of her eldest brother, Harry, who devoted what time he could spare from the family business to work among the 'roughs and toughs' who frequented the Coffee House he had opened near his home in Wimbledon. With her other brother, whose lodgings she shared, she attended the meetings and rallies of numerous missionary organisations; the Colportage Society (for the dissemination of Bibles); the CMS; the London City Mission; and latterly the Salvation Army. Once a week she journeyed down to Ipswich to give art and scripture lessons to the girls of Belstead, the nearest thing to an Evangelical finishing school, where she had herself briefly been a pupil; but she resisted persuasions to drop anchor permanently in that 'sweet landlocked harbour', being more certain than ever that her vocation lay 'with the rising flood of the world's best efforts in education.'

In February 1881, on attaining her thirty second birthday, Constance Maynard remarked to herself: 'Surely I am in "middle life" as people call it, yet I *cannot* feel it , only young with a sort of background of experience that makes me appreciate it and rejoice in it the more....' Probably she looked even younger than her years — it was only when she took to a cap at the age of forty that she felt finally safe from being mistaken for a student — and she was certainly the youngest by far of the party which gathered round Miss Dudin Brown's table a year later. According to the minute, the meeting had been called to consider whether there was 'room' for 'a College for Ladies, with all the high educational advantages of Girton and Newnham and others but founded on a scriptural basis, and conducted on distinctly religious principles.'[29] On the academic aspects of that subject she was

easily the most authoritative. When called on, after twenty minutes of preliminary discussion, she quickly made her case 'in defence of London, its degrees, lady teachers and many other things'. Her briskness no doubt appealed to the busy men who had given up a Saturday afternoon to be present,[30] and she for her part was struck by the swiftness with which the discussion 'flew to the mark at once — no side talking and scarcely any divergence of thought'.

Decisions were reached on two main issues, the best location for the college and its religious affiliation. After some debate on the rival merits of Cambridge, Miss Maynard's arguments in favour of proximity to London were accepted, Dr Barlow being deputed to seek out suitable accommodation in 'a healthy locality'. It seems more than probable that the other main head of agreement, to establish the College 'on the basis of the Church of England', represented something of a victory for Miss Dudin Brown and her clerical advisers: in all the previous discussions in which Miss Maynard and Colonel Petrie had taken part, the talk had always been of a 'Christian' college without further definition, though it went without saying that by 'Christian' was meant 'Protestant'. As the wording of the Trust Deed was to make clear, the intention of the founders was indeed to link the College with the most conspicuously Protestant side of the Church of England, but in so doing they tied the hands of their successors more firmly than they perhaps realised, or even wanted.

Detailed discussion of the financial aspects was deferred to the next meeting, Miss Maynard being asked to produce an estimate of the 'cost of the teaching power at first', together with a suggested scale of fees to be charged to students. The figures she actually produced (4 March) were more comprehensive, since she sensibly also took into account the initial cost of equipping rented accommodation for a notional ten students. On the assumption that these costs, and the rent charges, could be met from interest on the invested capital, she proposed a fee of £100 per annum.

Miss Dudin Brown had indicated at the 'First Meeting' her willingness 'to commence the work by a capital of £10,000'. To give opportunity for other potential benefactors to show their support, and to test the opinion of some of the Evangelical 'great and good' in regard to the scheme, it was decided 'to convene a meeting of Christian friends and lay it before them with a view to forming a Council who might appeal for funds.' That the small 'steering group' should have expressed the desire for a more formal arrangement is understandable. During March they had in fact already appointed an Honorary Secretary — Miss Maynard — and agreed to the nomination of Miss Dudin Brown's solicitor and bankers as their professional advisers. The 'meeting of Christian friends', which duly took place on 3 April, obligingly passed a resolution forming the original six, now augmented by the elder Miss Metcalfe, into a Council, 'with power to add to their number'. But in other respects, although to begin with the meeting seemed to go well, the outcome was less satisfactory.

The first of the invited guests to speak was Sir William Muir, who came out strongly in support. Well-known for his association with India, where he had combined a distinguished civil service career with voluntary work among native Christians, and himself a scholar, his commendation was of particular value.[31] More positively than the four gentlemen of the Council, who had dwelt on the earnest side of the College's objectives, Muir drew attention to the attractions of learning as a source of 'interest and pleasure'. Less encouraging were the few remarks from Mr FA Denny, noted for his benefactions to

From the Council Minutes of November 1882, in Miss Maynard's handwriting.

Evangelical causes,[32] who hinted that he could not see much practical use in working for degrees. But it was the octogenarian Earl of Shaftesbury,[33] the lion of the occasion, who poured the coldest water on the scheme. His disapproval of it was based on a statistic commonly regarded as supporting the case for more female education rather than less, the surplus of women over men, 'chiefly among the upper classes.' Shaftesbury insisted that it would be a sad mistake to throw yet more over-educated young ladies onto an already overstocked market, and implied it would be better, for those who might have to earn a living, to train them in work of the practical, useful kind that was being 'increasingly shunned'. On this discordant note the meeting came to an end — but not before Dr Boultbee had pronounced a benediction.

Lord Shaftesbury, the great proponent of humanitarian reforms and the doyen of Evangelical laymen, was a figure of such eminence that criticism from him, if it became widely known, could well endanger the project before it had fairly started. A vital piece of repair work was done by Miss Maynard over tea immediately after the meeting. Having seen Lord Shaftesbury comfortably installed in an armchair, and with herself settled on a stool beside him, she appealed to him not to speak against the plan in public. His response , as she reports it, 'Never mind what I said.....*You* have enthusiasm, you will succeed....' contained no direct promise; but it shows she had made an impression. Personally reassured, she was able to reply in confident terms to a stream of letters expressing fears that the scheme would fail through lack of outside support.

The failure of nerve proved to be short-lived. At the next meeting, early in May, the 'whole drift was for going on' and no one suggested modification of the scheme to take account of Lord Shaftesbury's criticism; somehow, as Miss Maynard long afterwards said, the objections 'melted away.'[34] Nevertheless, the conclusion that some damage had been done is inescapable. For one thing, the Council from now on fought shy of appealing for support to a wider public, and this made it

Canon James Fleming, Chairman of Westfield College Council 1882-1894.

difficult for the College to become better known. For another, the substantial subscriptions by which it was hoped to augment Miss Dudin Brown's benefaction failed to materialise. This meant not only that the capital available for building, when the time came, was on the small side[35] but also that Miss Dudin Brown was left in the controlling position; since she was in any case a little nervous about the project and not wholly in sympathy with its intellectual aims, there was for many years a constant danger that she might withdraw from the College its only means of support.

Now that the decision 'to go on' had been taken, the next step must obviously be the appointment of a principal. The position was formally offered to Miss Maynard on 15 May; Canon Fleming (who from the beginning had taken the chair at Council meetings) assured her that they had thought of no one else. Neither, of course, had she. She had advised them from the start on the educational aspects, winning most of them round to her point of view; and she had supplied, partly from guesswork, one suspects, but partly also from her knowledge of Girton affairs, essential details about staffing and other costs. Furthermore, knowing what was in the wind, she had brought with her to the meeting a paper setting out the 'Duties of the Mistress' — even the choice of title was hers, a borrowing from Girton. Yet although this was the moment she had so longed for, it would not be true to say that she greeted it without misgivings. A few days earlier she had attended the University's Presentation Day ceremony at Burlington House. The thought then went through her mind that this 'world of hard work and ambition' was not precisely what she had imagined as the setting for her life's work. Nevertheless, if this was the vocation to which God called her, she would accept it, while half regretting that she was not permitted to seek out 'simpler ways' to do His will. Never as self-possessed as she appeared, when she found herself before the Council on the fateful day her emotions almost overcame her: 'I shook when they called on me to speak, but they did not see it.'

The Council at once demonstrated their faith in her capabilities by setting an astonishingly early date for the opening of the College: on or about the first of October, only a few short months away. The multitudinous tasks that immediately descended on Miss Maynard

the hunt for accommodation, arrangements for the entrance examination, appointment of the one full-time lecturer which was all that the Council could allow, to name but a few — heralded the beginnings of the College proper, which is the subject of the next chapter. So, too, did the drafting of what became in effect the first College prospectus, whose content may more fittingly be mentioned here: for in this 'rapid outline of the work before us' we have the outcome of the two years of debate and effort with which this chapter has chiefly been concerned.

Under the heading *Proposed College for Women for the preparation of students for the London University degress*, the prospectus presents a scheme of education which reproduces in almost every detail the recommendations of the CWEU conference of January 1881. The tuition is to be in the hands of academically qualified ladies (alumnae of London or Cambridge), who will be resident; supplementary teaching, as needed, will be supplied 'from University College'; eighteen is to be the minimum age of entry; the only deviation is in the entrance requirement, which is now pitched rather lower than the standard of London Matriculation. 'Training' for the serious work of life is mentioned, coupled with a reminder that 'work....abounds among the young and cultivated as well as among the poor and ignorant' — a skilful dovetailing of Miss Maynard's line of reasoning in her paper *The Cultivation of the Intellect* with the definition of missionary work as more commonly understood, say by Miss Dudin Brown, Dr Barlow, or for that matter Major Malan. The religious purpose of the College is several times referred to, but a specific religious affiliation is not made a condition of entry; intending students and their parents are left to draw their own conclusions from the remark that 'the religious teaching will be in accordance with the principles and doctrines of the Protestant and Reformed Church of England'. The issue of compulsion is thus carefully avoided, its place being taken by the more difficult, if nobler, aspiration to 'direct the life and practice of the College by the precepts of living Christianity'.

The brochure went through one or more revisions before reaching its final form, perhaps an indication that a number of divergent viewpoints had still to be accommodated. At the end of June it was at last ready for despatch. Its issue, to friends thought likely to be interested and to enquirers who answered advertisements placed in *The Record*, a journal found in all good Evangelical homes, and the more secular *Journal of Education*, met with a lively response: stacks of mail, some of it containing applications for the post of principal, pursued Miss Maynard into August. By this time, but only just, it was possible to honour the brochure's promise that the site of the College would soon be announced: it was to be in Hampstead, the Council having agreed on 3 August to the renting of two newly built adjoining villas in Maresfield Gardens, just off the Finchley Road.

Notes & references

Note: for an explanation of the distinction between the two diaries kept by Miss Maynard, referred to respectively as 'Diary' and 'Green Book', see Author's Introduction.

1 From May 1882 King's College was also empowered to make educational provision for women and the college was already in process of setting up a 'Women's Department' in Kensington. Opened in 1885, the Department continued to provide the programme of popular 'lectures for ladies' which had unofficially been in operation since 1871; degree work started in earnest only after the appointment of an Oxford graduate, Lilian Faithfull, as head in 1894. F J C Hearnshaw, *The Centenary History of King's College London*, 1929, pp 316 ff and 493 ff.
Royal Holloway College, although already in building in 1882 did not open until 1886.

2 'The inception of Westfield College' by Miss CL Maynard and 'Notes on the history of Westfield College up to 1913, and on some of its foreign connections since' by Miss A W Richardson. Westfield College Archive.

3 Mary Petrie, as Mrs Ashley Carus-Wilson, published a memoir of Irene: *Irene Petrie, Missionary to Kashmir*, 1900. Schooldays are described p 12 ff.

4 The Princess Mary Village Homes, started in 1871 on land donated by Miss Cavendish, anticipated by several years the cottage system made famous by Barnardo. They were an offshoot of a Prison Mission begun in 1866 by Mrs Susanna Meredith and her sister Miss M A Lloyd. The headquarters of the mission was Nine Elms House, Wandsworth, but the sisters lived in Bayswater, thus not far from the Petrie home in Holland Park; Miss Lloyd, according to Mrs Carus-Wilson (*Irene Petrie*, p 211) was Mrs Petrie's 'dearest friend'. MA Lloyd, *Susanna Meredith*, 1903. K Heasman, *Evangelicals in action*, 1962 and more fully in her thesis, *The influence of the Evangelicals upon the origins and development of voluntary charitable institutions in the second half of the nineteenth century*, presented to the University of London

(PhD) in 1960. The Homes were under the patronage of Princess Mary Adelaide, Duchess of Teck (mother of Queen Mary).

5 In his pamphlet Malan asked enquirers to direct communications on educational aspects to Miss Cavendish, who at the time of writing was envisaged as the head of the proposed institution.

6 Mary Petrie mentions working on a book list and prospectus, and that she sent Miss Cavendish a copy of the London University regulations, but says nothing about the appointment of a principal.
Miss Maynard's introduction to the project was by way of Mrs Rundle Charles, author of the *Chronicles of the Schönberg-Cotta Family* and other historical novels, who knew both herself and Miss Cavendish; but it could just as well have come about through her elder brother, Harry Maynard, a friend of Malan's and at a later stage his ally in bringing pressure to bear on Constance.

7 Cambridge did not at the time (1875) formally admit women to the tripos examinations, let alone to the degree. It required only five more years to remove the former disability, close on another seventy to remove the latter.

8 She records enquiries or offers in respect of Norwich High School (1875), St Brandon's Clergy Daughters' School, Clevedon, (1877) and her own old school, Belstead in Suffolk, (1880).

9 What she read is not mentioned. A biography of Mary Lyon by a former pupil, Fidelia Fiske, was published in England in 1872 (*Mary Lyon. Recollections of a Noble Woman*. London: Morgan, Chase and Scott); there was also the pamphlet by Mrs Ranyard, founder of the 'Bible Women', to which Malan drew attention in his *Higher Christian Education* etc: this had the arresting title *Wanted: More Working Ladies; or Mary Lyon and her Training School*.

10 In 1875 she had described as 'curious' a paper on 'Gentlewomen as Domestic Servants' which she heard read at the annual meeting of the British Association for the Advancement of Science.

11 Miss Lumsden was one of the friends whose free-thinking outlook had so much distressed her at Girton.

12 These objectives are printed in full in a brief report of the formation of the CWEU which

appeared in the *Englishwomen's Review of Social and Industrial Questions* (new series), 15 December 1880, p 560.

13 Mary Petrie records that she made Miss Maynard's acquaintance on 11 December 1880, at one of the CWEU fortnightly meetings, and it is from her that we learn of the subsequent correspondence. In June 1881 Constance Maynard was present at the University College prizegiving and saw 'MGL Petrie' receive 'five magnificent ones'. The teashop meetings were recalled by Miss Maynard in her (unpublished) autobiography, in the passage quoted by CB Firth, *Constance Louisa Maynard*, 1949, p 181.

14 A copy of the printed report of the conference, which was held at Nine Elms House, was preserved by Mary Petrie, although she was not present at the meeting.

15 B Stephen, *Emily Davies and Girton College*, 1927, p 367f.

16 The work for this built up rapidly in the second half of 1881: between June and December Mary Petrie dealt with nearly 1600 letters to and from students and tutors.

17 The Christian Women's Union had been formed the previous year to bring together 'all classes of women' to discuss 'all subjects' of concern to Christians. *Englishwomen's Review*, October 1881, p 471. Topics covered at the Liverpool conference included emigration; schools in Asia Minor; women's social influence; preventive work among women and girls in moral danger.

18 First published in 1881, it was re-issued, with a Postscript, in 1888 and again in 1899.

19 Mary Petrie's diary: 26 October 1881.

20 The expression is Miss Maynard's: Green Book, 12 February 1882.

21 Mary Petrie's diary: list of recipients of one of her compositions, end pages, 1879.

22 CB Firth, *Constance Louisa Maynard* p 181, quotes the somewhat romanticised account of these events given in Miss Maynard's unpublished autobiography.

23 Unlike Miss Maynard, Miss Dudin Brown left no personal records, nor did she commit her views to writing.

24 ARM Finlayson, *Life of Canon Fleming*, 1909, p 116.

25 CL Maynard, *Ann Dudin Brown*, 1917.

26 CL Maynard, op cit: she repeated the assertion in 'The inception of Westfield College' (1927), adding details that cannot be correct, for example that Major Malan, who died in May 1881, sent a letter which was read out at the first 'Council' meeting in February 1882.

27 *Calendar* (i e Report) *of Westfield College (University of London)*, 1908.

28 E Stock, *History of the Church Missionary Society*, III, (1899), pp 321 ff.

29 Probably Miss Maynard's formulation; the report of the meeting (and of all subsequent meetings until she was succeeded as Hon. Secretary by Miss Clive Bayley in 1884) is in her hand.

30 Fleming, writing to his schoolboy son on the same day, refers to a 'very busy week' just past. 'Our school examination has taken place...... Mathew Arnold and I have been chained by it.' Finlayson, *Life of Canon Fleming*, p 187. The letter makes no mention of Westfield; neither does the biographer, who concentrates on Fleming's parochial activities.

31 In 1885 Muir was to embark on a second career as Principal of Edinburgh University. He was noted for his knowledge of Hindustani and Arabic, and was the author of a four volume life of Mahomet. Sir William Muir agreed to be listed as one of the college's 'Referees'.

32 He had recently contributed handsomely to the re-opening, under the auspices of the YMCA, of Exeter Hall, the meeting hall in the Strand especially associated with Evangelical functions.

33 Shaftesbury, in his Diary (unpublished), recorded that he took the chair at 'Miss Dudin Brown's meeting' but made no comment.

34 On 24 April Miss Dudin Brown was sufficiently undeterred to entertain Canon and Mrs Fleming, Colonel and Mrs Petrie, Miss Maynard and several others not of the 'Council' to 'rather a grand little dinner at the Buckingham Palace Hotel.'

35 Decidedly so when compared with the close on £600 000 expended on the building and furnishing of Royal Holloway College: D Paul, *Royal Holloway College Archives: a Guide* (unpublished: copy in University of London Library), 1973, p v; and cf David Owen, *English Philanthropy 1660-1960*, Cambridge, Mass., 1964, p 399 and n 12.

LONDON COLLEGE FOR LADIES,

FOR THE PREPARATION OF STUDENTS FOR THE LONDON UNIVERSITY DEGREES.

Present Address—WESTFIELD, MARESFIELD GARDENS, SOUTH HAMPSTEAD, LONDON, N.W.

Council

REV., CANON FLEMING, B.D., *Chairman.*

REV. W. H. BARLOW, B.D.	MISS METCALFE.
REV. T. P. BOULTBEE, LL.D.	LIEUT.-COLONEL PETRIE.
MISS DUDIN BROWN.	MRS. POWER.
MRS. ALEXANDER BROWN.	J. ROUND, ESQ., M.P.

MISS C. L. MAYNARD, *Hon. Sec.*

Mistress

MISS CONSTANCE L. MAYNARD, Cert. Stud. in Honours of Girton College, Cambridge.

The announcement that a College for Ladies has been founded in the neighbourhood of London, immediately calls to mind similar institutions at Cambridge and at Oxford, which are doing work so excellent that it may seem uncalled for to add another to the list. It must therefore be clearly understood that it is in no way a duplicate that is now originated, but one to supply a want that is known and felt by many.

The only Degrees in Literature and Science at present in England open to women (excepting those of Durham, which have not, as yet, been taken) are those granted by the University of London—the charter of March, 1878, allowing them to take the examinations on equal terms with men. These privileges are, year by year, more valued and more eagerly sought after, and offer good scope for the establishment of a College where students may receive preparation.

While the greater number of girls will, when schoolroom days are over, naturally be needed in their homes, a smaller portion will have the means, the desire, and the opportunity of continuing their studies in any special line that may be congenial to their tastes, or fit them for some definite sphere of work they have in view. The course of study involved by taking any of the Degrees granted by the University of London is acknowledged to be one that needs very thorough and full preparation, and that at the same time offers an admirable training for the mental powers, both as to the extent and accuracy of the knowledge required. Work abounds on all sides for those who have eyes to see it and hearts to feel its pressure, and this among the young and cultivated, as well as among the poor and ignorant, and for work of this kind such a training as can here be obtained is most useful.

With a deep conviction of the influence which in all departme[...] will be exercised in coming years by women whose powers have [...] an

Miss Ann Dudin Brown.

education, Miss Dudin Brown has devoted £10,000 for the purposes of such a College. This munificent gift offers a sure basis for a commencement, and it is hoped that in a few years worthy results, intellectual and spiritual, may command the confidence of a wide circle of those who are like minded.

It may be said that at University College, London, offers excellent teaching for all these degrees, and that students by residing in the immediate neighbourhood might avail themselves of its advantages at less cost; but merely intellectual exercise is only a part of "Education" in its true sense, and other and higher ends are in view which need the fullest recognition. On three chief points—the physical, mental and spiritual welfare of the students—solicitude may well be felt, and these require the most careful attention.

There is, in the first place, an evil to combat that was foretold by many as the dark shadow attaching to the cause of the higher education of women—a warning that has not altogether proved false—the evil of over-pressure and consequent loss of health. Stimulated, sometimes by ambition, sometimes by genuine interest in the work before her, one left to choose and to attend her own lectures, scarcely awakes to the thought of any resulting harm, until it is too late, and health is seriously impaired; but, under careful guidance, this danger is almost obviated. Air and exercise are steadily attended to, and the situation of the College at Hampstead allows healthy recreation in the form of games and country walks to be enjoyed without restraint.

Another point to be observed is the practical benefit of having the Staff resident, for, though the teaching power is supplemented by lectures attended in University College, the object in view is to leave it principally in the hands of ladies who are qualified for the post by holding either one of the Degrees granted by the University of London, or a certificate of one of the Tripos Examinations of the University of Cambridge; lessons are also given by visiting lecturers. The advantages of these arrangements are that the students can be classified in many different ways, according to their attainments in each subject, and, where necessary, can be taught singly; those who are backward can be helped, the slow can be encouraged, and the hasty shown how to work accurately and solidly.

But the chief gain and constant aim is to conform the arrangements of the household and to direct life and practice by the precepts of living Christianity, so that many a student may go out from thence with a new and enduring motive, ready to spend all in the service of the Lord. The religious teaching is conducted on Protestant principles, in accordance with the doctrines of the Church of England, though students need not necessarily be members of that Church.

For admission to the College an Entrance Examination is required, but this is not very difficult. Before entering on the courses of study by which the different Degrees may be obtained, an examination has in every case to be passed, which is called "The Matriculation Examination of the University of London." This examination, embracing as it does a large number of the most important subjects, and necessitating a thorough knowledge of the groundwork or elements of each, has been selected by several of our schools as a suitable final test of the merits of their teaching, and the boys or girls of the "sixth form" or "first class" are annually prepared and brought forward to this examination at seventeen, eighteen or nine-

teen years of age, as the case may be. Everywhere the demand arises for a better and sounder education for our girls; but although their inclusion in this scheme of instruction is a great step in the right direction, to attain to the standard of the "Matriculation," within the limits of ordinary school life, is found as a rule to be most undesirable, experience showing the constant tendency to hurried and superficial work on the one hand, or to an undue mental strain on the other. The Entrance Examination required for admission to the College is, therefore, laid on the lines of the "Matriculation," but at a considerably lower standard. Those who have passed the "Oxford or Cambridge Local Examination for Senior Students," [o]ther examinations that are judged to be equal in merit, are qualified to enter without [oth]er test. Students are not admitted below the age of eighteen.

The Session is that of University College, London, extending from the beginning of [Octob]er to the close of June, broken into three terms by vacations of about three weeks in [each] at Christmas and at Easter. The fees are £35 a term, but there are no extras, this [inc]luding board, tuition, and everything save personal expenses. Scholarships are, [from tim]e to time, attainable by those whose means are insufficient for this outlay. The whole [course] occupies about three years, but students on entering are in no way bound to take the [degree. T]hose who enter having already passed the "Matriculation" can, if desired, take [the B.]Sc. degree in two years, but as unlimited time is granted by the University of [London it w]ill usually be found wiser to allow a longer period. Students entering before [passing the] Matriculation," are encouraged to take it carefully, and without what is usually [te]rming," that they may derive real benefit from it, and that the mind may be [...] further labour rather than weakened by a mere burden on the memory.

[...] to the experience of former undertakings of a like nature, it is believed [...] moderate scale of fees the number of students must reach fifteen or [... The] College can be self-supporting. The temporary hired house, "Westfield," [is pleasa]nt and commodious, will only accommodate fourteen students when full, [and] it is hoped, as soon as possible, to erect a building suitable in every way [for the purpo]se. The sum of £10,000 before mentioned is reserved (with the [interest]) toward this outlay; but as at least £10,000 more will be required, [it is earn]estly desired from those who sympathise with the object now laid [...]

[... arra]ngements are most carefully and liberally made, each student having [...] fitted up as both study and sleeping-room, as well as the use [...] They are each left also in some measure to the arrangement of [...] and punctuality are expected in all those points on which [depends the] household.

[...] of the work before us. All who are at present engaged in it [...] they have, and it is believed that those for whose benefit it is [... take adva]ntage of the help now offered, truly fit themselves for sharing in [...] life in any form of it to which they may hereafter be called.

[... For f]urther particulars apply to the Hon. Sec.; address:—

WESTFIELD, MARESFIELD GARDENS, SOUTH HAMPSTEAD,
LONDON, N.W.

CHAPTER 2 MARESFIELD GARDENS TO KIDDERPORE HALL

1882~1891

It was almost by chance that the search for accommodation 'in a healthy locality', in or near London and with easy access to University College, ended where it did: for when first inspected, early in May 1882, Hampstead had yielded only a 'fine old military barracks' with no garden. But as house after house in other suburbs proved unsuitable by reason of their remoteness or ineligible surroundings (in one case proximity to a foundry), the lure of Hampstead became stronger. Numbers 2 and 3 Maresfield Terrace (now numbers 4 and 6 Maresfield Gardens), viewed by Miss Maynard together with Dr and Mrs Boultbee on 1 August, had nearly everything in their favour: closeness to the Finchley Road railway stations and the 'omni' terminus at Swiss Cottage, the gentility of the immediate surroundings and the availability of a seven year lease. Semi-detached, they required only piercing with communicating doors on all three floors and the removal of the paling fence between the two gardens to turn them into a workable unit, capable of fostering the beginnings of a corporate life.[1]

It was again more or less by chance that in acquiring its temporary home the College also acquired its permanent name. Although the subject had been discussed briefly at one of the earliest meetings of the 'proto-Council', when someone ventured to mention that there was so far 'no College for Ladies named Victoria', it was not raised again until December 1882, by which time the College was already a term old and in urgent need of an identifying label, if only in order to register students

Miss Maynard (middle row, right) with students and staff in 1885.

for forthcoming examinations. The Council's first, hasty, choice, 'The London College for Ladies', was quickly superseded by 'St Hilda's', chosen in commemoration of 'the great Englishwoman who was so early a reformer of education'. But although popular with staff and students - it inspired the latter to address a birthday ode to the Mistress as 'Queen of St Hilda's' in February 1883 – the name lasted a bare six months. Ostensibly it was abandoned in deference to objections from the proprietor of a neighbouring girls' school, who claimed priority of use; these might have been outfaced had not Miss Metcalfe, always a forceful figure on the Council, denounced 'St Hilda's' (she had been absent when it was decided) as likely to be thought 'by some....Ritualistic, by others fanciful, by others common, it being the kind of name....adopted by small local schools.' In its place the Council fell back on the formula 'The College for Ladies at Westfield', borrowing as a temporary expedient the name chosen by the landlord for the villas in Maresfield Gardens, with the intention of fixing on a more distinctive name once the College was established in permanent premises. But by the time that happened, in 1891, the name Westfield was already too 'full of memories and meanings' for any change to be acceptable.[2]

The College opened on Monday 2 October 1882 with a complete absence of ceremony. On this 'day of arrivals', as Miss Maynard described it, the students had their rooms apportioned to them and gathered for the first time at dinner. Afterwards the Mistress talked with them for half an hour in the Library and then ended the evening with Prayers. On the following day she sent them all to the University College Introductory Lecture with her assistant, Miss Katherine Tristram,* who afterwards 'gave them some lessons and set them off at work'.

Miss Maynard had hoped to recruit her first Resident Lecturer from her own college, Girton; but by the time she was in a position to make the appointment, in June 1882, the most eligible of that year's leavers were already bespoken.[3] Miss Tristram, a former pupil of Miss Beale's at Cheltenham Ladies' College (where Miss Maynard had first met her, during a brief stint on the staff) was a young woman of

whose 'Christian character' and background the Council need have no doubt: her father, a Canon of Durham, was an active supporter of CMS and her mother was a regular attender at the annual Mildmay Conference - it was there, indeed, that in the summer of 1882 Mrs Tristram met Miss Maynard and agreed to 'give her Katie'. Industrious and biddable, Miss Tristram possessed many of the qualities desirable in a second-in-command; but she was not a graduate - a defect she immediately set out to remedy by reading for a degree along with her first pupils - and she had had no previous experience of college life.

The next Resident Lecturer to be added, in October 1883, was Frances Ralph Gray*; she came fresh from the Cambridge Classical

No. 4 Maresfield Gardens as it is today (1982); probably its appearance has altered very little over the past 100 years.

Tripos and brought with her the bracing aura of her own college, Newnham. Miss Gray's 'character reference' was supplied by Anne Richardson, a fellow Newnhamite and classicist, not yet a member of Westfield but already well known to Miss Maynard as someone whose views on religion and education coincided at many points with her own. Miss Richardson's direct connection with Westfield started in January 1884 when, from a desire to associate herself more fully with Miss Maynard and her aims, she enrolled there as a student for the London degree and was permitted, 'by the special courtesy of both Colleges', to spend the next three years 'between Newnham and Westfield'. In April 1887, having graduated with First Class

Honours, Miss Richardson was appointed to the resident staff, the Council 'having taken into account that she was a member of the Society of Friends'.[4] In the meantime yet another Newnhamite, this time a scientist, had joined the staff: Josephine Willoughby (afterwards Mrs Adams Clark)* was appointed initially to relieve Miss Tristram of some of her classes but she was soon placed in charge of all the elementary teaching in science for the B Sc degree. The fifth and last Resident Lecturer to be appointed during the Maresfield Gardens era was Mabel Beloe; she had entered the College in 1883 as a student and was the first completely 'home-grown' product to be promoted to the staff.

It was on the students that the success or

Back row, left to right: Miss Richardson, Miss Maynard, Miss Grey. Front row: Miss Willoughby (later Mrs Adams Clark) and Miss Beloe; 1889.

otherwise of the College would depend. Miss Maynard, surveying the first entrants, felt a glow of satisfaction: 'so warm, so bright, so enthusiastic....they would make *anything* succeed'.[5] But she regretted that they were so few. Only seven had presented themselves (at admittedly short notice) for the entrance examination, of whom five had been admitted;[6] four further admissions in January and another two in April brought the total for the year up to eleven. This pattern, or something close to it, was repeated year by year; but since it was rare in the early days for students to stay for the full course the search for new students was a constant preoccupation.

That students were recruited only with difficulty is not really surprising. At the time the College opened the demand from women for university education, although growing, was still very limited. It has also to be remembered that secondary schooling for girls of a kind to provide suitable preparation for advanced work was far from fully established. Only twelve years had passed since the 'Taunton Commissioners', appointed by the government to enquire into the state of endowed and proprietary schools, had drawn attention to the 'want of thoroughness and ...system', the 'slovenliness and showy superficiality' they had found in the generality of existing schools for girls.[7] Exempted from this condemnation were the schools conducted by the two great headmistresses who gave evidence to the Commission, Miss Buss of the North London Collegiate School and Miss Beale of Cheltenham Ladies' College, both of whom prepared their pupils for the newly established Oxford and Cambridge Local Examinations (forerunners of the modern G C E). Educationally speaking, these were the models followed by the founders of an impressively large number of new schools for girls during the 1870s, amongst whom the most prominent single agencies were the Endowed Schools Commissioners and the Girls' Public Day Schools Company (GPDSC) who between them had been responsible, by 1882, for the the establishment of some forty schools of the new type;[8] to this reckoning several more could be added, for example St Leonards School, St Andrews,

where Miss Maynard had gained most of her teaching experience and Plymouth High School, where both Miss Gray and Miss Willoughby had been pupils.

But such schools were still quite thinly spread and many parents were in any case quite content, or indeed preferred, to keep their daughters at home under the care of a governess or to send them to small private schools where, although the secular teaching might be inadequate, the religious teaching was known to be in conformity with the parents' wishes. The previous education of Westfield's earliest students had in most cases been of this type, as is made plain in the Report issued at the end of the first year: 'The Students . . . are not forward in the main subjects to be learned. They come for the most part from quiet country homes, and scarcely one has had a systematic education such as is usually given to girls intending to study beyond schoolroom days'.[9]

Two out of the original five, Emily Thompson and Alicia Bleby, overcame their initial handicaps and took their degrees, Alicia Bleby with Honours in Classics. But this creditably high proportion of graduates, amounting to half if Miss Tristram is included, as she surely deserves to be, was not typical of the early years: the intake of 1885, for example, produced no graduates at all. Even when the number of more suitably qualified entrants began to increase, as it did in the early 1890s, there were still students who departed without taking a degree.

Ideally an entrant should have already passed the London Matriculation examination: the first to be in this happy position was M G White, in 1889. Since the University would accept no substitute, even those who came armed with a Certificate from one of the Local Examination Boards had to spend time during their first year working up the six subjects London required for Matriculation: Latin, two other languages (Greek, French, German were the only ones offered at Westfield). English, English History, and Modern Geography (all in one paper), Mathematics, Natural Philosophy (Physics) and Chemistry, all of which had to be passed. Next came the

Intermediate, with an only slightly smaller spread of subjects, and finally the more specialised examination for the B A or B Sc (Westfield undertook to prepare students for both). These were Pass degrees; Honours in single subjects could be obtained by sitting yet another examination.[10]

COLLEGE ENTRANCE EXAMINATION.

The Entrance Examination will be held in September next. No fee is charged. Forms of Entry may be obtained from the Hon. Sec. Application should be made for these forms in time to return them, filled up, not later than September 18th.

The Examination is conducted in writing. Every Candidate is required to satisfy the Examiners in :—

PART I.—PRELIMINARY.

1. Scripture History—the Old and New Testaments.
2. English History—A general knowledge of the leading facts.
3. English Grammar and Composition, with questions on the construction of sentences and meaning of words.
4. The principles and practice of Arithmetic.
5. Physical and Political Geography.

PART II.—OPTIONAL SUBJECTS.

Every Candidate is also required to satisfy the Examiners in two of the following subjects, of which one must be a language. No Candidate will be examined in more than four.

1. Latin—Easy passages for translation into English, and easy English sentences for translations into Latin, with questions on the Grammar.
2. Greek—An easy passage of Attic Greek for translation into English, and easy English sentences for translation into Greek, with questions on the Grammar.
3. French.
4. German.
5. Elementary Algebra—Addition, Subtraction, Multiplication and Division of Algebraical Quantities, Fractions, Square and Cube Roots, and Simple Equations.
6. Elementary Geometry—Euclid, Books, I., II. and III.

Those Candidates who enter their names as desiring to win a Scholarship will have an additional and more advanced paper in the Optional Subjects they select, and also in Nos. 2, 3 and 4 of the Preliminary Subjects.

To begin with there was obviously little call for specialist teaching. Accordingly, as Miss Richardson recalled, the Resident Lecturers (Miss Maynard included) 'contributed all we could to the common stock of instruction, elementary or otherwise'.[11] The students received much individual attention, being 'taken up at any point at which they happen to stand'. Roughly a quarter of the regular tuition was given by Visiting Lecturers: young women who had recently completed degree courses at Cambridge, Oxford or London and men who made free-lance coaching their profession.

SCHOLARSHIP.

A Scholarship of £51 a year for Three Years is offered for Competition at the Entrance Examination to the College, to be held in September next, by H. W. MAYNARD, Esq,, of Wimbledon.

The Candidate must be not over 21 years of age on the 1st October, 1883, must come into residence at the College at the commencement of that Session, must read for the B.A. degree of the University of London, and must be eligible by the Council of the College.

C. L. MAYNARD, Hon. Sec.

June, 1883.

From the 'Annual Report'.

Among the former was Miss Mary Petrie, who from January 1887 was responsible for most of the teaching in History and English: her well-prepared lectures, whether on Constitutional History ('wonderfully condensed') or on Grimm's Law were a tribute to her own erudition and to the thorough training she had undergone while reading at University College for the London B A. Male tutors were called on in particular for help with the Physical Sciences and Mathematics, but also for advanced work in Classics: a good example is Reuben Saward, a Cambridge classicist and former Fellow of St John's, who taught regularly at Westfield from 1882 until well into the 1890s. Although not invited to the informal meetings at which the Resident Lecturers discussed the students' progress, the Visiting Lecturers were treated to an Annual Dinner, followed by parlour games in which even the unlikeliest joined in with some zest.[12]

For practical work, especially in Chemistry, the students went at first to University College. With the fitting out of the basement of one of the Maresfield Gardens houses as a laboratory this ceased to be necessary, at least for a while.[13]

These somewhat piecemeal teaching arrangements were well-suited to the needs of a small College in process of building up its academic work and were probably the most economical that could have been devised. In February 1887, in her termly report to the Council, Miss Maynard commented on the very wide range of teaching being carried on, 'from the very highest for the Classical and French Honours . . . to an elementary stage considerably below the Matriculation' and went on to claim that four times as many students could be taught for scarcely any added expense. In the following year, with the advent of the first students wishing to read for the B.Sc, resources had to be stretched still further and the Council hinted that unless more sparing arrangements were made they would have to raise the fees. Miss Maynard successfully resisted this proposal, arguing that even a small increase 'would certainly keep some students away and therefore result in a loss'.[14]

The finances of the College were in truth very finely balanced—but no less so than the finances of the some of the students. Miss Maynard, together with members of her family, gave assistance privately in a number of especially deserving cases, as did Miss Richardson, and individual members of the Council. In addition there were scholarships, awarded on the basis of a competitive examination (a harder version of the entrance examination). The first two scholarshps (of £40 for three years) were donated by Miss Dudin Brown and by a Girton contemporary of Miss Maynard's, Amy Mantle (afterwards Mrs Sanders Stephens),[15] and were awarded to Emily Thompson and Alicia Bleby. Miss Dudin Brown favoured 'her' scholar with an invitation for a two-day visit to her private apartments in Belgravia, at the end of which she was reported to be 'entirely charmed' with her protégée.[16]

Although provision for cases of financial hardship could not be lavish, ways were nearly always found to prevent students from withdrawing because they lacked the means to continue. Reasons must therefore be sought elsewhere to account for students who stayed for only a short time or for whom a pass in

Matriculation or Intermediate examinations apparently sufficed.

Some short-stay students must have been attracted by the welcome extended in the College's annual report to those able to spare 'perhaps no more than 3 or 4 terms from other claims' who might be glad 'to have this short time of advanced teaching and of pleasant companionship'.[17] These tended to be the more comfortably off: such, for example, was Cicely Alexander, daughter of a prosperous business man and art connoisseur, who as a child had been the subject of one of James Whistler's most celebrated pictures, *Harmony in Grey and Green*.[18] She, and others like her (Ethel King, for example, already engaged to Miss Maynard's nephew, Henry Maynard) had no thoughts of a career and saw no need for formal qualifications. On the other hand, the example of Mary Douglas shows that it was still possible in the 1880s for a woman to embark on a successful career in education without benefit of a degree. After five terms at Westfield, where she studied Constitutional History and Logic, she left without taking any examination and was appointed soon afterwards to the staff of Worcester High School (afterwards the Alice Ottley School), to become in 1890 headmistress of the Godolphin School, Salisbury, where she proceeded to make a name for herself as one of the leading headmistresses of the day.[19] When admitting such students (many of whom became Westfield's staunchest supporters) the College did not lower its standards: all were required to take the Entrance Examinations[20] and to work alongside the rest, at whatever most interested them.

There were also students who came intending to read for a degree but who got no further than Matriculation or Intermediate. They need not be regarded as failures. For them, success in the first examinations, often after more than one attempt, may have been as great an achievement as a pass in the BA or BSc for girls better prepared. There were others again who broke off their course at Westfield in order to transfer to Medicine, the first to do so being Mary Cornford in 1888. Several who followed her example later worked as medical missionaries and perhaps owed to Westfield not only their grounding in the basic sciences but also their vocation.[21]

Illness, whether of the student or a relative, was an all too frequent cause of withdrawal. Opponents of higher education for women were apt to dwell on the damage it might do to women's health and physique. College authorities, and Miss Maynard was certainly no exception, were therefore particularly sensitive on this issue. From such incidental accounts as we have of student illnesses at Westfield it seems unlikely that the stress of academic work was itself the prime cause, although it may well have been an exacerbating factor. One suspects that students who had to leave on health grounds (poor eyesight was often the problem) were already ailing when they arrived, so that if the College was at fault it was for having admitted them in the first place. The same is probably true of the one or two recorded instances of severe mental illness. Against the illness or death of a near relative no precautions could be taken: at a time when daughters were expected to place 'home duties' above their own interests, the death of a mother could bring a college career to an abrupt end.[22]

Miss Maynard's concern to protect her students against the 'evil of over-pressure' is reflected in the regime she prescribed for their daily lives.

After Prayers at eight, followed by breakfast, the morning was to be spent either at lectures or in private study. Luncheon, 'spread on the dining table', could be taken at any time between twelve and two-thirty. The afternoon was devoted to outdoor recreation, either a walk in twos or threes to Hampstead Heath or tennis on the lawn. Tea was at three-thirty and all dined together at six. The evening was divided between private study and a period of socializing, the beginning of which was marked by the sending up of tea to each room at eight. Evening Prayer was at nine forty-five and at ten the gas in the passages was put out.[23] A poor sleeper herself, the Mistress set great store on going to bed early and took it very ill when Miss Gray and Miss Richardson set a bad example by staying up late.[24]

In thus mapping out the students' programme the Mistress had two complementary aims in view: to ensure a healthy balance between work and recreation and to provide opportunity for the growth of a corporate spirit - something not to be taken for granted in a college where newcomers might arrive every term. It is surely significant that the earliest group photographs show the College and its activities *in toto*: the conjunction of caps and gowns, blackboard, tennis racquets and tea-table, although an intentionally comic contrivance, is nonetheless emblematic.

Tennis was played almost from the start, green dresses embroidered with the honeysuckle motif adopted as the College emblem being worn for the purpose.[25] Miss Maynard enjoyed the game (as she did most forms of physical activity) and Miss Richardson was something of a champion, having played for Newnham. The annual 'tennis ties' were entered by staff and students alike and the students played matches against the London School of Medicine for Women, and in due course Holloway College. Even men were on occasion invited for an informal game. Winter or bad weather did not stop play, use being made of an 'indoor rink' somewhere in the neighbourhood. For other indoor physical exercise advantage was taken of the gymnasium opened in Hampstead in 1885 by Madame Bergman-Osterberg, who introduced 'Swedish drill' to England, and of the Finchley Road swimming baths (opened 1888), Miss Maynard being among the first to take the plunge.

The Mistress found it harder to devise suitable mental and social recreations which did not in her eyes 'open the doors to worldly tastes'. Under this rubric theatre-going was rigorously excluded, but not 'platform readings': Henry Irving's reading of *Hamlet* at the Birkbeck Institute in February 1887 was 'too good a chance for us non-theatre-goers to miss'. Amateur theatricals in the seclusion of the College were positively encouraged, provided no outsiders were present. So were Debates, to which the Visiting Lecturers and other friends were invited. Usually they dealt with a loftily abstract theme, thus that 'Art is more influential than Music' or 'The Work is of more importance than the Man'. but in January 1887 the subject of Women's Suffrage reared its head. From Miss Maynards's account it is not clear whether the proposition was for it or against: all we know is that the motion, whichever it was, was carried by eleven votes to five and that the tone of the debate was

beginnings in the Maresfield Gardens era. One was the garden party, first held (on a pouring wet day) in June 1884 and annually thereafter. The guests—as many as 270 in 1890—included family and friends of staff and students together with interested and distinguished patrons in the wider sense: on one occasion Miss Emily Davies, the founder of Girton, on

'... a very amusing group with the blackboard and caps and gowns and tea all set out together'. CL Maynard, Diary, 21 June 1889. As London graduates, Miss Beloe and Miss Richardson had the right, denied to the Mistress and Miss Willoughby (both Cambridge), to wear academic dress.

'most animated and nice'.[26] The resident staff were participants in all College entertainments and of most appear to have been the instigators; only in music-making did the students take the lead, with the very early formation of a 'Glee Club' and the contribution of £42 towards the purchase of a piano.[27]

Two events which became an established feature of the Westfield calendar had their

another Miss Buss, on a third, linking the present with the College's 'pre-history', the widow of Major Malan. Preparations ranged from filling the houses with flowers (fetched at 5 a.m. by the students from Covent Garden) to filling the 'bottles and tubes' in the laboratory: a forerunner of 'Open Days'. The other event destined to become part of Westfield tradition was the College's private celebration of 'capping day', the day on which the University conferred its degrees. In 1887, the first year in which Westfield had graduands to present, this took the form of a 'grand dinner', forerunner of the later 'Banquet'. The Mistress described it thus: 'The Council's health was drunk and then I proposed our three BAs amid a storm of clapping. Then the Ode was triumphantly sung (tune Marching thro' Georgia and I wrote the words) and gave much amusement through the introduction of their names in the Chorus. E. Thompson thanked for them and the three bridal bouquets were presented ... In the Library we had singing and then a perfectly impromptu charade, 'mistify'. Truly, a happy evening'.[28]

'A free, happy, truthful, energetic life that will last all my days': such was Miss Maynard's summing up of her own experience as a student, written just after she came down from Girton for the last time in 1875[29]. Wanting no less for her students, Miss Maynard preferred to rule by example rather than through prescription. The simple rules which governed the students' comings and goings were only such as might be expected given the social climate of the time, the proximity of London and the unsophistication of the young women to whom they applied: a student wanting to go out alone had first to seek permission, and the same was required of a group of students who might wish to 'take the train or go into London'.[30] Looking back, Miss Gray was of the opinion that Westfield students had all the freedom Newnham or Girton gave students in their early days'.[31] Inside the College, every student had one freedom probably denied to the great majority of her contemporaries: the freedom of a room of her own. This was a feature stressed in publicity about the College.[32] Miss Maynard's insistence on it shows that she had not forgotten her delight as a student on returning each term, from a spacious enough home and parents not unsympathetic to a daughter's studious pursuits, to 'this pleasant free life with its solitude and work'.[33] The large families and straitened circumstances that can be glimpsed in the background of some of the Westfield pioneers make entirely credible both the report in

1883 that the first students 'were delighted with their pretty rooms'[34] and the reluctant response of their successors to an appeal in 1889 to share rooms in face of a temporary shortage.[35]

The tone of Westfield as it became established during the first decade of the College's existence was set chiefly by the Mistress. This was especially so during the first year, when the unqualified Miss Tristram was her only resident assistant. The coming of Miss Gray and Miss Richardson signified more than a welcome addition to the teaching strength; for although younger than the Mistress, and without her experience, they were her intellectual equals and not afraid to express views which, 'although not antagonistic' were 'somehow altogether different' from her own. For example, the Mistress found herself in disagreement with Miss Gray (whose freshness of mind and character, and even her 'daring', she greatly admired) over the kind of reading matter to be placed in the Library, of which Miss Gray had charge. Miss Maynard's conception of a college library was that it should contain not 'what girls *may* read, and many had better not, but rather all they *ought* to read'. Miss Gray thought room should be made for books that '*really* educate', by which she seems in part to have meant works that were currently the subject of public debate, for example Matthew Arnold's *Culture and Anarchy* and George Eliot's *Adam Bede*. On the issue of novel-reading the two women were again on opposite sides, Miss Maynard scoring a victory in a Debate in 1885 on the proposition 'That the fiction of the nineteenth century has done harm to the mind, morals and literature of the age', which was carried by eleven votes to four (with four abstaining).[36]

Miss Richardson, first as a student and then as a lecturer, was apt to be ruled by impulse in a way that could upset the even tenor of

Right: From The Girl's Own Paper, July 1882. Miss Maynard also attended this ceremony: 'Went to Burlington House, where crowds were pouring in for "Presentation Day" ... some 200 young men and 15 girls — 11 graduates in full costume looking so neat and nice ... Saw M Petrie get her prize'. Five years later, the first Westfield degrees were conferred.

(Drawn by Madena Moore.)

SWEET GIRL GRADUATES.

A Scene at the University of London, May 10th, 1882

But a much more serious topic awaits me, to which I must hasten on, and that is the subject of the illustration of the " Sweet Girl Graduates," which portrays three out of the eleven ladies upon whom degrees were conferred at the London University on May 10th, 1882, nine of them being graduates in arts and two in science. The subject of the hood and gown has been discussed in intellectual circles for some time past, but so slow has been the action in our midst that New Zealand took the precedence of us, and more than a year ago not only accepted the position claimed by the ladies, but at Christ Church

the Chancellor of the University himself invested the candidates with their hoods in public, with the warmest compliments on their diligence and conduct.

The young ladies entered the Senate House at Burlington House last May in a body, with heads uncovered and gloved hands carrying the square college cap, robed in the flowing black silk gown yclept "the appropriate Academical costume," which they wore over black short walking dresses of simple make and style.

The London hood for a graduate in arts is of black silk lined with russet brown, and that

for science is of the same material and form, with a lining of golden yellow of a bright hue. Those of our readers who desire a full description will find it in an article called "University Hoods and How to Make Them," at page 554, vol. i. I hear that the hoods worn on the occasion of which I write were all made by their fair wearers, who were determined to show themselves at home in the employment of those implements long supposed to be peculiarly dedicated to the use of women, but with which, it seems, the other sex is now to be armed as well.

College life—for Miss Maynard, the ideal day was one when nothing out of the ordinary happened.[37] As an instigator of impromptu parties and expeditions Miss Richardson was second to none and the radiance of her personality cast its glow over colleagues and students alike. But hers was an intermittent presence. For several years she remained undecided about where her future should lie: with her father's textile factory and its model village for the workers at Bessbrook, County Armagh, or with Westfield. Even when the latter finally prevailed, she was not ready to undertake full-time work being anxious, as Miss Maynard reported to the College Council, to retain some 'leisure to keep her knowledge up to the highest point and to exercise it in the best and more useful way ...'[38] What took Miss Richardson so often away from the College was her popularity as a speaker on behalf of two causes in which she ardently believed, Temperance and Liberal Unionism. Her involvement with contemporary social and political issues added another dimension to College life and was perhaps at the back of the formation of a

'new political club' of which there is mention in 1888[39] The Irish question had to be handled delicately since Miss Gray, as a 'Tipperary Nationalist', was on the opposite side to Miss Richardson and the Mistress felt obliged to ban all mention of the subject from the dinner table.[40] But the Temperance movement, especially when it set out to stress the sufferings endured by the wives and families of habitual drunkards, was a cause particularly suited to the feminist and evangelical concerns of Westfield, where it met with a generally sympathetic response.

The religious teaching of the College was the particular care of the Mistress who was in truth its very 'life and soul'. Through her weekly Bible classes, of which in time there came to be several, each tailored to meet the needs of a particular group of students, and through her private walks and talks with individuals, the Mistress ensured that the spiritual and evangelistic purposes of the College were kept constantly in view. Finding the right approach was not easy; Miss Maynard felt

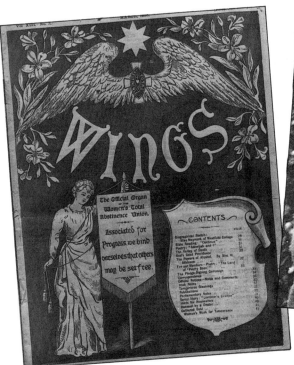

Miss Richardson and 'The Official Organ of the Women's Total Abstinence Union': she contributed an article on Miss Maynard to this issue.

with some students, as with some classes, she never succeeded. Whatever it was, her approach to her Bible classes was not static. In 1884, for example, she noticed that while the students were easy to interest in Philosophy, 'simple Religious teaching' fell flat, in consequence she set about the reworking of her material - as she never ceased to do throughout her time at Westfield.[41] The Bible classes took place on weekday evenings. Sunday evenings at Maresfield Gardens were marked by a less formal gathering which under the name 'Function' became one of Westfield's most distinctive institutions. The programme might include poetry reading, discussion of the day's sermons (all were expected to have attended some suitable place of worship, not necessarily Anglican), news of fields in which former students were active - one or two were often present in person - and ended with hymn-singing. Attendance was voluntary but the Mistress made it known that she would be 'very much disappointed if anyone regularly absented themselves'.[42]

The nine years in Maresfield Gardens (1882-1891) saw the inauguration of a mode of life which was to remain basically unchanged for the next twenty and more years, and the establishment of traditions which lasted much longer. During the same period the College's form of government settled itself into a pattern which endured, with minor modifications, until 1919.

Under the terms of a Deed of Settlement[43] executed on 21 May 1883 the government and administration of the College became vested in a Council whose membership was fixed at a minimum of seven. All the seven persons named as the founder members of the Council[44] had already shown their interest in the College by serving on the 'proto-Council'. In adding to their number they were required to observe certain conditions. First, 'every person proposed.....must be a member of the Church of England and ...approved by Miss Dudin Brown while living'. Second, evidence had to be produced that new members were prepared to 'further and promote the objects of the College' as set out in the Deed in two inter-related clauses (3 and 4):

3. The object of the College shall be to provide residence and instruction for ladies preparing for the examinations of the University of London or other Universities of the United Kingdom in conformity with the principles stated in the 4th clause of these presents.

4. The religious teaching of the College shall be strictly Protestant in conformity with the principles of the Reformation and in harmony with the Doctrines of the Church of England (as now by law established), which are defined in the 39 Articles and which are to be interpreted according to the plain and natural meaning thereof.

Although there is no precise record of the discussions which must have preceded the drawing up of the Trust Deed, it seems more than likely that the formulation of the religious clause owed much to the advice of Dr Boultbee, since it closely resembles a corresponding clause in the Trust Deed of St John's College, Highbury, of which he was the head.[45]

The Deed also names the persons appointed as the first Trusteees of the College (the four male members of the Council) and the first holders of the offices of Treasurer (Mrs Alexander Brown)* and Secretary (Miss Constance Louisa Maynard, also named elsewhere in the document as the first Mistress).

New members were very soon appointed, partly to fill up two unexpected vacancies (brought about by the resignation of Colonel Petrie for personal reasons in January 1884 and the death in the same month of Dr Boultbee), and partly by way of enlargement. The Trust Deed prescribed no fixed term of office for Council members and several of those appointed during this first decade continued well into the next century: Mr Sydney Gedge served from 1884 until his death in 1923, and almost equally long periods lay ahead of Mrs Emma Power (resigned 1915), Mr James Round[46] (1916) and Mr John Henry Master[47] (1917). It is noteworthy that two of the newcomers, the Reverend Frederic Edward Wigram and Mr Sydney Gedge, had a close connection with the Church Missionary Society: Wigram served from 1880 to 1895 as its Honorary Secretary;[48] Gedge, a solicitor whose practice included work for the London School Board, was a member of the Executive Committee of CMS and from 1891 held the Bishop of London's commission as Diocesan Lay Reader with a special brief for missions. [49]

MR. SYDNEY GEDGE, M.P.

Between them the Council members were well versed in the ways of the Church and the world, but all were new to the responsibility, in itself still a novelty, of running a college for women — or as they preferred to say, ladies. Definition of the social standing of the College was a task to which the Council early addressed itself, arriving after much anxious debate at a formula which was incorporated into the first Byelaws (November 1884): 'the Council shall not admit to the Entrance Examination any candidate who is in their judgement likely to be an undesirable inmate of the College by reason of her character, previous education, social position or personal surroundings'. There is evidence that Miss Maynard would have preferred a more positive restriction to the 'professional and private classes'. [50] The Council's scrutiny of applicants' credentials became a regular part of its business, and one it took very seriously.

In 1884, no doubt in order to relieve Miss Maynard of one of her many duties, it was decided to look for someone else to fill the office of Secretary. In appointing Miss Georgiana Clive Bayley the Council acted more wisely than they knew. Through her 'unremitting attentions' Miss Bayley brought the work of the Council into 'really good order'[51] before leaving in November 1886 to marry Edward Chapman, currently Quarter Master General in India. As Mrs Chapman she was appointed in 1889 to the Council on which she remained until 1937, serving from 1907 as Deputy Chairman. Throughout that time there was scarcely a Council subcommittee or College deputation to the University or other public body of which Lady Chapman* (her husband was created KCB in 1905) was not a leading member. Her exceptionally long and always active association with Westfield has its commemoration in the Lady Chapman wing of the main buildings, erected in 1926 and named in her honour.

The appointment of a Secretary other than herself was welcomed by Miss Maynard, and for the abilities of Miss Bayley and of her successor, Miss SM Smee, she had nothing but praise. Much less welcome was the Council's bland assertion that on ceasing to be Secretary she lost her entitlement to be present at meetings of the Council and that henceforth she would attend only if specifically invited. Miss Maynard's understandable resentment at such treatment, combined with her apprehension at the prospect of 'being ruled without protection by these people who know *very* little of what they are ruling', brought her close to resignation. [52] For the sake of the College she bore the affront, but relations between Mistress and Council inevitably became more distant, especially since the Council preferred to hold its meetings (of which at this period there were about ten each year) in central London and the members, with one or two exceptions, rarely found opportunity to visit the College. The Mistress was obliged to communicate with the Council by correspondence and through the submission of a written termly report; only rarely was she called in to speak on some particular issue (once for as little as five minutes). In time the Council came to recognise the awkwardness of this arrangement; in 1895 they agreed the Mistress should attend one meeting each term, in 1898 that she could be allowed an advance copy of the agenda, in 1899 that she should attend all meetings of the Council and its Committees.[53] But full membership of the Council was not conceded until 1913, and then only in respect of Miss Maynard's successor.[54]

The most crucial question facing the Council during the first decade of Westfield's existence was the provision of a permanent building. The original houses in Maresfield Gardens were soon discovered to be too small, and although augmented by rooms leased in the vicinity, as domestic premises they did not provide rooms of sufficient size to accommodate with dignity the essential needs of a collegiate foundation: even when it became possible in 1888 to lease the two adjacent houses, the Dining Hall and Lecture Rooms (not to mention the Laboratory and the Library) could not be adapted to accommodate a student body twice as large as the fifteen provided for at the outset. The search for a permanent site, or at any rate for larger premises, began in fact as early as 1883, the net at first being cast even more widely than in the previous year; by 1886 the field had been narrowed to the 'north side of London'.[55] Two years later it was recognised by most of the Council that no existing property was likely, as it stood, to be adequate for present and future needs and that they must therefore be prepared to build.

The first building site investigated was at Neasden, where the Metropolitan Railway had surplus land to offer. Although considered to be in a good position—'standing high, with very good views' and only ten minutes walk from the nearest station—the site had countervailing disadvantages: the need to build from scratch, the proximity of railway workshops, the mushrooming development of adjoining sites, and the suspicion that a new church, intended to serve the neighbourhood, was 'unlikely to secure an Evangelical Ministry'.[56] The Council's decision to wait for a better prospect proved wise. Less than six months later, in May 1889, the land comprising the Kidderpore Hall Estate,[57] again 'just off the Finchley Road', and within a mile or so of Maresfield Gardens, came on the market. Included in the sale was a lot containing the 'Mansion' together with about two acres of ground. From almost every point of view—familiarity of surroundings, scope for expansion, architectural distinction—Kidderpore Hall far exceeded in attraction any of the properties previously under consideration, as the Council was quick to appreciate. Progress thereafter was swift. In December of the same year, 1889, the Council authorised the Trustees to sign the purchase agreement, in the sum of £12,000, and at the same meeting decided to make the design of the necessary additions and alterations the subject of an open competition, in the judging of which 'most consideration' would be given to plans 'showing economy combined with good effect'. The winner was Robert Falconer MacDonald, son of the writer George MacDonald. He succeeded in keeping not only to his budget[58] but also to the time limit: Kidderpore Hall, the Dining Hall and the New Wing (named afterwards the Maynard Wing) were ready for occupation on Lady Day 1891, the date when the (extended) leases on the Maresfield Gardens houses expired.

The exchange of its temporary dwelling for a permanent abiding place marked the emergence of the College from a period of probation. Miss Dudin Brown, although a rare visitor to the College in Maresfield Gardens (according to Miss Maynard's diaries she came once at the very beginning and again in November 1884, when the Glee Club sang to her and she 'really seemed pleased'), had been keeping a close watch on the progress of her foundation. An infrequent attender at Council meetings, she was nevertheless consulted on every issue (whereas the opinions of other absentees were expressly excluded from consideration)[59] and usually exerted her influence on the side of caution. In effect Miss Dudin Brown had a controlling interest, since the fifty-fourth and final clause of the Trust Deed provided for the return of her capital endowment, should it appear to her impossible or inexpedient to continue the College.

Miss Dudin Brown attached great importance to this clause and was not easily persuaded into any course of action which would require its emendation: for she regarded it as a means of ensuring that her wishes in regard to the conduct of the College, as set out elsewhere in the Trust Deed, would continue to be observed. So long as Miss Dudin Brown remained the sole benefactor the question did not arise; but from 1888 the case was different, since by then it had become clear that Miss Dudin Brown's capital endowment of £10,000 would need to be augmented if the College was to build, and build with an eye to the future. The chances of appealing with success to other benefactors (the Baroness Burdett-Coutts was mentioned as a possibility) were restricted on the one hand by the entrenched position accorded Miss Dudin Brown under the Trust Deed and on the other by Miss Dudin Brown's initial refusal to agree to any relaxation of the provisions contained in Clause 54.[60]

Finding a way out of this impasse must have called forth from Canon Fleming, who continued as Chairman of the Council until 1894, all the 'unfailing tact and ability' for which he was gratefully remembered after his death.[61] The alteration to the contentious clause was at length secured by a new agreement between Miss Dudin Brown and the Trustees, made on 24 July 1890.[62] Later that year, as a further sign of her good will, Miss Dudin Brown voluntarily released for the building work more of her capital than she had originally intended and in so doing acknowledged 'the courtesy of the Council in their recent monetary pressure, as shown by refraining from an appeal to me for the further release of any portion of my gift'.[63]

These gestures on the part of the Foundress were a demonstration of her 'full confidence in the present members of the Council'—by which she meant in particular her assurance that they would 'themselves maintain the College in accordance with the religious principles set forth in the fourth clause' of the Trust Deed—and more generally of her satisfaction 'with the progress and success' of the College 'up to the present time'.[64]

Signs that Westfield was achieving what it set out to do are in truth plentiful. In the nature of things, the success which weighed most with Miss Maynard—the effectiveness of her so long-desired 'Christian college' in changing for the better the lives of individual students— is the one least easy to measure, the more so since direct testimonies are sadly lacking. The only place where the voice of the earliest students can be heard is in conversations noted in Miss Maynard's diaries. Particularly striking is the tribute from Frances Synge, academically the least successful of the first five students and the one on whom Miss Maynard worked hardest: 'You don't know what College *means* to a hopeless, helpless failure such as I'.[65] On leaving Westfield Frances Synge went to work with Miss Cavendish at the Princess Mary Village Homes and became the first of many to embody Miss Dudin Brown's hope that her college would be in some sense a training ground for missionaries. The first to go overseas, in 1888, was Miss Katherine Tristram; she was appointed, under the auspices of CMS, to the headship of the Bishop Poole Memorial School at Osaka in Japan, where she was later joined by some of her former pupils. Margaret Brooke, another of the first entrants, had married her cousin Graham Wilmot Brooke and accompanied him in 1890 on one of his missionary journeys on the Upper Niger.[66] At much the same time Mary Shields (entered Westfield October 1883) and May Walford (entered April 1887) were preparing to leave for mission stations in widely separated parts of India.[67]

Westfield would stand or fall, however, by its proven success as a teaching institution of university standing. Of the dozen or so who had graduated by 1891, more than half had done so with Honours, three in Classics, two in French, one in Physiology and one in Geology.[68] Of these, Anne Richardson and Mabel Beloe were Lecturers at Westfield; a third, Marie Pechinet, was appointed in 1887 to a resident Lectureship in French at Royal Holloway College.[69] But the former students able to contribute most immediately to the College's future were the ten or more (not all of them graduates) already teaching in schools. In 1891, the year in which Westfield moved to Kidderpore Hall, no less than three entrants out of a record total of eighteen came from

Kidderpore Hall, not long after Westfield moved from Maresfield Gardens in 1891. The dark paintwork seen here is probably the 'good beef red' chosen by Miss Maynard to match the brickwork of Falconer Macdonald's additions.

the school in Gloucestershire, Brownshill Court, where Emily Thompson was on the staff: here, and increasingly in other schools up and down the country, was seed-corn from which the College could grow, in reputation as well as in numbers.

Notes
&
references

1   Council Minutes 3 August 1882; CLM Diary 1 August 1882. More than thirty houses had been inspected, in places as far apart as Ealing and Stamford Hill; the house near the foundry was 'The Cedars', West Hampstead.

2   Council Minutes 25 February, 12 and 19 December 1882 and 31 January, 19 March, 6 June 1883; A W Richardson, 'Notes on the history of Westfield College...' p 15: 'The indistinctive name of "Westfield", now become so full of memories and meaning, was that of the house first taken...'.

Miss Maynard's recollections of how Westfield came by its name, as set out in her unpublished Autobiography (quoted by C B Firth, *Constance Louisa Maynard*, p 192) and in her paper 'The Inception of Westfield College', were somewhat different. She recounts a conversation at Maresfield Gardens in which she and Miss Metcalfe discussed what name to adopt in place of St Hilda's: 'Looking out the window she [Miss Metcalfe] remarked "The front aspect is West – Westleigh sounds a little too like John Wesley – what do you say to Westfield"?'. This conversation can only have taken place, as recounted, at some time after March 1883, the date when the school first objected; yet there is clear evidence that the name 'Westfield' was already attached to the Maresfield Gardens property at the time the College first rented it (or very soon after): Miss Maynard herself alludes to it under that name in a Diary entry for 22 September 1882.

The style 'Westfield College' was finally adopted by the Council in 1887 and appears in the title of the Annual Report for that year.

3   CLM Diary 24 June 1882. Details of Miss Maynard's soundings at Girton are given CLM Green Book 25 June 1882.

4   Council Minutes April 1887 and A W Richardson, 'Notes on the History of Westfield College...', p 16.

5   CLM Green Book 19 February 1883 (her birthday and the day she was feted as 'Queen of St Hilda's').

6   They were: Alicia Bleby, who, before coming to Westfield had spent some time in America; Margaret Brooke, educated at Belstead; Frances Synge, educated at Belstead and (briefly) Blackheath High School; Emily Thompson, educated at 'private schools', possibly in Cornwall where her father was a Congregationalist minister and schoolmaster; and Annie Tristram, younger sister of Katherine, previous schooling not known. All were daughters of clergymen, not all of them Anglican. Aged 25, Alicia Bleby was about six years older than the rest.

7   *Schools' Inquiry Commission, Report of the Commissioners*, 1868, Chapter 6, (Girls' Schools), p 548-9.

8   For the efforts of the Endowed Schools Commissioners, and subsequently of the Charity Commissioners, to secure a larger share of ancient endowments for girls' schools see S. Fletcher, *Feminists and Bureaucrats*, 1980; the Tables printed as Appendices show that by 1882 about 18 schools educating girls up to the age of eighteen had been set up in consequence of these efforts. For the 22 High Schools established by the GPDSC (subsequently GPDST) prior to 1882 see Josephine Kamm, *Indicative Past*, 1971, Appendix II.

9   *College for Ladies, at Westfield, for the preparation of students for the degrees of London University, Report of the First Year*, 1883.

This annual publication appeared subsequently under a variety of titles; for convenience it will be referred to hereafter as *Annual Report*.

10   Details of the examination requirements are given in the *University of London Calendar*, e.g. for 1883. For the Intermediate BA the subjects were: Latin and Roman History (2 papers); Greek; English Language, Literature and History (2 papers); Mathematics (2 papers); a modern language. For the Intermediate B Sc: Mathematics, Mixed Mathematics; Inorganic Chemistry; Experimental Physics; General Biology. In either examination a pass in each subject was required. For the BA three out of five subjects had to be offered: Latin and Roman History; Greek and Grecian History; English; a modern language; Mathematics, either Pure or Mixed; Mental and Moral Science.

For the B Sc there were ten subjects, of which three had to be offered: Pure Maths; Mixed Maths; Experimental Physics; Chemistry; Botany; Physiology; Zoology; Animal Physiology; Physical Geography and Geology; Mental and Moral Science.

For Honours in single subjects the examination was by and large similar to that for the BA or

BSc, the difference being that the subject had to be treated more fully; in the case of arts subjects, additional texts had to be studied and in some of the sciences more advanced practical work was expected.

11   A W Richardson, 'Notes on the History of Westfield College...'. p 18. Miss Maynard's teaching programme included classes in Introductory Logic, Greek for Beginners, German, and in the first year (1882–3) Physical Geography, one of the subjects she had taught at St Andrews.

12   Thus Mr WC Coupland, Visiting Lecturer in Mental and Moral Science, who 'joined in well in Adverbs', CLM Diary, 10 November 1886.

13   By 1890 students were again regularly attending outside lectures, at Bedford College, University College and the London School of Medicine for Women.

14   Council Minutes 4 July 1888.

15   Among others who donated scholarships were Miss Maynard's brother, Henry, and an old student, Alexandrina Peckover, who gave £150 for a scholarship on leaving the College in 1887.

16   CLM Diary 12 November 1883.

17   *Annual Report*, 1883, 1884.

18   Now in the Tate Gallery: see Denys Sutton, *James McNeill Whistler*, 1966, Pl 56 and p 189. Cicely Alexander (afterwards Mrs B W C Spring Rice) was at Westfield from January 1884 to March 1885; her parents' home, Aubrey House, Campden Hill, was on several occasions the scene of Westfield gatherings.

19   Co-editor with Sara A Burstall of *Public Schools for Girls*, 1911 and in 1912-13 President of the Association of Headmistresses. Mary Douglas entered Westfield in January 1884; she was a distant cousin of Miss Maynard's.

20   Ethel King, whose forte was tennis, prepared for the entrance examination by learning 'most minutely' the History of England from 400 to 800: 'No more use to her than Hebrew' was Miss Maynard's sardonic comment.

21   Others qualified afterwards as nurses.
Lectures in hygiene, home nursing and first aid were regularly arranged for the students and staff, perhaps as preparation for intending missionaries.

22   As happened in the case of Olivia Day, summoned home after less than six months at college to care for three younger sisters: CLM Green Book 20 May 1884. She never returned.

23   Regime described *Annual Report* March 1884, p 6.

24   CLM Green Book 31 December 1884 is one of several references.

25   Several mentions in CLM Diary March – May 1883.

26   CLM Diary February and March 1887.

27   Thus CLM Diary January 1887; as reported to the Council in February the amount collected was £32, which the Council agreed to augment,

28   CLM Diary 11 May 1887. The three graduands (all BA's) were: Anne Richardson, Emily Thompson, Marie Pechinet.
The text of the 'ode', the first in a long series of College songs, appears not to have survived.

29   CLM Green Book 26 December 1875.

30   From 'Rules for the Students' copied into Council Minutes Volume I, pp 61-62 (October 1882).

31   F R Gray, *Gladly....Gladly....*, London, 1931.

32   'Each student has a room to herself...' *Annual Reports*, 1886 and following.

33   CLM Green Book 2 February 1873.

34   *Annual Report* 1883.

35   CLM Diary December 1889.

36   CLM Green Book 15 June 1884 and Diary 9 February 1885; F R Gray, *Gladly....Gladly....* p 49.

37   Thus CLM Diary 11 November 1889: 'I love nothing to happen save just what *should* happen.'

38   Council Minutes 20 March 1889; as the price of her freedom Miss Richardson was willing to be content with a smaller salary. In this same year, 1889, Miss Richardson was being urged by friends to apply for two other posts, the Principalship of Somerville (suggested by Mrs Henry Sidgwick of Newnham) and the Headship of The Mount School, York, which in fact was offered to her: CLM *Diary* April and October 1889.

39   CLM Diary October 1888.

40   CLM Autobiography, Part VII, p 304.

41   CLM Green Book 10 February 1883 and 21 December 1884; cf. CB Firth, *Constance Louisa Maynard* p264-5.

42   CLM Green Book 6 October 1884.

43   Original at Westfield College; several times printed and reprinted with additions: *Trust Deeds. Westfield College, Hampstead N W.*

44   In clause 6: Ann Dudin Brown, Mrs Alexander Brown, Miss Anna Metcalfe, James Fleming, Thomas Pownall Boultbee, William Hagger Barlow, Martin Petrie.

45   Cf the extract from the Trust Deed of St John's Highbury printed in Finlayson, *Life of Canon Fleming*, p 131; 'The teaching and government shall always be strictly Protestant and Evangelical, in conformity with the doctrine of the Church of England as expressed in the Thirty-Nine-Articles, interpreted according to the natural meaning thereof'. The draft of the Westfield Deed was presented to the Council on 19 December 1882 when Colonel Petrie undertook to 'put in their right form' the 'many verbal corrections' before returning it to the solicitor.

46   Of Birch Hall, Essex; Conservative M P for Essex constituencies 1868-1906.

47   Of Montrose House, Petersham, Surrey. From 1884-1905 Mr Master was Treasurer of Westfield.

48   A Hampstead resident (Oak Hill Lodge). He resigned from the Council in 1886 but remained as Trustee until his death in 1897.

49   Conservative MP for Stockport 1886-1892, and for Walsall 1895-1900. Council meetings were frequently held at the offices of his firm, Messrs Gedge, Kirby and Millett, 1 Palace Yard, Westminster.

50   Council Minutes 29 September 1884.

51   CLM Diary October 1886.

52   For Miss Maynard's omission from the Council, see Council Minutes 1 August 1884; for her resentment see CLM Green Book 26 March 1884, the wound was slow to heal, being re-opened by a related incident which occurred in the autumn of 1885 (CLM Green Book 11 and 17 October). Miss Maynard was now able to contrast her position with that of the Mistress of Girton who, in the person of her old friend and contemporary Elizabeth Welch, had just been granted a seat on the Executive Committee: cf. B Stephen, *Emily Davies and Girton College*, London 1927, p 341.

53   Council Minutes June 1895, November 1898, June 1899.

54   Council Minutes 9 July, 1913.

55   Council Minutes 22 March 1886. Dr Barlow, who was now vicar of St James's Clapham, had suggested a house in that neighbourhood.

56   Discussions about the Neasden land are recorded in Council Minutes October–December 1888.

57   For the history of the Estate and Mansion see Appendix.

58   As seems to be implied by a Council Minute of 22 July 1891.

59   Trust Deed, clause 21. Miss Dudin Brown, moreover, was the one irremovable member of the council (clause 12).

60   Contributions to a Building Fund which it was hoped would match Miss Dudin Brown's initial donation of £10 000 were invited almost from the start (*Annual Reports* 1883 and following) but by the end of 1887 had reached only £1 384. The Council's plan to attract benefactions by appealing directly to individual philanthropists and City Companies was dropped in consequence of Miss Dudin Brown's refusal to alter clause 54 of the Trust Deed (Council Minutes 15 February 1888).

61   *Annual Report* 1909, p 17.

62   The sum due to be returned to Miss Dudin Brown should it appear to her 'impossible or inexpedient to continue the College' was reduced by half.

63   Having agreed initially on £5,000, she now volunteered to release another £3,000: Council Minutes 29 October 1890.

64   Preamble to the revocation of the original clause 54.

65   CLM Green Book 8 June 1884.

66   Graham Brooke died in Africa in 1891. His service with the CMS Niger Mission is described E Stock, *History of the Church Missionary Soc-*

iety III, p 362 ff, where his wife and her connection with Westfield are briefly referred to.

67 M Shields to the Santhal Mission in North India. M Walford to work as a Zenana Missionary (i.e. among women in purdah) at Palamcottah in South India.

68 Classics: Anne Richardson (Class 1), Alicia Bleby, Annie Abernethy. French: Marie Pechinet (Class 1), Mabel Beloe.

Physiology: Sara White (she later qualified as a doctor): Geology- Sarah Lowe.

69 Marie Pechinet is said on good authority to figure as 'Miss Lemaitre' in the novel *Dolores* (1911) by Ivy Compton Burnett, which is partly set in a women's college alleged to be in Oxford but based in all likelihood on the author's own college, Royal Holloway. See Hilary Spurling, *Ivy when young*, London 1974, Appendix II.

CHAPTER 3 THE 'NEW WESTFIELD' & THE 'NEW UNIVERSITY'

1891~1913

Miss Maynard's first reaction to the 'New Westfield' was one of disappointment: 'It is an institution....and so it does not suit'.[1] Yet it was quickly evident that Kidderpore Hall and its appendages furnished a setting in which the College could develop without detriment to its familial character. The Neo-Grecian mansion (built in the 1840s) and Falconer Macdonald's southward extension, which formed the Dining Hall, came close to reproducing the 'country house' atmosphere which had been sought for in vain when

The Mistress c 1895.

the College first opened, while in the purpose-built residential wing (today's Maynard) there was generous accommodation for up to forty-four students and the small staff of Resident Lecturers: everyone, students no less than lecturers. had two rooms. It was even possible to set aside a small room for the use of Old Students, who had a tendency, as Miss Maynard once noted, to 'run to the College as a home'. The more spacious surroundings were an enhancement to the College's private and public festivals: the rituals of the Banquet became more elaborate as the 'caps and gowns multiplied round the table' year by year, and the entertainment at the Garden Party more lavish: in June 1891 close on a thousand guests came to see the new abode and to be regaled with icecream by the quart and the music of a small string band.

Another factor making for continuity between the Old Westfield and the New was the stability of the leadership. As it happens, each of Miss Maynard's two remaining decades has a distinct character. The first was a time of in-ternal consolidation. The second was largely occupied with adaptation to the changes entailed by the admission of Westfield in 1902 as a School (in the Faculty of Arts) of the reconstituted University of London.

As part of the process of consolidation the Council set up the first of its permanent subcommittees. The task of this Household Committee was twofold: to control all aspects of domestic management, always with a view to economy; and to keep in good trim the substantial freehold property for which the Council was now responsible. This last was the particular concern of a new Council member, Maurice Hulbert,[2] who as an architect could give expert advice. Otherwise it was the lady members who took the lead: Miss Dudin Brown, who on a rare occasion took the chair, Mrs (Lady) Chapman, and most of all Miss Anna Metcalfe – 'energetic, knowing and very magnificent'.[3] It was thanks to a recommendation of the Household Committee that Miss Maynard was at last permitted to have a housekeeper to relieve her of day-to-day domestic cares. Precisely what type of person to appoint was not easy to decide. 'Lady housekeepers' – Miss Maynard's preference – often turned out, sadly enough, to be too decrepit or too diffident to exercise proper control over the servants; 'working housekeepers', belonging neither with the academic nor with the domestic staff, found their position intolerably lonely. The satisfactory solution of a Domestic Bursar who was both ladylike and professional emerged only after Miss Maynard's time.

With drains to see to, redecoration schemes to approve, worn-out furnishings to inspect, the members of the Household Committee were quite frequent visitors to the College. But in the eyes of the residents the Council's most familiar embodiment was Miss Smee, Secretary

> ❝ I appreciated Miss Smee's coaching from the balcony after lunch as we practised on the grass 'best' tennis court below. She insisted that I, being tall, should serve overhand after the then famous Miss Sutton, who introduced this at Wimbledon, for women as well as men. Miss Smee was then secretary to the Council and herself a well-known hockey player. We thought her very progressive. ❞
>
> D Reid (Stewart, 1905).

from 1887 to 1917 (and from 1897 also Garden Steward). The importance of Miss Smee's position as go-between is underlined by the frequency with which she replied to the Toast to the Council at the Banquet, on one occasion likening its members to the stokers of a vessel, labouring below decks to keep the College going. Non-resident and part-time, Miss Smee's self-identification with the College nevertheless extended well beyond the methodical and authoritative performance of her official duties. As well as coaching hockey teams, Miss Smee spoke in College Debates, to which she was able to contribute the view, not otherwise represented at Westfield, of a woman active in Local Goverment: her election in 1912 as Chairman of the Acton Public Health Authority was only the first of several public distinctions.[4]

Although the Secretary to Council dealt with all official business, the routine of admissions included, the Mistress was still left with a mountain of correspondence. On developing rheumatism in her right arm she was allowed, in 1894, to engage an Old Student to act as amanuensis, and thereafter was never without part-time secretarial help, drawn always from the same source and apt to be a

little amateurish since the post, which carried board and lodging but no salary, was often filled by former students awaiting permanent appointments in some quite different field.

An increasingly large part of Miss Maynard's correspondence arose from the system she had

From the Minutes of the Household Committee, 1890, in Miss Smee's writing as Secretary.

devised as early as 1887 for keeping former students in touch with herself and with each other. Those who joined the plan, which was known from the start as 'The Budget', were in honour bound to contribute their own news to a packet of letters in constant circulation. As the number of Old Students grew, so did the groups or 'Rings' multiply, until by the time Miss Maynard retired there were eight Rings 'whirling around'. At some point in its travels the Budget of each Ring came to the Mistress whose own often lengthy contribution, of which many examples survive, touched on a wide variety of topics. Since the Budget was in essence a personal (though not private) correspondence, its function was not usurped by the instituition in 1892 of the College Magazine, *Hermes*, in whose columns news of the marriages and appointments of former students, culled as often as not from the Budget letters, regularly had a place.

The initiators of *Hermes* (there were four) were all current students. In the first printed issue they appealed to 'past and present Westfieldians' to send in their literary efforts and announced they would also like to hear from those already 'engaged in earnest and concentrated work....or who have entered on wide and varied spheres of life and thought'.[5] Contributions of both kinds duly figure in the succeeding numbers, but of no less interest to us, and one hopes to the Council members and other well-wishers named in the List of Subscribers, is the closely printed 'Kalendar of Events'. Here are recorded, often in minute detail, the debates, meetings and sporting activities which developed in more systematic fashion the programme of extra-curricular activities begun at Maresfield Gardens.

The most obvious area of growth was in organised sport, which was given a powerful boost with the establishment in 1895 of a Hockey Club.[6] With more and more matches (tennis as well as hockey) being played against other colleges and local clubs, the practice was soon adopted of rewarding Westfield's champions with 'team colours', that is to say a Col-

lege hat band and tie. These proved so popular with the students in general that a variant of them, complemented by a blazer, eventually became a kind of Westfield uniform.[7] Indoors, more old-fashioned games like battledore, played in the Conservatory then attached to Old House, vied with newer inventions: in 1901 a pingpong tournament was staged in the Hall. But the recreational innovation which made the most stir was undoubtedly the bicycle.

Miss Maynard, always eager to try out new inventions, began her prolonged love affair with the machine in the autumn of 1893. Two years later, in October 1895, she noted that there were six bicycles in College and, recognising that here was a matter on which the Council might well hold strong views, sought from them a permission which, she alleged, had already been granted at all other colleges. The vote in favour of cycling as a student activity

Cover of the second issue of Hermes, *and an article by 'HB' from issue No 14, March 1899.*

was a narrow one – 'poor Miss Dudin Brown would as soon have us dancing on tight-ropes

> ❝We played cricket on a field which belonged to a boy's school. But they played in the day time, and we went after dinner, so it was quite nice and proper. The field was just below the College, and we used to tear down the road in an untidy, hatless procession, and climb over the paling; such was our zeal for the game . . .❞
>
> *Anon* (Hermes, *1899*).

as see us on cycles' – and was only carried on the understanding that certain rules were observed: 'The dress of each student shall be approved by the Mistress'; 'No student shall ride into or towards London, nor beyond an area which shall be indicated by the Mistress on a map...in the cloakroom'; 'No student shall go out alone or after dark'. After an accident in which a student badly injured her knee, a prohibition against coasting was added. The Mistress, who was of course exempt from the rules, used her bicycle not only on the lengthy vacation tours for which she was famous but also, for several years, as her ordinary mode of transport into and across London.[8]

The games clubs and other student societies now had formally elected officers and committees. The principle of election was also applied to the appointment of the 'JPs' and Orderlies, the students whose task it was to 'keep the peace' during silence hours and to maintain a satisfactory level of tidiness. At Maresfield Gardens there had apparently been

THE LEARNER

Bike, bike, bike,
   On my anxious, wobbly course;
But I would that my hand were surer
   In guiding my wild steel horse.

Oh, well for the thoughtless and gay,
   That they jeer at my fate from the well.
Oh, well that the bike was not
   Quite broken to bits by the fall.

And the experts cycle on,
   Displaying a wondrous skill.
But oh! that my steed would allow me to mount
   By standing both upright and still!

Bike, bike, bike,
   On the friendly asphalt court,
But the day I shall ride on the Hampstead roads
   Is further away than I thought.

Left: The Mistress "In holiday attire, – shovel hat, motor veil, kaffir-head stick, spectacles, fountain-pen, – all complete!" inscribed on this photograph of January 1906.

Right: A poem from Hermes, *January 1896.*

no need for such officials (closely resembling school prefects) and their introduction in 1891[9] perhaps bore out Miss Maynard's prediction that the 'New Westfield' would have an institutionalizing effect. The student Fire Brigade, also begun in 1891, was another matter.[10] The danger of fire was ever-present in buildings lit at the outset entirely by oil lamps, so it was only common prudence to see that the residents were drilled in the use of the canvas chute and other equipment procured by the Household Committee on the advice of the Hampstead Fire Chief. The serious burns suffered by two students when a lamp overturned at a fancy dress party in 1894 brought home to the Council the need to in-

    ✖ Two important events ... were Picnic on the River organized by Miss Whitby, and marmalade cutting ... 'volunteers' gathered in the dining room after dinner and thinly sliced hundreds of oranges while lustily singing all the College songs. The staff went about sharpening our knives and the maids removed the cut oranges in huge bowls and brought fresh ones. ✖

*I Stephen (*Hermes, 1903).

stall the safer alternatives of incandescent gas and electricity; the major part of the programme was completed by 1896, but several more years elapsed before every nook and cranny was made safe.[11]

A fancy dress party (needless to say no outsiders were present) was a most unusual occurrence. The staple programme of 'Evening Amusements' at this period consisted of Glee Club performances, privately arranged readings of Shakespeare plays or other literary works, and an occasional auction of student possessions to raise funds for amenities, for example a movable platform for the Dining Hall. On some evenings more serious fare was provided. For several years Mrs Clara Goslett, who held the certificate of the Sanitary Institute, gave a short course on aspects of public hygiene;[12]

Miss Richardson continued her talks on Temperance, laying especial stress on the social ill-effects of alcoholism; Saturdays, as before, were dedicated to the College Debate. Towards the end of the decade (in about 1898) a Social Club was formed, not for convivial purposes but to promote, through reading and discussion, the factual study of topics such as poverty, housing, and other allied matters of public concern. Among the outside speakers invited was Miss Margaret Bondfield, Secretary of the National Union of Shop Assistants (and afterwards the first woman to sit in the Cabinet).[13]

Although it was Miss Maynard's earnest wish that her students should engage in 'useful work' outside the College, she felt obliged to disallow 'general visiting among the poor.... for fear of infection'. The kind of work she encouraged is illustrated by the account in a Budget Letter dated 1899: 'The students are allowed to have one person each, either old, crippled, blind, or in some way cut off from public worship, to whom they may read every week. Some 15 or 16 have these, and 3 others have a [Sunday School] class, and 2 more go to the East End to teach little boys to sew shirts (of all funny things!) and 2 more have a singing class for our 11 maid-servants, and others do other isolated works, so that nearly everyone has *one* little bit in the week of real effort for the good of others....'. The College's main corporate 'good work' was to entertain a party of Factory Girls to games and refreshments every Whit Monday.[14]

As is clear from the figures just quoted, the College was still very small. In fact it was not until 1897 that the 'New Westfield' was filled to capacity, and then only for a short time. More encouraging was a gradual but noticeable improvement in the academic standard.

Of the students at College during the 1890s almost one half eventually obtained degrees (in some cases after completing their studies elsewhere). The majority of these did not proceed to Honours, but they could still do the College credit: in 1895 Westfield candidates made up a quarter of the women placed in

Right: Fire Drill (early 1900s). On the left, Miss LJ Whitby supervises the evacuation from the Old House. Note the College ties.

the First Division of the BA (Pass) Examination, earning for themselves a mention in the daily press.[15] The proportion attempting the Honours Examination was much smaller, but some who did so entered in subjects not previously taken from Westfield: for BA Hons. in German, Mathematics, English and History; for BSc Hons. in Physics and Botany. Four First Classes are recorded: two in English, one in History,[16] one in Botany. Students who chose subjects not covered by the Resident or Visiting Staff, or for which the Westfield laboratory was inadequately equipped, attended lectures and classes at other insititutions, principally University College and Bedford College.

A brief glimpse of lectures at Westfield at the beginning of the decade is provided by Miss Maynard's account of a visit from Dr

---

❝ People have such funny ideas about the College. One lady ... said she was so glad to meet me, and to hear what Westfield really was, — a college just like Girton, was it? Oh, she had thought it was a kind of a home with a gentleman at the head.❞

Anon (Hermes, 1899).

Barlow and 'a clerical friend' to observe 'the working of the College' in 1891. The Classical teaching of Miss Gray and Miss Richardson was pronounced 'accurate and delicately shaded and above the ordinary Oxford lecture in refinement and taste': since the author being expounded by Miss Richardson was Juvenal this was a tribute indeed. Also seen in action were Miss Willoughby (Geometry) and Miss Beloe, 'who put on cap and gown to amuse us'.[17]

Three of these four Resident Lecturers, who in 1891 made up the total full-time strength, left the College in the course of the next ten years. Miss Gray and Miss Willoughby both departed in 1894, the former on appointment as Head of St Katherine's School, St Andrews, the latter on her marriage, after a six-year engagement, to William Adams Clark, MD. Quite apart from the soundness of their

teaching, both had contributed to the well-being of the College in ways not easily measured. Miss Gray had been the person Miss Maynard had turned to at moments of emotional crisis, whether her own or a student's. Miss Willoughby, with her scientific training, was regarded as the great authority on all practical matters: it was to her, for example, that the heating engineer explained the hot water system of the 'New Westfield', 'pouring facts upon her which she absorbed with the intuition of real genius'.[18] Both Mrs Adams Clark and Miss Gray remained in close contact with Westfield, Miss Gray being appointed in 1897 a member of the Council.

Miss Beloe, after thirteen years spent teaching a subject (Mathematics) not really her own (she had taken Honours in French), left in 1901 to become Headmistress of Howell's School, Denbigh.

The vacancies in Classics and Science left by Miss Gray and Miss Willoughby were filled by a succession of well-qualified representatives of the rising generation of university women, some of them so young and untried that Miss Maynard privately called them 'babies'. Only one, Edith Simey,[19] Lecturer in Classics 1894-1898, was a Westfield graduate. The Lecturers in Science were all Cambridge trained: Minnie Baldwin, a Girtonian with a First in both parts of the Tripos, who left after a couple of years to marry Dr J.C. Willis, Director of the Peradeniya Botanical Gardens in Ceylon; another Girtonian, Jessie Vinter; and finally Florence Strudwick, a Newnhamite who had taken First Class Honours. Appointed in 1899, Miss Strudwick remained in the post until 1905 and so restored a degree of stability.

But the two most lasting appointments of this period both had their origin, as is often the way, in short term engagements.

Lilian Janie Whitby had entered Royal Holloway College in 1890 and was a London graduate (BA Pass, First Division); but whilst there, under an arrangement currently in force, she had also taken Oxford Honours Examinations in Mathematics, securing a First in both Moderations and Finals. Miss Whitby first came to Westfield in October 1895 as a temporary replacement for Miss Beloe, absent through illness. This was so successful that in the following year she was made permanent as an additional Resident Lecturer. From 1901 until her retirement exactly thirty years later Miss Whitby was Westfield's only full-time lecturer in mathematics, and as such might be thought to have occupation enough. But she undertook in addition, and did so almost from the moment of her arrival, all the routine academic business of the College (time-tabling, registration of students for examinations, correspondence with the University) and acted in short as an unofficial Registrar.

Caroline Anne James Skeel* joined Westfield in January 1896 as Visiting Lecturer in Classics, having completed the previous summer a student career at Girton which had astonished even Cambridge by its brilliance: from a First Class in part one of the Classical Tripos in 1894 she had proceeded in the following year to repeat the performance in the first part of the Historical Tripos. Testimonials[20] from her teachers in both subjects testify to qualities likely to lead to sucess at a more advanced stage in either: an exceptionally quick grasp of both facts and principles, extreme accuracy, enthusiasm, and a fine sense for usage and style. For a time (starting 1897) Miss Skeel lectured at Westfield in both History and Classics; but from 1901 she taught only History, confirming that this was her preference by enrolling at the London School of Economics to work on the thesis in sixteenth and seventeenth century conciliar government for which she was awarded in 1904 the degree of D Lit.

The lecturers of this second generation were noticeably more assertive than their predecessors. They dared to protest, for example when the Council, alarmed at the many failures in the previous year's Matriculation, proposed in 1899 to invite an external examiner to re-

The resident staff in 1905, in the Conservatory which was demolished in 1914. Back row, left to right: Miss Richardson, Miss Whitby. Seated, left to right: Miss McDougall, Miss Maynard, Dr Skeel, and Miss Strudwick.

view the staff's marking of papers written by the students in a 'mock Matric.'. They made their feelings known in a letter signed by all five Resident Lecturers: 'We, as Lecturers at Westfield College, while desirous of aiding the enquiries of the Council in every way, respectfully protest....against such inspection of our work by any outside teacher whatsoever. We represent various Colleges and Universities and think a scrutiny of this nature is purely unparalleled. We should be quite content that our classes should be examined by any person regarded as competent should such a course be thought useful; but that our own work should be so examined....is not consistent with the dignity of our position'.[21]

❛ I felt no particular necessity for a hearty bread-and-butter tea at half-past eight, but when an old student came to my door to tell me that that was what the gong meant, I meekly trotted down after her ... I remember that I asked the girl next to me if she was going in for the matric, and also my feelings when she said she was a lecturer ... ❜

Anon (Hermes, 1899).

Quite apart from the professional affront, it is clear from subsequent correspondence between the Chairman, Dr Barlow, and Miss Richardson (who although of the older generation often identified herself with the younger) that also in issue was the College's policy in regard to the admission of unmatriculated students. Miss Maynard had already suggested to the Council (in 1898) that Matriculation was an examination which could now more conveniently be taken from school. The Lecturers, while applying themselves conscientiously to this more elementary form of teaching, no doubt felt that their real work lay with the more advanced students. Since the College had so few scholarships with which to attract better qualified students, they perforce had 'more difficult material to work on than that

existing at other colleges'.[22] The twin solution to the problem - more financial support for well-qualified applicants and better schooling all round - took time to materialise. The College continued for some years yet to admit unmatriculated students, and to do well by them: one such was Catherine Firth - entered 1901, BA Hons History Class I 1905, MA History 1910, D Lit 1912.

The episode of 1899 was not without positive outcome. In one of her letters to Dr Barlow, Miss Richardson had suggested that it would be better 'if Council and Staff could be more closely connected....as at all other Colleges'. It so happened that at the suggestion of a new member, Dr Henry Wace, who had just resigned from the Principalship of King's College, the Council had recently set up its own Education Committee.[23] This Committee's initial terms of reference extended no further than consultation with the Mistress over appointments to the non-resident staff. But under Dr Wace's forceful chairmanship the Education Committee did not shrink from proffering advice on a wider range of topics (the failures in Matriculation being one), without having among its members, as Miss Richardson pointed out, any representative of those actually engaged in teaching. The Council's solution was to sanction the formation in July 1899 of a parallel committee, composed of the Mistress and all the Resident Staff, to 'advise the Council, when consulted by them, respecting the educational work of the College; and to have power to offer suggestions to the Council on educational matters'. The link between this body (the 'Educational Board')[24] and the Council's committee was the Mistress. The introduction of these new arrangements could hardly have been better timed, in view of the repercussions on the 'educational work of the College' of the changes already afoot in the University of London.

Writing of the University of London in 1869, Matthew Arnold had decried it as 'a mere *collegium*, or board, of examiners'.[25] As things stood, the University was in fact in no position to offer the 'first-rate systematic instruction' which Matthew Arnold and other critics considered should be an essential part of a university's role. Under the charter granted to it in 1836, the University of London had been empowered to award its degrees to persons summarily defined as: 'Pupils from University and King's College' and from 'any other Bodies for Education....from time to time named by the Crown'.[26] Over the next twenty years the number and variety of institutions seeking and obtaining nomination became so great that efforts to control the quality of the candidates' preparation through production of a certificate of satisfactory study were admitted to be useless. From 1858, when the rules in respect of certification were abolished, London degrees were open to candidates irrespective of their place of study (and from 1878

The College from the road, about 1929.

also irrespective of their sex); hence it followed that the Senate's 'sole means of influencing the course and character of the teaching was ....in its schemes and regulations for examination'.[27] While on the one hand it gave hope of a degree to private, unattached students and on the other offered a reliable standard against which aspiring new colleges (Westfield for example) could quickly test their performance, this system was frustrating to teachers who were interested in advancing their subjects, since in the interests of fairness the syllabuses had to be reduced to the narrow range of what could be regarded as common knowledge.[28]

Growing dissatisfaction in some quarters with a University which amounted, in one flippant description, to little more than 'a measuring rod and a note of interrogation',[29]

led to the formation in 1884 of an Association for Promoting a Teaching University for London. For reasons which cannot be entered into here, this seemingly simple objective was attained only after years of controversy and the investigations of two Royal Commissions. It was only with the passage into law of the University of London Act of 1898 (after four years of legislative delay) that the way was at last clear.

The task of drawing up Statutes was entrusted under the Act to seven Statutory Commissioners, who were required to work within a framework laid down by the second of the Royal Commissions, the so-called 'Gresham Commission' (chaired by Earl Cowper, it had reported in 1894). Included in the report of the Gresham Commission was a list of twenty-one institutions, all already preparing students for London degrees, which it was proposed should form the 'Schools' of the reconstituted University; this list, with one or two additions, was endorsed by the Statutory Commissioners and incorporated into the Statutes published early in 1900.[30]

Westfield, although it had not given evidence to the Royal Commissions, had expected to be included; the revelation that it was not came therefore as a great blow.[31] Private enquiries by Dr Wace yielded the following somewhat sheepish explanation from Dr Mandell Creighton, Bishop of London, who was one of the Statutory Commissioners: 'I am very sorry about Westfield, but there is now no remedy. The Commission is officio functus: its Statutes, Schedules and Reports have been passed from it to Parliament. But I should like to explain that the Commission at an early stage decided that its function was to make an adequate University, not a complete one, and to leave the new University to shape itself and arrange details....Westfield must apply as soon as possible to the Senate. It is of course no real disability as several of its teachers are recognised and their pupils are internal students.'[32]

It appears to be the case that three Westfield lecturers, Miss Richardson, Miss Skeel and Miss Whitby, had already obtained Recognition as Teachers under the new Statutes, a status conferred in respect of qualifications and experience of preparing students for the London degree, and not restricted to teachers serving in Schools of the University.[33] Whether or not Dr Creighton was correct in claiming that their students ranked as 'Internal Students' is less certain. At all events, the College Council was not content to see Westfield left in an ambiguous position. Accordingly, in March 1901 application was made in due form to the Senate for the admission of Westfield as a School in the Faculties of Arts and Science.[34]

This first application was not successful; but the letter of rejection hinted that if 'certain deficiencies' were remedied the outcome of a second might be different. From an interview with the Academic Registrar, Dr Frank Heath, who had 'inspected' the College on behalf of the University, it emerged that the deficiencies were of two kinds. First, that subjects were being taught for which the College had no Recognised Teachers; second that both the Library and the Laboratory fell below the required standard. The Library was deemed by Dr Heath to lack many of the essential works needed for the study of Arts

subjects, let alone Science, while the College's one Laboratory, housed very unsuitably in an attic, was equipped only for the courses in Chemistry, Zoology and Botany prescribed for the Intermediate, so that at the very least a Physical Laboratory would need to be added.[35]

The matter of staffing was easily dealt with by the appointment as Visiting Lecturers of Recognised Teachers from other institutions.[36] However, to put right the other defects would obviously entail expenditure. Since the Council lacked the funds to develop the Arts and Science sides simultaneously, and since the improvement of the Library seemed the easier objective to attain, it was decided in January 1902 to make 'for the present' no further application in respect of Science and to concentrate all effort on the Library.

The office of Librarian at Westfield, as at many other colleges until well into the twentieth century, was filled by a member of the teaching staff. The College was extremely for-

Below: the attic laboratory, which was in use 1891-1921, and again from 1929-1935.
Right: the Application for Admission to the University of London.

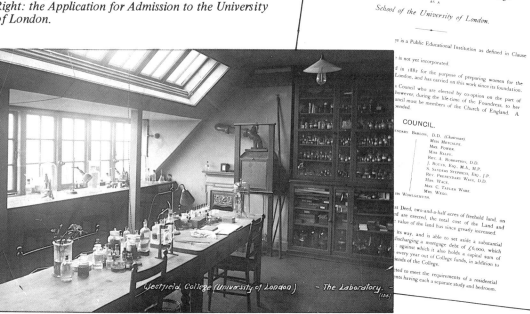

tunate to have as Librarian at this juncture Caroline Skeel, whose energy, persuasiveness and scholarly connections swiftly produced results. Between July 1901 and October 1902 the number of volumes in the Library more than doubled, bringing the total up to 3319. The College *Annual Report* for 1902 records gifts in kind to the Library from close on fifty individuals and publishers and from seven learned societies; the Early English Text Society donated a complete set of its publications. Successive issues of *Hermes* and the *Annual Report* tell a similar tale.

Miss Skeel's efforts were complemented by the launching of an appeal to Old Students and other friends. In March 1902 the ad hoc committee in charge of the appeal (which had been set up when Science was still on the agenda and was therefore known as the Equipment Committee) was invited by the Council to consider the College's building needs. These it had no difficulty in identifying as a purpose-built Library to replace the room on the first floor of Old House, which was now full to overflowing, and two additional Lecture Rooms. It took less than a month for the Council to make up its mind to proceed along these lines. Armed with this declared intention, and with the proof of what had already been achieved, the College made a second application to the Senate, this time confining its request for admission to the Faculty of Arts. On the evening of 26 June 1902 a telegram reached Westfield with the news that the Senate had resolved that same day to grant the application.[37]

The Council's pleasure in at last achieving the goal was made greater by the public recognition thus accorded to Miss Maynard and to the 'valuable work she has now carried on for so long a period'.[38] The tribute was thoroughly well-deserved. But as the Mistress was the first to acknowledge, the credit for having turned the University's rejection into acceptance belonged in part to the Council, for its persistence, but still more to certain of her colleagues: to Miss Whitby, whose orderly mind saw its way clearly through the tangle of University regulations; to Miss Skeel, who was perhaps the person most deeply committed to

the safeguarding of Westfield's future as an academic institution; and pre-eminently to Miss Richardson who, in the absence on leave of Miss Maynard[39] when the blow first fell in 1900, alerted Council and Old Students to the gravity of the situation, canvassed support for Westfield's case from influential friends, set in motion the collection of the necessary information to sustain it, and guided the Mistress through the final stages.[40]

It was characteristic of Miss Richardson to draw attention in 1900, when the outlook seemed dark, to a brighter side of the current 'difficulty about the new University'. As she pointed out to students past and present at the Banquet: 'More interest has been aroused in Westfield than, perhaps ever before. Many have heard the name of the College for the first time, others have been obliged to recognise for the first time what excellent work it is doing'.[41]

Among Westfield's most passionate advocates were some of its former students, half a dozen of whom had written jointly to the Council in the previous March (1900) to protest at the exclusion of the College from the first list of recognised Schools.[42] This group became the nucleus of Westfield's formal association of Old Students (the Westfield

WCA minutes of September, 1901.

College Association or WCA) which was founded later that same year. Since membership was (and is) on a voluntary basis, the Association was not all-inclusive in the manner, for example, of the Girton Roll. But the WCA soon attracted a sufficient cross-section for it to reflect the composition of 'Greater Westfield' with some accuracy; and with two leading members of the Council, Lady Chapman and Miss Gray, as President and Vice-President, it was kept in close touch with current developments. Hence the WCA was well able to bring the needs of the College to the attention of the Old Students, whose generosity has never failed. By 1902 the WCA had already collected £200 for the Equipment Fund, the first of many such donations.[43]

The work of both Staff and Students was much affected – for the better, most would have said – by Westfield's new status as 'part of a great whole'.[44] The *Annual Report* for 1904 shows that the Staff, both Resident and Non-Resident, was by then composed almost entirely of Recognised Teachers, of whom the majority were members of their respective Boards of Studies. These last were of great importance in the functioning of the reconstituted University: through them teachers had a voice in the shaping of syllabuses and degree requirements, met each other on the ground of a common discipline and worked out means of collaboration, whether in teaching or research. In order to maintain a common standard of instruction, the University reserved to itself the power to approve the 'Schedule of Courses' taught in individual Schools, details of which had to be forwarded for publication in the University Calender. Westfield's lecture programme was also printed in the College's *Annual Report*, appearing in it for the first time in the issue for 1903; in 1904 there is the first mention of participation by Westfield Lecturers in the University's programme of Inter-Collegiate courses.

The degree regulations of the reconstituted University made it possible for students aspiring to Honours to bypass the more broadly based Pass examination. At Westfield the opportunity for greater study in depth opened up by the introduction of the single sub-ject Honours degree was clearly welcome: it took less than a decade for the balance between Pass and Honours graduates to tilt decisively in favour of the latter. Because of its small size, the number of subjects Westfield was able to teach for Honours was restricted. For many years the choice the College offered to intending BA Hons. students was confined in effect to Classics, History, English, French and Mathematics.[45]

In this first decade the most popular, by a narrow margin, was Classics. Both Latin and Greek had been taught at Westfield from the outset; necessarily, because of their compulsory status under degree regulations, but also out of respect and affection for the classical world as a fount of goodness second only to Christianity. Even those students not aspiring to degrees – categorised from 1892 as 'General Students' – were required from 1900 onwards to attend classes in either Greek or Latin. Greek plays, whether witnessed at Bradfield or in Cambridge or enacted by Westfield students, were exempt from the general ban on the theatre, while the very title of *Hermes*, not to mention the classical tags and allusions scattered through its (or, as its early editors preferred to say, 'his') pages is indicative of the extent to which the small change of classical studies had currency among the students. The centrality of the Classics was further underlined by the preference accorded to classicists in the appointment of Resident Lecturers. Eleanor McDougall,[46] a Royal Holloway graduate who joined the College in that capacity in 1902, had spent some time on archaeological research in Cambridge and developed the teaching at Westfield on that side. Miss McDougall clearly had the power to leave a lasting impression: one former student recalled long afterwards that her lectures on Alexander the Great contained 'the spice of life', another remembered evenings in Miss McDougall's room when 'the origins and meanings of Greek myths and their influence on modern philosophy and creative thinking' were eagerly discussed.[47] On her departure for India in 1915 Miss McDougall handed over the department to a colleague who was to remain in office as Senior Classical Lecturer until the

1930s and who belonged to a distinguished company of long-serving Lecturers from whom the College of the post-war years took its tone: Constance Emily Parker.[48]

History as an Honours subject was of comparatively recent origin in London and to begin with candidates for the single subject Honours degree were few: so it is remarkable that in the first examination held under the new regulations (1905) four out of the five candidates were from Westfield and that these included the only one, Catherine Firth, to be placed in the First Class. At this stage Caroline Skeel was Westfield's only Lecturer in History; she was also Librarian; and in pursuit of her own research she spent all her spare time in the Public Record Office and the British Museum. In 1907 Dr Skeel was obliged by ill health to resign her position. Her place as director of studies in History was taken by her own former teacher and source of inspiration at Girton, Ellen McArthur. Since Dr McArthur continued to live in Cambridge and could only spare one night away each week, a former Somerville student, Alice Sergeant, who had been research assistant to the great medievalist, Paul Vinogradoff, was appointed Resident Lecturer and was retained to support Dr Skeel on her return, as a Non-Resident, in 1911.[49]

The Lecturers in English and French were all Non-Resident and often held a comparable post at some other institution. Thus Miss Charlotte Paquier, Lecturer in French at Westfield, was also responsible for all the French teaching at the East London College (now Queen Mary College), while Miss Kate Warren, the senior of two English Lecturers at Westfield, was on the staff both of the East London College and of the Northern Polytechnic Institute. In these subjects, as in History, much benefit was derived from the system of Inter-Collegiate courses: it appears, for example, that all the teaching in Old French (which figured large in the syllabus) was concentrated at University College. It was under the auspices of the Inter-Collegiate programme that men students first appeared at Westfield, to attend a course given by Miss Paquier.[50]

Of the five subjects offered at Westfield

for BA Honours under the new regulations, Mathematics took the longest to become established, producing its first graduate only in 1911. This does not mean, however, that Mathematics ceased temporarily to be of importance in the years immediately following 1902: students reading for the BA Pass might choose to take Mathematics as one of the components; and Mathematics played an important part in the restructuring of the College's provision for Science.

Although not admitted in 1902 as a School of the University in the Faculty of Science, Westfield had not been obliged to give up all preparation of students for the B Sc. Miss Strudwick, while not a Recognised Teacher, was qualified to teach for the Intermediate B Sc; students who wished to proceed further remained attached to Westfield but were registered, for University purposes, as External Students and went (as before) for their advanced work to other colleges. This arrangement, while satisfactory for existing BSc students, was unlikely to attract new entrants. The departure of Miss Strudwick in 1905 (to become Lecturer in Biology at the newly established Goldsmiths' College) might thus have been seized as an opportunity to bring all science teaching at Westfield to an end. The case for its retention was put, most forcibly, by Miss Richardson: she argued that without Science the College would be in danger of losing touch 'with the more modern and progressive side of University education'; and that without B Sc students to make up the numbers the College might prove difficult to fill, as Westfield science graduates teaching in schools, (thus far roughly equal in numbers to arts graduates), would no longer be able to recommend Westfield to their pupils. In accepting Miss Richardson's advice, which had the backing of the staff's Educational Board, the Council also accepted the implication that at least one science subject, in addition to Mathematics, would have to be taught at Westfield up to Final B Sc standard. The Science Lecturer appointed would therefore need to be of the calibre to obtain Recognised Teacher status; and the subject chosen would have to be one which did not tax unduly the very limited capabilities of the College's attic laboratory or 'involve any very great expense in apparatus'.[51]

The choice very quickly fell on Botany, which was seen to meet both these requirements: any idea that Botany won approval as the most 'ladylike' of the sciences can quite certainly be ruled out, and would have been scoffed at by the young woman appointed in 1906 to the vacant Resident Lectureship in Science.

Ellen Marion Delf* was twenty-three when she arrived at Westfield, fresh from a distinguished undergraduate career at Girton and having already made a brief start in research. She had been warned by Miss Richardson that 'apart from a modest allowance for petty cash (amount unspecified and obtained in small sums on application) there was no provision for apparatus or other items of equipment', but even so was unprepared for the sight of the 'eight or ten bottles with bits of plants, mostly in very poor condition' which represented the botanical collection. It took Miss Delf a year to acquire the basic equipment (microtome, auxanometer, palaeobotanical specimens etc., for which the Council made a special grant) and to amass plant material of a suitable type. Miss Delf's next major request to the Education Committee, submitted in 1908, was for a laboratory assistant: this was met by the release of one of the domestic servants daily from twelve to one to 'wash up and dust'. In 1910, when the foundations for advanced work had been laid and small improvements to the Laboratory were in prospect, it was at last possible for the University to approve the Laboratory for 'work up to the standard of the Final B Sc Pass Examination' in Botany and to grant Miss Delf the status of Recognised Teacher.[52]

Marion Delf, like Caroline Skeel, regarded her work as teacher incomplete if it did not 'at least awaken the desire amongst students to follow some line of investigation for themselves'. Opportunity for research was thus as essential to Miss Delf's educational purposes as it was to her own inquiring disposition: and to be told, as she was by the Principal of another college (in a shameless attempt at poaching) that at Westfield she would 'never get any research done', only strengthened her will to succeed. Westfield, it is true, was not ideal for research that required the control and conduct of observations over a long period: the academic staff were not permitted to reside during the vacations and in the summer the maids used the Laboratory as a sitting-room. Fortunately, the work on the physiology of saltmarsh plants and succulents which Miss Delf had already started under F F Blackman in Cambridge could be done outside the Laboratory. By 1912 it was sufficiently advanced to be worked up into the thesis on transpiration for which she was awarded the London D Sc. Dr Delf's first published paper had appeared the previous year, and she was soon followed into print by one of her own pupils, Alison Maybrook.[53]

In 1903 the Council had identified in its *Annual Report* two fields in which they fore-

Marian Delf in 1912, in DSc robes.

saw 'great efforts' would have to be made if the College was to meet the 'increased responsibilities involved in its closer relations to the University': the provision of adequate scholarships and extension of the College buildings. These objectives were pursued in parallel, but precedence was given to honouring the Council's already expressed intention to provide a larger and more suitable home for the Library. The architect was again Falconer Macdonald, who designed the extension to match the Dining Hall. He linked it to the Old Wing at first floor level with the romantically conceived 'Bridge of Sighs'. The upper room, furnished with fumed oak and with shelving running round three walls, made a fit place — still more so when the gallery was added in 1911 — in which to ascend the 'steep and toilsome road to learning' (as Miss Gray put it on the occasion of the opening in 1904).[54] The ground floor was divided between two lecture rooms, bringing the total up to four — or rather five, since the Laboratory, as Miss Delf was to discover to her dismay, was often commandeered for lectures quite unconnected with Science.

The next project, for an adjoining residential wing, was started almost before the Library was complete. From 1903 onwards the number of students needing to be accommodated was regularly in excess of the forty-four for which the 'New Westfield' had been designed. To some extent the 'bulge' was an artificial one, caused by a timelag in adjusting admissions to take account of the 'three years of continuous study' which the University insisted on as a qualification for the Internal Degree: rooms which under the old system might have been vacated after one or two years now remained under the same occupancy for three. Experience of working the College with this slightly larger number of

Westfield's first purpose-built Library (afterwards named 'Skeel'), photographed in the 1920s.

students (the overflow having been accom-modated in a house rented in the neighbour-hood) suggested that the maximum could safely be increased to sixty. The wing pro-viding the additional sixteen places was ready by October 1905 and its occupation was in-augurated by a service of thanksgiving held the Library — the first instance at Westfield of a clerically-conducted act of worship. The reason for this unprecedented solemnity was that the occasion was held to mark the comp-letion not only of the recent additions but of the College in its entirety — at least so far as the Founders were concerned.[55]

The combined cost of these two projects, the Library and its annexed south wing, am-ounted to something over £9000. Three gifts of £1,000 apiece — from Miss Dudin Brown, Mrs Sanders Stephens and an anonymous friend - made up the bulk of the £4000 need-ed for the Library.[56] The residential wing was paid for almost entirely by Miss Dudin Brown (with a contribution of £4000) and thus it is with obvious justification that this part of the College now bears her name - except in so far as later generations may be misled as to the extent of the contribution made by the Foundress not merely to one small portion of the College but to the whole.[57]

The Council's efforts to enlarge the funds for scholarships were rewarded by further offers from generous past donors (Miss Dudin Brown amongst others) and from new bene-factors: the Westfield College Association, which donated two scholarships, one for Arts and another for Science, almost before it had come into existence; and two city companies, the Drapers and the Goldsmiths. With help from these and other sources it was possible to offer five or six Entrance Scholarships each year in amounts equivalent to one-third or slightly less of the fees. Yet the situation re-mained precarious since, with the exception of the scholarship founded by Mrs Sanders Stephens and awarded for the first time in 1908, none of these carried an endowment. It is true that since 1890, when County and Bor-ough Council Scholarships had become avail-able,[58] a few students had entered the College with support from public funds; but compet-

A student's room in the Dudin Brown Wing, taken in 1929.

ition for such awards was fierce, and even those who succeeded might still need a Col-lege Scholarship as supplement. The Council's summing up of the position in its *Annual Re-port* for 1912 shows that the provision was still far short of the need: 'For the last two or three years, from 22 to 35 candidates have competed each year for five or six scholar-ships, and of those who were unsuccessful, not more than five or six could hope to enter the College without substantial pecuniary help, although many were promising students, and eager to enter on a University course'.

Scholarships were deemed important on academic as well as charitable grounds. Having been accepted by the University, the College had no wish to see its standards slipping be-low those of other Schools. Intellectual prom-ise, of the kind tested by the more searching Scholarship Examination introduced in 1909, therefore became an increasingly important desideratum in a potential student. The girls' High Schools and Boarding Schools founded in the last quarter of the nineteenth century were still the main providers of well-prepared university applicants, so it is not suprising that the Westfield Scholars of the early 1900s were supplied, almost without exception, by schools of this type: the Girls' Public Day School Trust, with its wide spread of schools, always had at least one representative in the annual list.

Once arrived, these and other entrants

ODE, 1898.

I.

O, Hockey is the game for those
Who cast aside their cares,
And do not fear the knocks and blows
Which each one bravely bears.
The whistle blows, the ball it goes,
And all rush on pell-mell ;
The backs they mingle with their foes,
And do their part right well.
All hear the cries of "foul" and "sticks,"
But yet they do not stay,
With mighty slogs and hearty kicks,
They rush into the fray,
The cowards all may stay at home,
And play their tennis calm,
But Hockey is the game for those
Who have no fear of harm.

II.

...t when the ball comes whizzing down,
Pursued by one and all,
...! then it is a joy to see
...ur centre brave and tall.
...e takes the ball just as she should,
...nd keeps it till she sends
...n, right o'er the keeper's head,
...th a long and swinging hit.

Off-side ! Off-side ! the field resounds,
The umpire smiles serene,
And gently blows the whistle loud ;
A goal for Westfield team.
The cowards all may stay at home
And play their tennis calm,
But Hockey is the game for those
Who have no fear of harm.

III.

Oh ! Comrades dear, and did ye hear,
The news that's going round ?
That hockey sticks no more exists,
Since summer suns abound.
No more the ball will fly around,
The paint will not come off,
For it is in the cupboard now,
And feeling very lone,
But till we have got so old and stiff,
And till we've got so grey and gaunt
And cannot limp about,
And cannot move from gout,
Oh, till that day we'll ever play
The game we all adore,
And never fear, but give a cheer,
For the Westfield Hockey Team.

E. M.

Above:
"Ode" published in Hermes,
1899, and right: the Second Eleven Team of 1902 or 1903.

found that life at Westfield presented features already familiar from their schooldays: 'uniform' (worn admittedly from choice), competitive games (interest in which was made the keener by the formation in 1906-1907 of University Hockey and Tennis Teams), 'prefects' in the shape of JPs and Orderlies. From about 1904, when a Senior Student — 'appointed by the Mistress after consultation with the staff and elder students' — first appears on the scene, there was even a species of Head Girl. One effect of the new degree regulations was to accentuate the division of the College into distinct 'years': each year's intake now entered at the same time (termly admissions being almost a thing of the past), followed a similar programme and graduated together.

Non-resident students, although regularly admitted from 1903 onwards,[59] made up only a small proportion of the student body, on average perhaps one in twelve.[60] But their freedom to come and go unaccompanied must have been a factor in securing the release of resident students from the rule obliging them to seek permission from one of the resident staff before venturing out alone. The recollections of students there at the time suggest that this act of emancipation was desired as much by the younger lecturers (to whom

requests to go out were most frequently addressed) as by the students. The latter did not fail, however, to mark the moment when it came: 'On the first day of the relaxation almost every student could be seen walking down the Finchley Road ALONE'. Bicycling 'in the direction of London' had also by this time ceased to be a crime: for many, with inter-collegiate lecturers and special classes to attend, it had become a necessity. To continue with the recollections just quoted: 'Nothing was done about chaperoning us when we went off to lectures on a bicycle — or by bus. I even remember, when I was nearing my Final, going in the late evening for a private tuition from a man....at Bedford College and coming back alone about ten at night.'[61]

University-wide student committees and societies were at this date still in their infancy. In 1904, however, Westfield sent a delegate to the conference which led to the formation of the Students' Representative Council (forerunner of the University of London Union); in 1912 the Westfield representative was Vice-President of the Council and was one of London's delegates to the grandiose-sounding Congress of the Universities of the Empire.[62]

This decade (1902-1913) also saw the launching in College of subject-oriented societies. An Archaeological Society and a

Nature Study Union did not survive, or at least did not survive under those names, but the line of descent of a third, the History Club, has remained appropriately unbroken. It was inaugurated in 1909 by Dr McArthur, a keen suffragist, with her paper 'Women petitioners and the Long Parliament'.[63]

The issue of women's suffrage in the twentieth century was naturally one that attracted increasing attention. The subject came up in College Debates three times between 1893 and 1907, and on each occasion the voting showed a clear majority in favour of extending the franchise to women on equal terms with men. However the desire among Westfield lecturers and students to see Westfield

---

❛ It was Miss McDougall who prevented me from joining Christobel Pankhurst's famous suffragette march when she said, 'Miss Moy-Evans, you look so very young you would add nothing to the dignity of the occasion .❜

B Moy-Evans (1907).

---

playing a public part in the campaign, which was now entering its more demonstrative phase, was not shared by the Council. Miss Maynard, who was personally in no doubt about the justice of the cause, explained to Old Students with some care the attitude adopted in regard to a suffrage procession in the summer of 1908: 'It was not thought well that our College should take the prominent part the others did — Girton, Somerville etc. marching under their distinctive banners. Neither did we forbid it as Holloway authorities did to their present Students. The result was that all the Staff (save of course Miss Whitby) and five of the elder Students went. I am too much identified with Westfield to be able to go. Miss Dudin Brown was staying with us — she has paid us three separate visits of six days each this Term — and I don't think she approved, but wisely held her tongue. It was all most orderly and quiet and those who went enjoyed it very well, seeing Miss Fawcett, Miss

Emily Davies, and all the other celebrities concerned.'[64]

In its religious life Westfield allied itself, as might be expected, with the efforts of the Student Christian Movement (SCM) to evangelise the student world at large. The SCM, when formally constituted in 1905, represented the convergence of two separate but related organisations which had been in existence since the mid-1890s, the Student Volunteer Missionary Union (SVMU) and the British Colleges Christian Union (BCCU).[65] The branch of the BCCU established at Westfield in 1896 was regularly host to the combined annual meeting of all London branches for women students. The College was also represented by a sizeable and enthusiastic contingent of past and present students at the summer camps held by the BCCU (and later SCM) in Derbyshire. Inside Westfield itself, however, the BCCU must have had less scope for evangelisation than in Colleges and Universities where the Christian tradition had worn thin or was non-existent. The methods of the BCCU were no novelty so far as Westfield was concerned, the main difference being that at Westfield the meetings for Bible study and the exploration of missionary and allied questions were directed not by students, which was the BCCU style, but by the Mistress (and in the case of devotional meetings for Quaker students by Miss Richardson).

The Student Volunteer Missionary Union had the more specific purpose of enrolling students as future missionaries. Its activities were thus of obvious interest to Westfield and it is not surprising to find that the College received regular visits from SVMU travelling secretaries and that it was well represented at the great quadrennial conferences mounted by SVMU between 1896 and 1912. Yet Westfield names are not found among the initiators and early leaders of the Union, several of whom were women. There is in fact evidence that Miss Maynard was not at first wholly in sympathy with SVMU. She had been present at one of its earliest gatherings (at Keswick in 1893) and had witnessed 'the rush of volunteers, both men and women': while she admired their 'happy courage', she could not suppress the thought that it was 'born of ignorance'.[66] From her own former students in the field Miss Maynard knew enough of the difficulties of the missionary's life — isolation, depression, illness, physical danger, uncongenial society, dearth of tangible results — to wish her present students to be as mature as possible before making a declaration as firm as that required from the Student Volunteers: 'It is my purpose, if God permit, to become a Foreign Missionary'. Miss Maynard also had her doubts, and these applied equally to the BCCU, about the wisdom of leaving such potentially important movements in the hands of a largely undergraduate leadership. This objection was removed with the appointment around 1908 of more experienced men and women to the permanent secretariat of the SCM. The General Secretary, the Reverend Tissington Tatlow, although something of a heretic in Miss Maynard's eyes, became a trusted friend.

The progress of former students in their chosen work, whether as missionaries or otherwise, was followed in the College with keen interest. The results of systematic attempts to collect information are to be seen in a printed 'Classified List of Public or Professional Workers who were Students at the College between its foundation in 1882 and 1913'.[67] Out of two hundred or so, just over fifty figure under the heading 'Missionaries'. The largest number, thirty, had gone to India; China and the Middle East follow with eight apiece, Japan and Africa with four; one, a Dutch student, had gone to Java and another, with her husband, to South America. Several more, including some prevented by domestic ties from going overseas, are known to have worked in various capacities for Missionary Societies at their home base.

There can be little doubt that in proportion to its numbers — and perhaps absolutely — Westfield produced more missionaries during the first thirty years of its existence than any other college of comparable standing. The expectations of Miss Dudin Brown were thus fulfilled. But a greater number by far entered the teaching profession: some in order to prepare for missionary service, but the majority with no such evident intention. Miss Maynard looked on her schoolteachers at home and in the colonies with as much pride as on her missionaries proper. In some ways she prized them more, as the extension of her own mission to the 'world of Education'. Out of her desire to see trained minds, backed by a sincere and well-instructed faith, at work in the places where they could exert the greatest influence, Miss Maynard openly encouraged her students to aim at Headships and helped them on their way with sound advice: 'Dear friends, ...do *not* stay too long in one school.... Two

WESTFIELD COLLEGE
(UNIVERSITY OF LONDON).

Classified List of Public or Professional Workers who were Students at the College between its foundation in 1882 and the year 1913. MISTRESS (1882 to 1913) MISS CONSTANCE L. MAYNARD (Mor. Sci. Trip. Cam.) The Names of deceased Students are printed in Italics.

MISSIONARIES.

HEAD MISTRESSES.
K. A. S. Tristram, B.A., C.M.S., Bishop Poole Memorial School, Osaka, Japan.
G. M. Walford, C.M.S., Sarah Tucker School, Palamcottah, India (1910-1916).
M. Price, C.E.Z.M.S., Girls' School, Quetta, Baluchistan.
B. S. Fowler, C.M.S., St. John's School, Agra.
M. S. Impey, B.A., F.F.M.A., Friends' Girls' Boarding School, Tungchwan, West China (1916-1921).
R. Mosscrop, B.A., Girls' Schools, Jaffna and Barrakpur (1903-1909).
A. E. Leslie, M.A. (Durham) (Mrs. Marshall Fox), F.F.M.A., Girls' School, Brumana, Syria (1899-1914).
W. A. Coate, B.A., C.M.S., Girls' School, Cairo.
O. C. Cocks, B.A., C.M.S., Acting-Principal, Alexandra High School, Amritsar.
W. L. Crabbe, B.A., C.E.Z.M.S., Girls' School, Kutien, Futien, South China.

COLLEGE LECTURERS.
A. R. Brutton, Lady Muir Training College for Teachers, Allahabad.
W. M. Fisher, B.A., Lecturer in History, Women's Christian College, Madras (1915-1920).

MEDICAL MISSIONARIES.
J. Lamb, M.B., B.S. (Lond.), C.E.Z.M.S., St. Catherine's Hospital, Amritsar.
M. Townsend, M.B., B.S. (Lond.), (Mrs. M. E. Wigram), C.M.S., Bannu, India.
R. H. Western, M.D., B.S. (Lond.), Kangra, Punjaub.
S. E. Hill, M.B., B.S. (Lond.), C.M.S., Baghdad (1911-1915).
E. M. Lea-Wilson, L.R.C.P. & S. (Mrs. Saywell), Z.B.M.M., Nasik, India (1904-1914)

ASSISTANT MISTRESSES IN SCHOOLS.
D. Stubbs, B.A., C.M.S., Girls' School, Foo-Chow, China.
L. Grubb, B.A.(Mrs. O. Hodgkin), F.F.M.A.,Tananarive, Madagascar (retired 1922).
C. Bryant, B.A., C.M.S., Women's Normal School, Foo-Chow, China.
A. W. Jemmett, B.Sc., S.P.G., St. Margaret's School for Girls, Ranchi, Behar.
J. I. Holland, B.A., C.M.S., Girls' School, Cairo.
B. M. Davis, B.A., Sarah Tucker College and Blind School, Palamcottah, India, (1914-1918).
I. Stephens, B.Sc. (Mrs. W. A. Stephens), Z.B.M.M. Manmad (1913-1918).
M. C. Sanctuary, B.A., S.P.G., English Lecturer, Queen Mary's School, Delhi.
E. M. Pearson (Mrs. Williams), C.M.S., Girls' School, Foo Chow, China (1912-1923).
M. Miyagawa (Mrs. Shinahara), Doshisha School, Japan (1915-1920).
F. M. Bickersteth, B.A., C.M.S., Queen Victoria High School, Agra.
E. Boothby, B.A., Universities Mission, Rhodesia (1914-1920).
M. P. Naish, B.A., F.F.M.A., Chungking, West China (1915-1920).
C. Gunning, Dutch Mission, Soekaboemi, Java.
E. Snowdon Smith (Mrs. Langdale-Smith) C.M.S. Emmanuel School, Bombay (1916-1922).
D. E. Olliff B.A. (Mrs. Gorrie) S.P.G., Cathedral High School, Lahore (1918-1921).
E. M. Mulholland, B.Sc., C.M.S., Girls' School, Foo Chow, China.
E. M. Ecroyd, F.F.M.A., Girls' School, Brumana, Syria (1916-1922), Trade School, Beirut.
M. A. Johnston, British Syrian Girls' School, Beirut.

OTHER MISSIONARIES.
M. G. Brooke (Mrs. Graham Wilmot Brooke), C.M.S., Niger Mission (1890-1892).
E. S. Fox, (Mrs. Elwin), C.M.S., Chinese Women Students' Hostel, Tokio (1900-1923).
A. M. Naish, B.A., Dobnavur, South India.
H. Newman, B.A., S.P.G., St. Hilda's Mission, Tokio (Retired).
C. L. Robertson, Gopal Ganj, Saran District, Punjaub.
M. E. Barker, C.E.Z.M.S., Palamcottah, South India.
E. P. Miller, B.A., Kano, West Africa.
M. L. Everard, C.M.S., Sierra Leone (1905-1914).
K. M. Strong, B.A., C.M.S., British Syrian Mission, Damascus.
L. M. Soltau, B.A. (Mrs. Cuthbert), U.F.C. Mission, Rajputana.
F. B. Hoyte, B.Sc. (Mrs. Lyle), I.P.M., Gogha, Kathiawar, India.
D. Holmes (Mrs. Rodwell), F.F.M.A., Tungchwan, China.
E. M. Kitching, B.Sc., M.S.U.W., Bombay.
H. de N. Walker, Y.W.C.A., Madras (1919-1922).
D. Turner, Nurse, C.M.B., B.M.S., Lady Hardinge Hospital, Dholpur, Rajputana.
H. R. Bradley, Nurse, B.M.S., Palwal, India.
G. Barbour (Mrs. Mathewson), B.M.S., Palwal, India.
F. E. Newton, F.R.G.S., Haifa, Palestine (1903-1919).
E. M. R. Swain, B.A. (Mrs. St. John), South America (1916-1919).

years is rather short — "Why did she leave? etc.," — three years is ideal and four tends to be a waste of your youth. The point is to get experience. The first post is always very hard (and necessarily), the second should be higher, a Second Mistress, or a Head of Department, or charge of a House,....and the third should be the HM or something very like it. Every profession is open at the *top*, and I love to see my people climbing there.'[68]

By the time Miss Maynard retired in 1913 a dozen or so had reached 'the top' and several more would shortly do so. Most had become the Head of a private school or of schools on a religious foundation such as the Quakers' Mount School at York, of which Winifred Sturge (entered Westfield 1887) had been Head since 1893. But the appointment in 1912 of Emma Hart (entered Westfield 1896) as Head of Hanson Girls' Secondary School in Bradford and in 1914 of Lucy Hall (entered Westfield 1893) as Head of Pontefract and District Girls' High School broke new ground, these being schools established in the wake of the Education Act of 1902, which was the first to bring secondary schooling within the scope of the public provision.

New entrants to teaching made up about a half of each year's graduands. They spread themselves over a wider variety of establishments than their seniors, going not only to places which already had Westfield connections but also into Elementary Schools, Pupil Teacher Centres and Teacher Training Colleges. The favourable impression made by Westfield graduates is shown by a remark once made to Miss Maynard by Mrs Eliza Woodhouse, Headmistress of Clapham High School (GPDST): 'Assistant Mistresses from other good colleges work hard to make their own departments a success but Westfield students work hard to make the whole school a success'.[69] That is not to say that specialist teachers were not in demand, especially for Science: as Miss Maynard noted in 1906, 'all England seems to have a taste for it just now'.[70] Westfield graduates, schooled in Miss Maynard's Bible Classes, had the further merit that they could usually be relied on to teach Scripture, a subject already causing concern

and in which few teachers had received any specialised preparation.

One or two in each year took up social work — in Settlements, with the Church Army, in Children's Homes — in a paid or voluntary capacity. But it appears that the only one to obtain a professional qualification was Eleanor Green (entered Westfield 1902) who, taking advantage of a new opening for educated women, trained as a Hospital Almoner. Exceptional in a different way were the very few who ventured outside the categories so far enumerated: for example, the student who threw up her scholarship to go on the stage (with no recorded success) and Gwendolyn Thomson (entered Westfield 1911) who as Astra Desmond was to have a most distinguished career as a mezzo-soprano.

Well under half of those who entered the College between 1882 and 1913 eventually married, the proportion in the second and third decades being somewhat higher than in the first. In 1908 Miss Maynard reckoned that out of 335 former students 62 were married and had between them produced 65 children (almost certainly an underestimate on both counts).[71] From the marriage announcements published in *Hermes* it is clear that few students rushed into matrimony straight from College: but whether the interval was short or long, Miss Maynard was likely to be present at the wedding.

In Miss Maynard's own evaluation, her five hundred students (with many of whom she continued to correspond and to exchange visits long after she had retired) represented the major fruit of her life's work: it saddened her, therefore, to have to confess that nowhere among them, or even on her staff, could she see a possible successor to herself.[72]

Miss Maynard announced her impending retirement to the Council in October 1912, just under a year before the date, September 1913, when she intended it to take effect. It was decided not to advertise. Instead the subcommittee set up to deal with the appointment, of which Miss Maynard was a non-voting member, would take steps 'to hear of desirable candidates'. The qualities looked for were: a degree or its equivalent; the 'right tone of Churchmanship'; personality; and 'power and experience of organisation', all to be embodied, in Miss Maynard's arresting image, in 'an angel in cap and gown descending from the sky'.

Agnes de Sélincourt* was already known at Westfield. She had been Dr Skeel's contemporary at Notting Hill High School, GPDST, and afterwards at Girton; whilst still an undergraduate she had visited Westfield on behalf of the Student Volunteer Missionary Union;[74] and in recent years she had become closely acquainted with Miss Richardson. More important, Miss de Sélincourt was both a scholar, reputedly with a working knowledge of fourteen languages, and a missionary. Not long after graduation she had helped to found the Bombay Missionary Settlement for University Women and she had served subsequently as Principal (the first) of the Lady Muir Memorial College, Allahabad. Invalided home from

Miss de Sélincourt in 1917.

India in 1909, Miss de Sélincourt had been appointed to a senior position in the SCM (as Secretary of the SVMU) and was thus currently in contact with English students. Just turned forty, she was of an appropriate age.

So acceptable was Miss de Sélincourt to the selection subcommittee that on 20 December she was seen by Miss Dudin Brown, whose consent was required under the terms of the Trust Deed. The Foundress was well satisfied. Since Miss de Sélincourt had already agreed, though not without some initial hesitation, to accept nomination, the formalities could be completed without further delay. On the evening of 9 February 1913, following the second of the two Council meetings needed to ratify the appointment, Miss Maynard was able to tell the students that the College had a Principal-elect.

Sadly, Miss Maynard was robbed by a passing illness of the delights of her final summer term. But although obliged to be absent from the Banquet, she was able to attend her farewell parties and receive in person the splendid parting gift of £800, which she immediately handed over to form the nucleus of a fund for needy students. For her last Bible Class she took the subject she had chosen for her first, the Parable of the Sower.

It is a truism to say that without Constance Maynard there would have been no Westfield. The uniqueness she ascribed to herself — in no spirit of boasting — was linked in her mind with the 'peculiarities' of her upbringing and temperament. The three causes to which she dedicated Westfield — vital religion, intellectual endeavour and feminine independence — were matched in her own life by the strong emotional attachment to Evangelical beliefs and Puritanical ways implanted during her childhood and the countervailing longing for intellectual and personal freedom which impelled her to break loose. Her vision of Westfield was of a place where these forces would come together in fruitful interaction. The balance she aimed at was so delicate that outsiders were apt to miss the point, as did the Headmistress who dismissed Westfield as 'all cant and prayer meetings'. Even those most closely involved tended to fix on one aspect to the detriment of the rest. The Council, long dominated by Evangelicals of the fundamentalist type against whom Constance Maynard continued inwardly to rebel, were unsympathetic towards any application of the 'Higher Criticism' to the study of the Bible.[75] The teaching staff showed greater understanding but sometimes distressed Miss Maynard by too patent a wish to make Westfield 'just like other Colleges'. The Mistress did not waver, but she was

'daughters' or 'nieces' with a warm embrace. She was remembered as 'approachable, kind and understanding' and she succeeded, for all her private misery, in making Westfield a conspicuously happy place: 'No one scolded, no one sneered....Pious, it did not insist that you should be pious; in effect a place where all the world appeared to be friends.'[77]

Although short and in later years quite stout, the Mistress bore herself with great dig-

Left: cover executed by the Mistress for her set of farewell verses. Above: one of her Ring letters.

acutely concious of being alone; for years she lived under a heavy cloud of depression, the full extent of which she confided only to her diaries.[76]

The side of herself the Mistress showed to her students was much sunnier. Newcomers would be greeted on the steps of the Old House with the eager question, 'Which are you?' followed in the case of Westfield

nity. The portrait of her, commissioned by the Old Students from George Joy to celebrate the College's coming of age and which now hangs in the Entrance Hall, shows the Mistress in her 'preaching dress' and accompanied by carefully chosen attributes: her red Greek testament, the dress-watch which timed her Bible Classes, the Westfield honeysuckle, the carved chair presented by Dr Barlow,[78] which is still part of the hall furniture in the original Kidderpore Hall (Old House). But the result, while it satisfied the sitter, did not please Miss Richardson: 'the slight, stiffly poised figure with so correct and elegant an air as might suit the conventional Head of a private school of seventy years ago' (she was writing c 1925) seemed to her to contain 'little or nothing to represent the strength and character of the Mistress.'[79]

Half in self-reproach, but also half in pride, Miss Maynard acknowledged that she had never bestirred herself to seek for the College 'money and position'. It is true that the circle of benefactors widened by only a little during Miss Maynard's time; and it was also true that the financial margin remained uncomfortably narrow. The fees, which had stayed unchanged, now had to support increasing expenditure on tuition, books and equipment: the amounts required were small, but large enough to make it essential that all sixty places were occupied. This last requirement was fortunately becoming much easier to meet, as the number of suitable applicants began regularly to exceed the number of places: although it was deflating for Miss Maynard to be told in 1907 by Mrs Sidgwick of Newnham that 'Every College was full just now, because times were better'.[80]

'Position', whether or not Miss Maynard consciously sought it, had in fact been achieved. In 1913 the educational and academic world was represented on the Council by two distinguished Headmistresses, Mrs Woodhouse and Miss Gray (who in 1904 had become the first High Mistress of St Paul's School for Girls), and a notable Oxford scholar, Dr A.J. Carlyle. The retirement in 1907 of Dr Barlow, the last surviver of Miss Dudin Brown's origional trio of clerical advisers, had brought into the Chair of the most eminent layman yet to serve on the Council, the Lord Chief Justice, Lord Alverstone.* In the University of London the Mistress naturally took her place beside other Heads of Schools and Institutions at public ceremonies and in 1907, somewhat to the astonishment of her Council, she joined an official delegation on a visit to Paris. Moreover dignitaries of the University came to add their weight to Westfield's own public occasions: the first Principal, Sir Alfred Rücker, was present at two ceremonies connected with the building of the Library wing and publicly congratulated the College as the first School to add to its provision for Arts.

When Miss Maynard became Mistress of Westfield, women's colleges were still in their heroic age; when she retired, more than thirty years later, they were an established part of the higher educational scene. She deserves to be remembered, and not only at Westfield, as one who demonstrated the capacity of wo-

Lord Alverstone, Lord Chief Justice of England 1900-1913, and Chairman of Westfield College Council 1907-1915.

men to govern. With little in the way of precedent or example to guide her, she was conscious in the early years of making many mistakes; indeed, it was only on her sixtieth birthday that she felt herself complete mistress of her 'complex profession'. She made no mistake in her resolve 'not to go near the College' whilst Miss de Sélincourt was finding her feet. 'When you leave a thing,' she wrote to her Old Students, 'never try to touch it afterwards...but set to work only on the part you do not say Goodbye to; and I have a goodly heritage.'

Notes
&
references

1 CLM Diary, April 1981.

2 Member of Council 1890-1927.

3 Miss Maynard often refers to Miss Metcalfe in such terms. Highfield, the school kept by Miss Metcalfe and her sister occupied a large part of what is now Golders Green Road. It was clearly a more luxurious establishment than Westfield aspired to be: 'all grandeur and collies...and soft carpets', was Miss Maynard's description after a visit in January 1889.

4 Miss Smee was later to serve as Chairman of Acton District Council and as Mayor of Acton. She was the first woman to be appointed JP in Middlesex and the first to be Chairman of Acton Juvenile Court. For her reply to the Toast to the Council, see *Hermes*, (the College magazine), April 1912, p 4.

5 The first issue is dated July 1892 but it had been preceded by handwritten numbers, from which the editors made their selection for the first printed version. Thereafter two issues appeared each year.

6 The rental of the hockey field (at Childs Hill, shared with South Hampstead High School, and subsequently at Golders Hill) was met chiefly from subscriptions. *Hermes*, January 1896 and March 1897.

7 A College 'ribbon' distinct in pattern from the tennis colours is referred to in *Hermes*, July 1893: ties are first mentioned in *Hermes*, October 1899. Irene Biss (at Westfield 1907-1911) recalled an incident on a bus in which an unknown gentleman, who turned out to be a member of the Council, identified her as a Westfield student from her blazer and hat band. Irene Biss, 'Reminiscences of Westfield College' c 1970. Typescript, Westfield College Archives.

8 Council Minutes, November 1895; the rules were published in *Hermes*, January 1896 and (the rule against coasting) January 1898. Miss Maynard reported Miss Dudin Brown's view to Old Students in a Budget Letter 22.1.1896. Her own cycling exploits are copiously recorded in Vacation Diaries: in 1896 she covered 2060 miles.

9 The date at which JPs and Orderlies were introduced is referred to in *Hermes*, July 1894.

10 First referred to in an entry CLM Diary, October 1891, where it is recorded that a party of students went to observe the rescue practices conducted by Captain John Shaw of the London Fire Brigade. At one time every student was expected to serve for at least one term in the Brigade but from 1897 it was composed solely of volunteers with a lecturer, Miss LJ Whitby, as permanent Captain: *Hermes*, January 1895 and September 1897. Purchase of equipment: Council Minutes, 3.1.1892.

11 Provision of a safer form of lighting was first discussed by Council in February 1895 but a start was made only following a second, less serious lamp accident, later that year: Council Minutes, February and December 1895. Once provided with electricity, the students were forbidden to use oil lamps or candles. However, since the current was switched off at 10.30 (for economy) this ruling was often disobeyed; it was therefore left on and students 'put on their honour' not to use the light after 11pm except in case of illness. Council Minutes, February 1896.

12 Illustrated by a conducted tour of the plumbing: *Hermes*, January 1895.

13 The Social Club is first mentioned in *Hermes*, October 1899, in a way which suggests it had been in existence for some time. Margaret Bondfield's visit is reported in *Hermes*, October 1901. The article on her, by M Miliband, in ed. J Bellamy and J Saville, *Dictionary of Labour Biography*, II (1974), notes her 'strong religious faith' (Congregationalist) and teetotalism.

14 Factory girls had also been entertained, in a field at Childs Hill, in Maresfield Gardens days.

15 *Hermes*, January 1896: 'It is pleasant to read in the daily papers that "Westfield College" heads the list and to see the faces of some of our new BAs meeting us in the pages of the *Lady's Pictorial*'.

16 Evelyn Savidge (Mrs Lees), who took Cl I Hons. in History in 1900, the first year in which Westfield entered candidates, was awarded the University's Derby Prize for an essay on Public Opinion, printed in *Hermes*, March 1901.

17 CLM Diary, November 1891.

18 CLM Diary, February 1891. Miss Willoughby further deserves to be remembered as organiser

of an annual river picnic for Matriculation candidates to which her fiancé brought some of his fellow medical students.

19 Student 1888-1892; BA Hons Classics and German; Gilchrist Prize Medal. Resigned her Lectureship in 1898 on appointment as Lady Tutor, Durham College of Science, Newcastle-on-Tyne. Subsequently took up social work.

20 Copies are preserved in the Westfield College Archives (Skeel Papers), along with a letter from Mrs Montagu Butler (Agnata Frances Ramsay, wife of the Master of Trinity) referring to Caroline Skeel's second success, in the Historical Tripos, as 'the honour of the year' (17.6.1895).

21 The full text of this letter is given in Council Minutes, 19 May 1899. The signatories were: A W Richardson, M T Beloe, L J Whitby, M H Ross (Miss Simey's successor: left to be married same year), F Strudwick. Visiting Staff were said to be in agreement but had not signed for lack of time. The Council did not withdraw their proposal; but there is no evidence that it was implemented.

22 Text of the subsequent correspondence: Council Minutes, 14 June 1899.

23 Council Minutes, 9 March 1898. The surviving minutes of the Education Committee start only in May 1900, but its earlier proceedings can be followed in the reports it presented to the Council.

24 No Minutes survive before May 1903.

25 Matthew Arnold, *Schools and Universities on the Continent*, ed RH Super, 1964, p 319.

26 University of London, *The Historical Record (1836 1912), being a Supplement to the Calendar*, 1912, p 9.

27 *Ibid*, p 12.

28 H Hale Bellot, *The University of London. A History*, 1969, p.8. (Reprint of article in *Victoria County History, Middlesex* Vol I, 1969).

29 T L Humberstone, *University Reform in London*, 1926, p 48.

30 Printed in full in *The Historical Record* cited n 26.

31 In 1892, when the Gresham Commission was appointed, no one at Westfield was in touch with University affairs. From the time the Commission reported in 1894 there is evidence of increasing interest at Westfield in the reconstitution of the University (articles in *Hermes*, references in speeches at the Banquet, mentions in the Council Minutes) but efforts to attract the attention of the Statutory Commissioners proved unavailing.

32 Text in full in minutes of a special meeting of the Council 5 April 1900.

33 University of London *Calendar* 1901-1902, for the following year shows that two further Lecturers, both Non-Resident, had secured recognition: Miss M Alford, Classics, and Miss K Warren, English.

34 A copy of this application is preserved in the Westfield College Archives.

35 Council Minutes, 10 July 1901.

36 In French: Dr Louis Brandin, of University College; in German, Professor Henry Atkins, of King's College. No Recognised Teacher was appointed for Science.

37 The preceding correspondence (June 1902), which is preserved in the College Archives, shows that the University first had to be satisfied that the College Council intended to make a recurrent annual grant for library books of not less than £50. For reception of the news by telegram see *Hermes*, October 1902. The immediate rejoicing was muted by public anxiety over the illness of King Edward VII which had delayed his coronation.

38 Council Minutes, 9 July 1902.

39 Miss Maynard was away from February to September 1900, visiting Egypt, the Holy Land and Switzerland; she was granted a second, shorter leave in 1910, which she spent in Canada. On both occasions her place was taken by Miss Richardson, who in 1895 had been given the title Senior Lecturer.

40 The members of the Council most active in the affair were Dr Barlow, Lady Chapman, Dr Wace and, from his appointment to the Council in January 1901, Dr A Robertson, Wace's successor at King's — in effect the Education Committee; as instructed by the Council; 5 April 1900, they worked 'in close communication with the Educational Board'. The Mistress of course took her share, even to the extent of once allowing University affairs to intrude on the sacredness of Sunday: CLM Diary, 24 March 1901.

41   *Hermes*, October 1900.

42   The letter (copy in the College Archives) was sent from St Andrews where all six signatories (AS Abernethy, H Wenham, A B Pearce, E F M Moor, HM Smith and H Borthwick) were working as school teachers; Miss Gray, although not entitled to sign herself, is known to have been closely involved. The writers express dismay at a possible consequence of the exclusion − 'the degradation of our college to the position of a hall of residence for external students' − and continue: 'We could not conscientiously recommend that our pupils...should (after this change comes into operation) enter Westfield with a view to obtaining such scholastic qualifications as earn for women places in the best schools and other good posts in the educational world.'

43   College *Annual Report* 1902: 'largest gift to date.' For the beginnings of the WCA see *Hermes*, 1951-2, pp. 20-22, from which it is clear that the initiative was indeed Miss Gray's.

44   Miss Maynard's description: Budget Letter, 20.10.1902.

45   The distribution of subjects taken by Honours BA Finalists 1905-1914 was as follows (number of First Classes in brackets):
Classics 23 (2); History 21 (5); English 14; French 8 (6); Mathematics 2 (1). Efforts to provide Honours teaching in Philosophy appear to have petered out. German, although taught for the Intermediate, was not an Honours School at Westfield.

46   Miss McDougall graduated with First Class Hons. in Classics in 1896. Immediately before coming to Westfield she had been Head of Classics at Bedford High School. She was the first Westfield lecturer to give an inter-collegiate course, on Myths and Cults at University College. Subsequently (1915-1938) Principal − the first − of Women's Christian College, Madras.

47   Recollections of (i) Mrs de Vere (IC Moule, entered Westfield 1903), letter to Ring 6 of the Budget c 1956; (ii) Margaret E Popham (entered 1914, subsequently Principal Cheltenham Ladies' College), *Boring? Never!* (autobiography), 1968, p.26.

48   Honours Lit Hum, (Somerville) 1901; Assistant Lecturer in Greek, Bedford College 1902-1906; Classical Lecturer Westfield 1906-1936. As well as being able to call on Miss Richardson, the Classics department had two Non-Resident Lecturers: Miss Margaret Alford (from 1904 also Head of Latin at Bedford) and the Reverend J W Coke Norris, a master at Harrow.

49   Ellen Annette McArthur: Historical Tripos Cl I, 1885; Litt D (TCD) 1905; Lecturer in History at Girton 1887-1907; FRHS and Vice-President in 1906.

Alice Sergeant (afterwards Mrs Henderson) obtained Hons in Modern History at Oxford and in the same year (1905) was awarded the London BA (External). She left Westfield in 1917 on appointment as inspector to the Indian Educational Service.

50   Miss Paquier lectured at Westfield 1899-1913, taking over as head of French on securing Recognised Teacher status in 1902. She resigned to become full-time at East London College.

Miss Warren lectured at Westfield 1898-1926: she was granted Recognised Teacher status in 1902 and in 1920 became Reader. Miss Warren had a succession of young assistants who specialised in the language work. Neither she nor Miss Paquier appear to have been graduates.

51   Educational Board Minutes, 24 November 1905 and 29 January 1906.

52   Much of the material in this and the succeeding paragraph is taken from the two unpublished memoirs by Dr Delf Smith written c 1969-70: 'Reminiscences of Westfield College mainly 1906-1914' and 'Botany at Westfield 1906-1948'. Although compiled so long afterwards and erroneous on points of detail, these accounts are invaluable first-hand testimony and can be supplemented from contemporaneous articles published in *Hermes* − eg, 'The Botanical Work of the College', March 1909.

53   E M Delf, 'Transpiration and Stomatal Behaviour in Halophytes', *Annals of Botany*, April 1911. A M Maybrook, 'Note on the Biology of Fegatella Conica', *New Phytologist*, vol 13, 1914.

54   *Hermes*, October 1904.

55   CLM Budget Letters, May 1904 and October 1905.

56   *Annual Report*, 1903, 1904; the anonymous donor was Miss Priscilla Hannah Peckover of Wisbech, aunt of a former student.

57   Donation to the 'south wing': *Annual Report*, 1908, p 17, where reference is also made to Miss Dudin Brown's assistance in paying off a mortage of £6,000 taken out in 1890-91 to

help finance the 'New Westfield'.

58 These Scholarships were administered by County and Borough Technical Instruction Committees (set up in 1889). Those awarded to university students were given principally for Science.

59 *Annual Report* 1903: 'Non-resident students can enter for single courses or for a complete University course. In either case they have full use of the Library, Common Room and garden and may join the College Clubs and Societies'.

60 Proportion as stated in the Report of University of London Inspectors who visited the College November 1909.

61 Reminiscences contributed 1976 by Mrs Lyle (F B Hoyte, entered Westfield 1906).

62 *Hermes*, March 1905 and 14 October 1912.

63 *Hermes*, October 1909; Dr McArthur's paper was published in the October 1909 issue of the *English Historical Review*.

64 CLM Budget Letter, 30 June 1908.

65 Details are given in Tissington Tatlow, *The Story of the Student Christian Movement*, 1933.

66 CLM Autobiography, (July 1893), p 326.

67 A circular was sent to Old Students in 1912 (Education Committee Minutes 14.11.1912). The list as we have it seems to be an updated version since it mentions appointments obtained well after 1912-1913, which for present purposes have been left out of account. Also extant is an earlier list, dated 1908, headed: 'Classified List of Past Students who engaged in Public or Professional Work'. Neither list is exhaustive.

68 CLM Budget Letter, July 1911.

69 CLM Budget Letter, October 1907.

70 CLM Budget Letter, September 1906.

71 Handwritten addition to 1908 List referred to n 67.

62 CLM Green Book, 18 March 1910. Miss Richardson, who was a Quaker, was excluded under the terms of the Trust Deed.

73 Council Minutes 14 November 1912 (follows report of December meeting) and CLM Green Book, 21 November 1912.

74 For the first time in October 1893.

75 These criticisms were most accute in respect of Miss Maynard's attempt (1901-1907) to set up a 'Divinity Faculty' at Westfield, references to which are to be found *passim* in the Council Minutes of the period, in Miss Maynard's Diaries, and in a special notebook, 'Westfield College Divinity Faculty'.

76 She had added to her burdens by the adoption in 1887 of the six-year old 'Effie', whose sad story is well told by C B Firth, *Constance Maynard*, chapter 10.

77 Mary Butts, *The Crystal Cabinet*, 1937, p 252. This tribute is the more remarkable in that the author (Mrs Rodka: entered Westfield 1909) was made to leave in consequence of a foolish piece of deception. A young non-resident lecturer who was implicated had her appointment terminated. The affair is referred to in E.M. Delf Smith, 'Westfield College ... 1906-1914'. (See n 52 above).

78 CLM Budget Letter, May 1903.

79 A W Richardson, 'Notes on the History of Westfield College', p 34.

80 CLM Vacation Diary, September 1907.

CHAPTER 4 'WE MUST ADVANCE, WE MUST EXPAND' 1913~1919

In her presidential letter to the members of the Westfield College Association dated January 1914, Lady Chapman reported: 'The first term under Miss de Sélincourt has passed most happily, and.... the transition from one regime to another has been carried out with the minimum of strain and difficulty'. But the equally happy future which Lady Chapman went on to predict was to be cut cruelly short. Appointed in 1913, Miss de Sélincourt had been in office less than a year when the horizon was darkened by the outbreak of the war: she died suddenly in

Miss Agnes de Sélincourt, Principal of the College from 1913-1917.

1917, and so did not live to see the return to more settled conditions. Yet although her time was so brief, and the circumstances seemingly so unpropitious, Miss de Sélincourt carried the College decisively forward in the spirit of her own injunction, 'We must advance, we must expand', and the momentum did not slacken during the nearly two years of interregnum which followed her unexpected death. This chapter therefore continues beyond that tragic event to the year 1919, which saw not only the appointment of Miss de Sélincourt's successor, but also the accomplishment of certain changes to the College's constitution which Miss de Sélincourt believed to be essential if Westfield was to 'live and prosper'.

Miss de Sélincourt remained loyal in all fundamental respects to the objectives for Westfield she inherited from Miss Maynard. But her ways of attaining them were different. Instead of shunning publicity for the College,

she courted it and was quick to seize on ideas for making Westfield, its achievements, and even its where-abouts, better known: within a year of her arrival notices of scholarship awards and other distinctions were being sent regularly to the press, direction boards had been posted at the turnings off the Finchley Road and the College's first illustrated prospectus (as distinct from the Calendar or Annual Report), was in preparation.[1]

As a way of enhancing the reputation of the College with the local as well as with the academic community, Miss de Sélincourt introduced a series of public lectures. The first lecture each year was advertised as an 'Inaugural Lecture', on the model of similar lectures given at other London colleges at the start of the session: in October 1913 the lecturer at Westfield was the Dean of St Paul's, Dr W R Inge, who took as his title 'Liberal Education: ideals and possibilities.' There were also contributions from inside the College, Dr Skeel speaking on 'Hampstead in the eighteenth century' and Dr Delf on the history of Botany. In some years the programme was built up around a particular theme, as in 1916-1917 when eminent historians were invited to speak on topics connected with the war and its probable after-effects.

The students, as they became accustomed to the occasional presence in College of well-known scholars and public figures, were emboldened to invite speakers of comparable standing to address the meetings of their societies. Thus in the first three years of its life the English Club, founded in 1913, otherwise known as The English Adventurers, was addressed in turn by J W Mackail (civil servant, classicist, and biographer of William Morris), Professor WP Ker,* and Edmund Gosse, man of letters, who treated his audience to a 'Causerie'.

In one of her few early breaches with established Westfield tradition, Miss de Sélincourt invited professional theologians to deliver some of the Divinity Lectures which she had substituted for Miss Maynard's weekly Bible Classes.[2] The first to give such a course, in the Lent term of 1915, was an old friend of the College, Tissington Tatlow. The next was William Temple,* whose six lectures on St Mark's Gospel in February 1916 made a deep impression on his hearers. Temple, although a new friend (but an old acquaintance of Miss de Sélincourt's, with whom he had worked in the Student Christian Movement), was already a familiar figure at Westfield. He had joined the Council in September 1914, and at the time he gave his Divinity course had just become its Chairman.

Miss de Sélincourt's idea of the dignity due to the College comes out most clearly in her decision to convert the annual garden party into a more ceremonious occasion. Commemoration Day, as it came to be called, was first observed in June 1916 and was soon acknowleged as the high point in the College year. The programme began with speeches (from the Chairman for the day, when possible the reigning Vice-Chancellor, from the Chairman of the Council, from the Principal, and from a Guest of Honour — one of the first was Dame Millicent Fawcett, leader of the non-militants in the campaign for women's suffrage), and concluded, after an interval for refreshment which preserved something of the garden party atmosphere, with a service, held at first in the neighbouring St Luke's and after 1929 in the College Chapel.

Although the first Commemoration Day anticipated only in its essentials the grander occasions of the postwar years, that it could happen at all is a reminder that during the 1914-1918 war it was possible for women's

colleges to carry on more or less normally. There is a hint that at Westfield, which contained a strong Quaker element, relations between those with pronounced pacifist tendencies, of whom Miss de Sélincourt, although not a Quaker, was one, and the rest, were not always easy.[3] The 'War Club' formed by Miss Sergeant, one of the History lecturers, in which 'thinking' and 'doing' were equally encouraged, was perhaps an effort to reduce the tension. The 'thinking' was directed towards the problems of postwar reconstruction, the 'doing' consisted of fruit-picking and other land work during the vacations, sweeping snow from the streets of Hampstead to earn money for the Red Cross, the despatch of letters and parcels to prisoners of war, and other such activity.[4] On graduating several students took work connected directly or indirectly with the war, and so added to the number of former Westfield students already serving as nurses, canteen organisers, relief workers with 'distressed aliens' or as replacements for men in Civil Service and other positions.

The College buildings suffered no damage from aerial bombardment, although the threat of it was real enough for zeppelin drills to be

---

❝ We never had any bombs very near, but used to pick up bits of shrapnel on the hard tennis courts after a raid . . . on the occasion of the first daylight raid, when bombs were dropped on Piccadilly Circus . . . we stood on the steps and watched the planes go over until we were hustled down into a boiler-room . . . ❞

Recalled by BM Baylis (1916) in 1976.

---

instituted alongside fire practices. Shortages and soaring prices made it essential to economise on fuel, light, and food; and to save labour, also scarce, some of the homely customs which still survived from Maresfield Gardens days (late evening trays, for example) had to be abandoned. No doubt there were grumbles, but the general impression is of a contented household, the credit for which belonged in large measure to Miss Roberta Black, appointed in 1913 to take charge of domestic affairs. Miss Black's experience, gained in posts at Bedford College and as Lady Superintendent of a Training College in Salisbury, differentiated her so markedly from the former housekeepers that Miss de Sélincourt insisted on a change in title to that of Bursar. Miss Black fed the College in wartime, nursed it through the serious influenza epidemic of 1918 (in which the house-boy died), and had the satisfaction, before she retired in 1928, of seeing the kitchens enlarged and improved. Miss Black's practical efficiency was united with a warmth of personality which made her 'beloved by many generations'.

Academic performance was not adversely affected by wartime conditions. The 'very studious' atmosphere in College reported by Miss Whitby[5] in 1915 is perhaps to be connected with the drop to zero in the number of failures, which in prewar years had averaged between three and four.[6] The only new development was the recognition of the Botanical laboratory for Honours work, which meant that from October 1915 it was possible for Westfield students to sit for the Honours B Sc as internal students. At the same time, the Council agreed to allocate another two rooms to Botany (both very small and known collectively as the 'horse box'), and in this way managed to satisfy the requirements set by the University for the teaching of research students. Dr Delf, around whom the department had been built up, had meanwhile resigned her position on election to a research fellowship at Girton; and it was only through a combination of unforeseen events, amongst them the all too early death of her successor, Dr Ethel de Fraine, that Dr Delf returned to Westfield to take up the threads again in 1918.

It is hard to say whether the position of students taking Botany Honours was strengthened or weakened by the concentration of virtually all their teaching at Westfield. As a small minority in a predominantly Arts College, the Botany School was to stand out in the 1920s and 1930s as a remarkably cohesive, self-contained group, proud to be the sole representatives of a scientific discipline. But the lack of contact with other experimental sciences was felt by some to be a real deprivation, for which the presence at Westfield of a Mathematics School was at best a partial compensation.[7] In 1916, when there were still a few students taking External Honours in science subjects not taught at Westfield, the B Sc students joined forces to found a Science Club 'to promote interest in Science among members of Art Schools'. Sad to say, within a few years the secretary was lamenting in *Hermes* that the Club was not fulfilling its aim: out of twenty or so members, nearly all were scientists.[8]

Westfield's financial position, already giving concern in the years immediately preceding 1914, was very much worsened by the economic effects of the war. In 1908, recognising that even when the College was full the income from fees was insufficient 'to maintain the necessary standard of efficiency in instruction and equipment', the Council had launched an appeal for an Endowment Fund; although the initial response was good, the amount contributed by 1914 fell far short of the £25,000 which had been recommended by the University as the 'minimum required to effect a reasonable measure of financial security.'[9] More disturbing still, from 1909 onwards the annual accounts showed a steady rise in household expenditure, put down to 'the students larger appetites', but also to increases in the cost of basic provisions.[10] Deficits on the year's working were at first small enough to be covered by fees from the conferences organised at Westfield by bodies such as the Church Missionary Society, and by anonymous donations. For the year ending December 1913, however, the gap was too large to be bridged in these ways, and recourse was had to a bank loan.[11]

The outbreak of war nine months later was followed not only by a further steep rise in costs but also by a fall in fee income, for which the sudden withdrawal of half a dozen students was partly responsible. Suspecting that this exodus had a financial cause, and

Right: excerpts from the May 1918 economy "News-sheet".

Westfield College Magazine.

MAY, 1918.

VACATION LAND WORK.

During the Easter vacation, seven of us, including Miss Parker, went for a fortnight to Studley Agricultural College in Warwickshire. Our work consisted chiefly in digging round fruit-trees in the orchard, but also included sorting potatoes (a horrible task, too, when they are rotten !), digging up brussel sprouts, double-digging, making a new fence, thinning out radishes, and other odd jobs. We slept in the rooms of students who were away having their holiday, and were given board and lodging in return for our work.

There have been two squads from WESTFIELD this vacation working on the land, while many other students have been fruit picking and gardening near their own homes. Owing to urgent demands for strawberry-pickers, a party of five went at the beginning of July to Mrs. Bomford at Salford Priors near Evesham, where we have been now for three years in succession. J. M. Abbot helped with flax-pulling near Yeovil. On September 1st, a party of eight are going to Suckley near Worcester to pick damsons and apples.

M. K. WAKEFIELD (Corresponding Representative).

FLAX-PULLING.

During the long vacation I have been flax-pulling in Somerset. About ninety girls, mostly from London, came down, and we made our headquarters at Barwick House, an empty mansion about one and a half miles outside Yeovil. The house was quite unfurnished, and we slept in rows round the rooms on straw mattresses. All the rooms were named by their occupants, and one met Arcadia close to Pandemonium, while the occupants of the Sardine Box and the Hotel Cecil carried on conversations across the passage.

The first day we were there we were given a lecture on flax, and learned that one acre of flax makes wings for from three to three and a half acroplanes. On an average, given fair weather and a good field, one girl should pull from half to three quarters of an acre of flax in a week.

J. M. ABBOTT.

CAMBRIDGE.

As it was impossible for me to arrange to go with a party from Westfield, I spent three weeks of the summer vacation fruit picking at a village, well known for its orchards, six miles out of Cambridge.

The man I worked for was not a large fruit grower, but had a big orchard and several acres of market garden. I cycled out from Cambridge every morning to begin work about 9 o'clock, and reached home again between 9 and 10 p.m. I was paid 4d. an hour.

Most of the fruit was taken to one of Chivers' depôts in the village, or to the factory itself. Every evening at the depôt a long line of carts was drawn up, closely packed with large wooden tubs, and baskets full of fruit to be weighed and registered.

E. A. WOLSTENCROFT.

SUCKLEY.

When our party of eight arrived at the cottage in which we were to stay during our fruit picking, we found it in a state of chaos, with dust and cobwebs everywhere. By degrees we were able to make it a suitable abode for civilized people. We did all the housework besides fruit-picking.

We began work by finishing a plum orchard, and found the work slow and heavy. Four of us pulled about 770 lbs. of Victoria and Pershore plums on the first day, and five of us the next day pulled twice as much. We were paid 3d. for every 24lbs. which we picked into large baskets called " sieves."

Most of our fellow workers were hop pickers. At first we were rather afraid of them and their language, but we found that they were kind-hearted and amiable. When we were apple pulling later, we worked by the day (7 a.m. to 5.30 p.m.), with an hour off for dinner. We took our alarm clock to the orchard, and it was a great joy when we heard it at half past five when we could go home and have our supper.

Y. SKIDACHI.

fearing that it might be repeated as more and more parents found themselves in difficulties because of the war, the Council let it be known that reduced fees could be arranged 'in special circumstances',[12] and so succeeded in keeping the College full throughout the war years. This policy was no doubt a wise one, but in November 1915 the Council found itself impelled to increase its debt to the bank and to reactivate the Endowment Appeal, in abeyance since September 1914. To emphasise the urgency of the situation, contributions were also invited to a 'War Time Maintenance Fund', which by December 1916 had attracted well over £1000, enough to tide the College over its immediate difficulties, but leaving the main problem — the inadequacy of the fee income to meet essential expenditure — unsolved.[13]

Since there could be no immediate prospect of increasing the fees, the alternative was to take in more students, a solution which Miss de Sélincourt had favoured from the first. 'Kingswear', a house opposite the College and capable of accommodating another ten students, had been on the market for some time, but earlier efforts by the Principal to interest the Council in its purchase had failed: as well as lacking the funds, the Council were not convinced that expansion was either feasible or desirable. However when Sir Joseph Maclay, a Glasgow ship owner who had made a substantial contribution to the War Time

---

CYCLING ACCIDENT AT ROBIN HOOD'S BAY.

Lady Visitor Succumbs to Injuries.

Coroner's Inquest.

On the afternoon of Tuesday, a cycling accident occurred at Bay, when a lady visitor, to journing at the neighbour Ravenscar, received serious which she, unfortunately, s Friday afternoon last week. Miss Agnes de Sélincourt, pi Westfield University College returning to Ravenscar, and, ing the bank near the n at Robin Hood's Bay, overturned, the rider heavily to the road, serious injuries, which resul at the Convalescent Hom Whitby, to which instif quickly conveyed. Her injut to by Dr. J. G. Ross, withi accident. The deceased l educationalist, and had l Westfield College since 4! brilliant scholastic career, years she did excellent wc educational missionary, the Lady Muir Memorial Allahabad, from 1901 to 1 cited at Girton and Som obtained a first class modern languages tripos inquiry into the end circ ducted by Mr. George E at the Home, on Saturd Dowson was chosen fore the following evidence.

Professor Ernest de ham, said he was Profe guage and Literature versity, and brother of de Sélincourt. She years of age, was unm cipal of the Westfield London—a large ladi sister had a house at accustomed to spend t knew she had been sta He was informed of and arrived in Whitt 28th. He found her Home, Chubb Hill, w veyed. Deceased believed she only lost a-half hours before she was very ill. N afterwards. did the So far as he knew s plaint against anyor dent. She was full had been done for which she had bee died on Friday afte o'clock, and he passed away.

IN MEMORIAM.

Agnes de Sélincourt.

THE death last week of Miss Agnes de Sélincourt—due to a bicycling accident, from the effects of which she was thought to be recovering—was indeed a severe blow to Westfield College. When, but a few years 'rincipal of that branch sity, she undertook n .... Her predecessor, Miss office from the foundation 'that fact, and the fine york, had given her a Vestfield comparable with iss Beale in the Ladies' a. Gratifying, in a sense, ice is, inevitably it tends successor. And to say ignore the loyal sup- Maynard consistently incourt. But there were s of what may be termed ffence the straitest Evan- iginators proposed that a ie college, and built at the also serve as the college le Sélincourt felt that the free to attend whatever ice they preferred, and that f Westfield, while defi- rch, should yet be parti- y Protestant repute of the ily changed. Moreover, ial difficulties. Miss de r from robust when she , and she hoped to strength upon educa- nistrative work, leaving nds. Owing to unforeseen d impossible. For these, sons, it was a most onerous ertook. wonderful. She gained the f her staff, and not least of rked for many years under ifferent régime. With the at once dignified and sym- ore of ways she brought ment into Westfield. Her ig presence seemed to per- She was an admirable ose merely to propose a inks, she was sure to say hings in perfect style. iant personality, however, bt that intense religious dominant factor. She had ork in India, and had learnt of patience and wide sym- radiantly vital person, and umanship was a living ce. And her intellectual r to read with understand- theological books—always nore useful to other people.

HAMPSTEAD. *Oct. 13/917*

THE LATE MISS DE SELINCOURT.

THE memorial service to Miss Agnes de Sélincourt, principal of Westfield College from 1913 to 1917, was held on Thursday afternoon at St. Luke's Church, Hampstead.

The service was conducted by the Rev. William Temple, chairman of the college council, assisted by the Rev. Tissington Tatlow. The lessons were read by Professor de Selincourt, and the benediction was pronounced by the Bishop of Willesden. A short address was given by the Rev. William Temple, in which he spoke of the loss of the principal as a bewildering calamity, but, after describing how the passion of her life had been to bring the knowledge of God to those who were without it, he suggested that consolation might be found in the thought that, at a time when so many were passing to the other side imperfectly equipped for the life beyond, her powers might be even more needed in their service than in her life here. He dwelt on her conception of the relation between the spiritual and intellectual life, the intellectual being the instrument for achieving the purpose willed by religious faith. It was her aim for the college to rear on the spiritual basis already laid a noble intellectual structure, so that all its members might be fitted to share in the great work of furthering the Kingdom of God. Nothing could better express her message to those whom she loved than the words just read from the second lesson (Philippians ii, 12-16, and iv, 8-9). The service concluded with the singing of the Gloria in Excelsis by the college choir, accompanied by Mr. Martin Shaw on the organ. It fittingly expressed throughout not so much the spirit of mourning as an inspiring message for life of faith, hope, and love.

Among those present, besides members of the council, were the Right Hon. Sir Joseph Maclay, Professor Hill (Academic Council of the University of London), Rev. Dr. Headlam (King's College), Miss Tuke and Miss Edgell (Bedford College), Miss W. Smith (University College), the Rev. Dr. Andrews (New College), Miss Seaton (Girton College), Miss Powell (St. Mary's College), Miss Brooks (London School of Medicine for Women), Mr. T. Hancock Nunn and Miss Topham (Hampstead Council of Social Welfare), Mrs. Chisholm (Hampstead Women's Local Government Association), Mr. W. Hind Smith (Council of Dr. Barnardo's Homes), the Rev. E. S. Carr (Zenana Bible and Medical Mission, with which the late principal was associated in India), Miss Boyd (representing the Missionary Settlement for University Women at Bombay (of which the late principal was one of the founders).

A brief dedication service was afterwards held by "Mr. Temple in "Selincourt Hall" to mark the opening of the new House. Thanks to the generosity of Sir Joseph Maclay, the college will always possess in this extension a vivid reminder of the work of its principal.

AGNES de SELINCOURT,

Principal of Westfield College
1914—1917

The Master is here, and calleth thee.

Strength and beauty are in this Sanctuary.

They go from strength to strength.

Your joy no man taketh from you.

Then, in such hour of need
Of your fainting, dispirited race,
Ye, like angels, appear,
Radiant with ardour divine.

Ye fill up the gaps in our files,
Strengthen the wavering line,
Stablish, continue our march,
On, to the bound of the waste,
On, to the City of God.

For so from out that cross flashed forth the Christ,
That no fit word I find to picture Him.
But whoso takes his cross and follows Christ
Will pardon me for all I leave unsaid,
When in that lightning glory he sees Christ.

So from the lights that on the cross outshone
Music was gathered up and caught my soul.
Paradiso xiv. 104–8, 121–2.

Love never faileth.

Maintenance Fund,[14] came forward in 1917 with a benefaction specifically directed towards the purchase of Kingswear, the situation was transformed.[15] By May 1917 negotiations were sufficiently far advanced for the Principal to be able to discuss arrangements for the official opening of 'Maclay House' (the name provisionally chosen) in October, and it was already becoming clear that, contrary to the Council's pessimistic predictions, all the rooms would be occupied.

Miss de Sélincourt's death, on 31 August, from a tetanus infection following a bicycling accident, came as a stunning blow. The opening ceremony nevertheless took place, and on the date she had planned; but it was preceded by her own Memorial Service, conducted by William Temple, who led the procession of gowned students and other mourners up the road from St Luke's to complete the act of commemoration by naming the new acquisition — the first addition to Westfield's stock of buildings — 'Sélincourt Hall'. Although its surroundings have greatly altered, 'Sélincourt' itself still stands, not the loveliest of College houses, but deserving respect as a monument to the 'wise optimism' of the second Principal.

So utterly without warning was Miss de Sélincourt's death, at the age of forty four, that the College possesses no formal portrait of her.[16] Verbal portraits agree in describing Miss de Sélincourt as small, dark, bright-eyed, full of vitality (notwithstanding her indifferent health, a legacy of her time in India). 'It is difficult', one account continues, 'to convey by description the....radiance of her personality, her quiet manner, lit by flashes of incisive speech, and her piercing glance softened at the call of sympathy'.[17] Miss de Sélincourt's liking for order and tranquillity was reflected in the white paint and plain coloured furnishings she chose for her own room — 'more like a drawing room than a study'. In place of Miss Maynard's clutter of pictures, Miss de Sélincourt had on her walls only 'a dozen Madonnas, all framed alike'. Former students remembered with appreciation their reception as 'freshers' in Miss de Sélincourt's 'tasteful and softly lighted private room',[18] and these same qualities were no doubt equally appreciated by the students who were allowed to entertain their fiancés unchaperoned in the Principal's room (in the afternoons), and by the Non-Resident Lecturers to whom it was lent for private interviews with students. By such unobtrusive, imaginative gestures, Miss de Sélincourt did indeed reveal that she had 'a certain creative touch'.

As *Hermes* truly observed (October 1917), 'in four short and difficult years the Principal ....lifted the College into a new career of progress.' Of all the changes in which Miss de Sélincourt had a hand, perhaps the most crucial was the revision of the Trust Deed, whose provisions regarding the governors of the College had remained unaltered since the foundation of Westfield in 1882.

Under the terms of the Trust Deed, membership of the Governing Body, the Council, was restricted to Anglicans (of a type carefully defined), and there was no provision for the Mistress or any of the academic staff to be appointed members. This was how things stood when Westfield was admitted in 1902 as a School of the University, and nothing was said at the time to suggest that any changes were desirable. The first hint of criticism appears in the Report of the University's 'Inspectors of Teaching and Equipment' who visited the College in 1909.[19] Their reference to the 'anomalous' position of the Mistress, who attended meetings of the Council but had no vote, and to the complete absence of representatives of the teaching staff, was taken up and expanded into a forthright recommendation by the 'Persons appointed to Report upon Organisation and Administration' who inspected the College for a second time in 1911:[20] 'We are of the opinion that it is desirable that the Principal should be ex officio a member of the Governing Body, and further that there should be on the Governing Body....representatives of the Teaching Staff to be elected by a Board of Principal Teachers ....and we would welcome a modification of the Trust Deeds which would render such representation necessary.'

After digesting these reports, (which were in general highly complimentary), the Council resolved in June 1913 to appoint Miss de

Sélincourt (due to take up her office as Principal in September) a full member of the Council and 'to consider the placing of a member of the Teaching Staff on the Council.' Under a separate resolution the Council also agreed to the setting up of a Board of Principal Teachers, with the Principal as chairman, and in doing so gave official recognition to a body, composed of Heads of Department and 'regular teachers of not less than one year's standing', which had been meeting once a term since 1909.[21]

Thus far it had been possible to comply with the wishes of the University without breaching the terms of the Trust Deed. In theory it would also have been possible for members of staff, provided they were Anglicans, to be appointed to the Council. But this solution was not acceptable, for reasons which Miss Richardson explained in a letter to Lord Alverstone. First, Council members were appointed for life, which in the case of staff would be inappropriate. Second, restriction of staff membership to Anglicans might exclude people whose presence on the Council was especially desirable, for example Miss Whitby (a Methodist), who had charge of all the University correspondence and business .[22]

Early in 1915, when the Council had still not found a way to 'place a member of the Teaching Staff on the Council', the Board of Principal Teachers drew attention to the still unresolved issue of representative membership and asked for it to be considered on a broader basis. To quote from the minute: 'It was unanimously resolved that application should be made to Miss Dudin Brown and the Council to admit representatives of the Board of Teachers, the University, and of the Old Students, to the Council, with the proviso that such representation should still leave a large majority, e.g. four-fifths of the Council, members of the Church of England'.[23]

The proposal to include University representatives was no doubt prompted by the Report of the Royal Commission on University Education in London (the Haldane Commission), published March 1913, which recommended, amongst other things, representation of the University on the Governing Body of each School.[24] Although implementation of the Haldane Report had been held up by the outbreak of war, some members of the Westfield Council were already convinced that provision for University representation would eventually have to be made. Since the Council had already been warned that the restrictive character of its membership would be an obstacle to the appointment of University representatives by the Senate,[25] and since the academic staff insisted on the principle of 'free election' for their own representatives, amendment of the Trust Deed was unavoidable.

It was at first thought that the Council itself had power to make the necessary alterations, provided that Miss Dudin Brown, now well over ninety, gave her consent. But although this was forthcoming, (in a letter written to Lord Alverstone in the summer of 1915, which was somehow mislaid),[26] legal opinion[27] cautioned the Council against proceeding on its own, 'even with the full approval of Miss Dudin Brown', and advised the College to make application to the Board of Education for a Scheme under the Charitable Trusts Acts.

The proposed amendments were forwarded to the Board of Education in April 1916. In November the official answer came that the Board was willing to approve exemption from membership of the Church of England only in respect of University representatives on the Council; similar exemption for representatives of the academic staff was deemed unnecessary, since they could be presumed to have been appointed 'in accordance with the denominational requirements of the Trust Deed'.[28] The second part of this reply was baffling, for it had been explained to the Board's officials that the Council had never felt themselves prevented by the Trust Deed from appointing non-Anglicans to the resident staff. What the Trust Deed required (clause 37) was that the Council should 'take care to ascertain' that the 'principles' of those appointed were in accordance with the 'principles' set out in clause 4, which reads as follows: 'The religious teaching of the College shall be strictly Protestant in conformity with the principles of the Reformation and in harmony with the

Doctrines of the Church of England (as now by law established), which are defined in the 39 Articles and which are to be interpreted according to the plain and natural meaning thereof'.

The Board of Education, fearful of 'unduly straining their powers under the Charitable Trusts Acts', refused to budge.[29] But since they were willing to allow the College to take its case to the Court of Chancery, the Council decided that it was worth one more effort to obtain the modifications to the Trust Deed which they now more than ever desired. For it had suddenly become obvious that to survive financially the College would need to have access to grants from public funds, and that the distributors of public money were likely to require some form of representation, unhampered by denominational restrictions, on the College's governing body.

There had been important changes in the leadership of the College between the time of the first attempts to secure modification of the Trust Deed and the institution of proceedings in the Court of Chancery. Lord Alverstone had died in December 1915, Miss de Sélincourt in August 1917. In their places were William Temple and, as Acting Principal, Miss Richardson, who was one of those most eager to see 'a more liberal' constitution.

The instructions given to the solicitor employed to draft the new application did not follow in all particulars the College's original submission to the Board of Education. The category of representative members was extended to bring in two appointees of the London County Council, whose Higher Education Committee was empowered to make rate-aided grants to University institutions. In line with the wishes of the University, clause 37, which regulated the appointment of academic staff, was amended to provide for a selection committee on which the University (through its members on the Council) and the Board of Principal Teachers would be represented. Agreement on these two items appears to have been unanimous. More contentious was the deletion of the reference to the 39 Articles from clause 4, in which 'the religious teaching' of the College was defined.

The matter of clause 4 was first raised, in November 1918, by Mr Arthur Sturge, who had joined the Council as Treasurer in September 1917. Now an Anglican, he came from a Quaker background; and he declared that 'if he was asked to satisfy the Council as to his position under that clause [as he should have been on appointment!], he would not be able to give a satisfactory answer.' Pointing out that the Trust Deed was unlikely to be revised 'for many a long year', Sturge hoped the opportunity would be taken to modify the clause, which in its existing form he could only regard as being 'to the discredit of any body of intelligent people.... engaged in fostering the education of young people.'[30] He found he had supporters not only on the Council but also among the resident staff. Miss Richardson, for example, foresaw 'difficulty in future' if 'literal assent' to the 39 Articles 'in their plain and natural meaning'

William Temple, Chairman of Westfield College Council 1916-1921, pictured here as Bishop of Manchester in 1920. He went on to become Archbishop of Canterbury in 1942.

was still to be required, and claimed that 'to her certain knowledge, neither of the first two Principals would for one moment have committed herself to this acceptance for some of the Articles'.[31] Lady Chapman, on the other hand, was for keeping clause 4 as it stood. In reply to the points raised by Mr Sturge and Miss Richardson, she denied that 'literal assent' had ever been demanded: the 39 Articles were mentioned, she supposed, because in their totality they represented the standard of orthodoxy in the Church of England. To attempt to remove them, Lady Chapman continued, might jeopardise all other reforms, since agreement to amend the Trust Deed had been won on the assurance that 'no attempt would be made to tamper with the fundamental religious basis' as defined by the Founders.[32]

Temple, better able than most to interpret clause 4 in the light of Anglican doctrine and practice, took its wording to be 'a way of saying: "Loyal to the traditional position of the Church of England as a reformed part of the Catholic Church and as barring out those who wish to get behind the principles of the Reformation." '. He was clear that the gist of clause 4 must stand; but he regarded the reference to the 39 Articles as inessential, and let it be known that its omission was the one change he was prepared to approve.[33] In the eyes of some this concession may have appeared disappointingly small; to make up for it, however, the obligation hitherto resting on the Council to 'ascertain' that the principles of the academic staff were in accordance with clause 4 was removed, and with it any suggestion that candidates for posts at Westfield might be subjected to a religious test.

The petition embodying the proposed revisions was submitted to the Court of Chancery, after approval by the University, early in 1919; on 27 May Mr Roger Gregory, a solicitor with experience of educational trusts (and into the bargain a 'strong churchman') who had acted for the College, wrote to tell Lady Chapman that the Judge had that day made an Order sanctioning the alterations in the Trust Deed, 'which for all practical purposes' were now effective.

When, two years later, William Temple resigned from the Council on becoming Bishop of Manchester, the valedictory notice which appeared in the College's *Annual Report* (1921) singled out for mention 'his wise judgment on difficult problems'; nowhere was that quality seen to better advantage than in his treatment, at once diplomatic and principled, of the problems posed by the amendment of the Trust Deed. As a relative newcomer, he had to win the confidence of such old-established Council members as Lady Chapman, since 1909 Vice-Chairman, who had been associated with the College almost from the first. While regard for his clerical status was undoubtedly a factor in his success — as someone said, 'Lady Chapman will never really fight against Mr Temple, she has too much respect for the clergy'[34] — so, too, was his native tact and kindliness, as when he consulted her before bringing a proposal of his own before the Council: 'You know them so much better than I do'.[35]

It should not be forgotten that Westfield's great good fortune in having William Temple as Chairman of Council at this critical point in its history came about through Miss de Sélincourt. They shared a breadth of vision from which Westfield was ready to benefit, although in the nature of things it was Miss de Sélincourt, through her day to day contact with students, who made the greater impact. A large part of Miss de Sélincourt's field of vision was filled by the educational and religious work overseas for which, in keeping with Westfield's traditions and with her own early commitment, she longed to train up leaders. So short was Miss de Sélincourt's span as Principal that she was able to achieve less in this direction than she must have hoped; even so, it was during her time that Westfield became linked, in the one case actually, in the other prospectively, with two overseas undertakings

---

Right: part of the correspondence concerning clause 4. Top row: to Miss Richardson from Lady Chapman; to Miss Richardson from Miss Gray. Middle: to Lady Chapman from Miss Skeel; to Miss Richardson from Miss Skeel. Bottom: to Lady Chapman from Mr Sturge; to Lady Chapman from Mr Temple.

Baltimore
Limpsfield
Surrey. Oct. 26ᵗʰ

My dear Miss Richardson.

We are doing our best to get on with the revision of the Trust Deed. I saw Mr Gregory on Monday, and gave him the Council instructions. He will prepare a scheme and bring it to a Special meeting of the Council on Nov. 8ᵗʰ if its then approved he will send it to the Board of Education for their approval, which will facilitate the work when brought into Court. I do not think it ...

ST PAUL'S GIRLS' SCHOOL,
BROOK GREEN, HAMMERSMITH, W. C.

Nov. 5th, 1918.

My dear Anna,

...

Nov. 6ᵗʰ 1918

My dear Lady Chapman,

It was most kind of you to write so fully as well as to telegraph. I will be at the Church House at 11.30 on Friday on the chance of some members of the Sub-committee being able to come.

I do not think that any one who has known the college intimately for many years has the slightest wish that its aim & character should be altered. What one does hope, however, is that the Trust Deed should be so modified as not to give — as it does at present — an impression of rigidity that is ...

Individual members of ... sympathy ...

Holly Hedge Cottage. Well Rd. N.W.3.
Nov 10ᵗʰ 1918.

Dearest Anna,

Friday had three committees & Saturday was spent in marking B.A. papers, so Sunday has come before your letter has been written. Miss Parker has told you the details of the Council meeting : we have got the point of representative members of public bodies — also an improvement of the ... of the clause about appoint- ... went to the ... . I proposed exactly what the University asked viz. that the University members [of your Council] & the Board of Principal Teachers should be representative on the Selection Committee. & that was carried.

... other minor improvements ...

TELEPHONE:
491 BROMLEY.

SHEPHERDS GREEN,
CHISLEHURST.

15. Nov. ⁹

Dear Lady Chapman

Since the meeting of the Whitfield Council last week I have been thinking a good deal about ... It was a surprise to me to find that no proposal had been made to deal with it because that clause had always appeared to me to be the most difficult one in the whole Deed. I wonder whether the members of the Council have become so used to it & so accustomed to view it that they hardly appreciate its ... When I first came became some little time after I had ... the position of Treasurer it quite st..

21, MELBURY ROAD,
KENSINGTON, W. 14.

...

W. Temple

with which it has been very closely connected: Women's Christian College, Madras, and I Fang Girl's Collegiate School in the Chinese province of Hunan.

Women's Christian College, Madras, which opened in 1915 with Miss Eleanor McDougall, Classics Lecturer at Westfield, as its first Principal, was an interdenominational enterprise, founded with the backing of a dozen or more missionary societies in this country and the USA.[36] Miss McDougall's interest in the educational needs of women and girls in India was first aroused when, with Miss Richardson, she attended the great international missionary conference held in Edinburgh in 1910, and it was deepened when, as a direct result of that conference, she was sent on a fact-finding tour of India in 1912-1913. The sponsors of Women's Christian College could thus be confident that in Miss McDougall, with her proven abilities as a university teacher and her first-hand knowledge of conditions in India, they had found the ideal Principal for their venture. With Miss McDougall at its head, and with Westfield graduates among the staff, the Madras College not unnaturally came to be thought of as Westfield's 'sister college in the East'.[37] To help start it, Miss Maynard had handed over to the sponsors the entire proceeds (about £1,700) of a collection she had organised for missionary purposes just before her retirement, and former Westfield students also contributed gifts in kind -- textbooks, a telescope, and an especially inscribed Bible, which a Westfield visitor to Madras in 1970 found still occupying an honoured position.[38]

Now amalgamated with two kindred institutions, Women's Christian College, (or, as it now is, Colleges), Madras, continues to flourish.[39] A more chequered fate was in store for I Fang Girls' Collegiate School, which was launched at Changsa in 1918 by a young Westfield graduate, Pao Swen Tseng, who had entered the College in 1913 and was the first Chinese woman to obtain a London Honours degree (in Botany). Miss Tseng set up her school in temple buildings donated by her family, an extremely ancient and illustrious one, and she hoped it would form the nucleus of a Christian University. China's constant state of turmoil in the decades following 1918 made this dream unrealisable and eventually brought about the closure of I Fang. As a

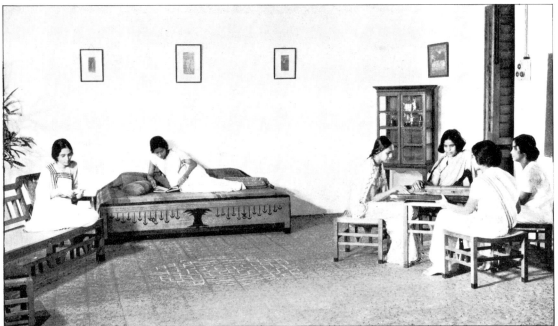

The Students' Common Room, Women's Christian College, Madras (about 1935).

school, I Fang, otherwise 'The Garden of Fragrance', offered pupils 'a life of free, joyous, strenuous fellowship', in place of the 'purposeless round of gossip and domesticity' which was the usual lot of girls in the families of the well-to-do (as it had been in England, when Westfield was founded). Miss Tseng's conduct of the school was so successful that she became an acknowledged authority on girls' education, and while China's national government lasted she was often called on for advice. Thereafter Miss Tseng took up residence in Taiwan, where for a time she did work for the United Nations Commission on the Status of Women.

I Fang's supporters in England included several people connected with Westfield, Miss Richardson in particular, and its fortunes were followed there with great concern. In the 1920s two Westfield graduates, Winifred Galbraith (who had been Miss Tseng's contemporary) and Violet Grubb, interrupted established careers to go as teachers to I Fang.

‘She was very calm, always. Those guilty of boorish behaviour in her presence felt the whole of China condemned them.’

Miss Tseng as a student, recalled by DA Belfield (Vernon, 1913) 1975.

The accounts they sent back[40] tell of desperate expedients to keep the school going in face of physical attack and local hostility, and also of Miss Tseng's great courage and determination.

I Fang Girls' Collegiate School.

Miss Tseng in 1915.

Pao Tseng's Westfield was the Westfield of Miss de Selincourt, whose example she acknowledged as the inspiration of her own dedication to a life spent in 'education and various Christian service'.[41] Many others no doubt could have said much the same: 'God buries His workmen', wrote Miss Maynard in an obituary tribute to her successor, 'but goes on with His work'.[42]

Finding a new 'workman' to take Miss de Sélincourt's place as Principal took longer than expected. The Council had hopes of attracting Winifred Mercier, Lecturer in Education in the University of Manchester; but Miss Mercier's heart was in teacher training and she went instead to be Principal of Whitelands College. When, in May 1918, the Council finally decided to advertise, they appear to have received only one reply worthy of consideration, but since it came from Bertha Surtees Phillpotts,* Girtonian, former research fellow of Somerville and an acknowledged expert in her field of Icelandic studies, the auguries at last seemed good. And so they were; but even when Miss Phillpotts accepted the appointment, in December 1918, there was still some delay before she could be released from the wartime post she held at the British legation at Stockholm, so that it was not until May, 1919, that Westfield received the new Principal who was to lead it — brilliantly — into the postwar era.

Miss Richardson, seen here as Acting Principal from 1917-1919.

Notes & references

1 Minutes, Resident Staff Meeting (formerly the Educational Board) 1913-1914.

2 Miss Maynard recalled in retirement that she never 'gave away her pulpit', whether to clergymen or other members of staff. Miss de Selincourt further broke with tradition by giving her own Divinity Lectures in the morning, in an ordinary lecture room. She is said to have shown in them a determination to take students 'to the roots of the subject'. *Westfield College 1882-1932*, p 36.

3 *Ibid.*, p 34.

4 *Hermes*, October 1915 and other wartime issues.

5 To Miss Maynard, living in retirement at Little Bookham, Surrey: CLM Diary, December 1915.

6 Failures, not normally mentioned, are recorded along with successes in a handwritten list of degree results for the years 1903-1918 preserved Westfield College Archives.

7 Until 1929, when biochemistry was introduced, Westfield BSc students were obliged to take Mathematics as their subsidiary subject in Finals.

8 *Hermes*, April 1916 and June 1920.

9 *Report of the Persons appointed to Report upon the Organisation and Administration of Schools of the University with Reference to Westfield College*, 1911-1912, p ii. At this date the Endowment Fund stood at just over £6000.

10 Household Committee Minutes, 2 February, 1910.

11 £300, as shown in the General Account for the year ending 31 December 1913, *Annual Report*, July 1914.

12 Principal's report of the arrangements made by Council with the Professional Classes War Relief Fund, Minutes, Resident Staff Meeting, 27 November 1914; cf Lady Chapman's letter to the WCA, December 1915: 'in several cases fees have been reduced'.

13 The accumulated bank loan of £1000 remained outstanding. The appeal for the War Time Maintenance Fund, managed by Miss Minna Gollock, a voluntary worker for the Church Missionary Society who had joined the Council in 1915, eventually raised over £2000.

14 Sir Joseph Maclay was Minister of Shipping, 1916-1922. The approach to him which resulted in his donation of £500 to the War Time Maintenance Fund was made by Miss Richardson's brother-in-law, Frederick Leverton Harris, MP, Parliamentary Secretary to the Ministry of Blockade 1916-1918.

15 This second benefaction, of £5000, was made on the prompting of Maclay's daughter, Janet (afterwards wife of Sir John Inskip), who had entered Westfield as a General Student in 1916. The information in this and the preceding note is based on the obituary of Lady Inskip, by EM Carus Wilson, in *Hermes*, 1974, and notes of an interview with Lady Inskip in 1973.

16 A posthumous pencil sketch was made by Amicia de Biden Footner from student snapshots and was photographed for display alongside the portraits of the founders: *Hermes*, March 1921.

17 *Westfield College 1882-1932*, p 34.

18 M E Popham, *Boring? Never!*, p 24.

19 The inspectors were the historian, A W Ward, Master of Peterhouse, Cambridge, and E A Gardner, Professor of Archaeology, University of London.

20 The 'Persons' are not named in the printed report, but according to Miss Maynard's Diary (June 1911) they were 'the Vice-Chancellor and Dr Bennett'. The Vice-Chancellor in June 1911 was MJM Hill, Astor Professor of Mathematics; Dr Bennett has not been identified. This second visitation may have had some connection with the activities of the Haldane Commission, for which see n 22.

21 Before its change of title this was known as the General Staff Meeting.

22 Written 22 February 1911, this letter antedates the second University visitation referred to n 20 above and was the reply to a letter from Lord Alverstone, who was preparing the evidence to be presented by Westfield to the Royal Commission on University Education in Lon-

don (the 'Haldane' Commission), which had been set up in 1909.

23   Minutes, Board of Principal Teachers, 29 January 1915. To meet the difficulty of 'life membership', the Board proposed the election of representative members for a fixed term, which was the solution the Council adopted.

24   For the later history of the 'Haldane' proposals as they affected Westfield see Chapter 5.

25   *Report of the Persons etc*, (see n 9), p i.

26   Miss Dudin Brown's letter, dated 30 June 1915, was forwarded to the College by Lord Alverstone the following day, but was apparently not available for presentation to the Council at a Special Meeting to consider revision of the Trust Deed held 13 October 1915, which Lord Alverstone was too ill to attend (he died in December). The loss of Miss Dudin Brown's letter was not too serious since Lady Chapman, after seeing Miss Dudin Brown in November 1915, was satisfied that the Foundress 'fully understood the scope and effect of the proposed changes and was eager for them to be carried through', and was thus able, when required to some years later, to swear an affidavit to that effect. The documents on which the above summary is based are preserved in a file of papers concerning revision of the Trust Deed compiled by Lady Chapman and now in the College Archives.

27   As well as consulting Mr Tomlin, KC, the Council had the advice of two lawyers among its membership, Mr Clement Montague Barlow, an authority on educational law (son of the former Chairman), and Sir Philip Barker Wilbraham, specialist in ecclesiastical law.

28   WR Barker, Board of Education, to William Temple, 23 November 1916. The Board 'saw no difficulty' about unrestricted University representation because of an amendment to the Trust Deed executed by Miss Dudin Brown in 1900, by which she released the Council from their contingent obligation to repay the £5000 still secured to her from her original endowment. She had taken this step in the belief that it was necessary to secure Westfield's admission as a School of the University, which she considered to be 'desirable'. The Board of Education argued that amendments necessary to enable the College to continue to comply with her wish were allowable.

29   The Board of Education was nervous, so Miss Richardson was privately informed, because revised Schemes which it had approved recently had been criticised in the courts.

30   Arthur Sturge to Lady Chapman, 15 November 1918, and to Miss F R Gray, 29 November 1918.

31   Miss Richardson to Lady Chapman, 29 November 1918 and to Mr Sturge, 24 November 1918.

32   Lady Chapman to Miss Richardson, 27 November 1918.

33   William Temple to Lady Chapman, 18 November 1918.

34   Miss F R Gray to Miss Richardson, 4 November 1918.

35   William Temple to Lady Chapman, 20 August 1918.

36   For its origins and early history see *Women's Christian College, Madras, 1915-1935* (no author's name, but compiled and largely written by E McDougall), and *Westfield College 1882-1932*, pp 76-78.

37   Winifred Fisher (Mrs Finch), a Westfield History graduate, was on Miss McDougall's original staff; by 1932 she had been followed by three more Westfield graduates, and three Madras graduates had entered Westfield as students.

38   G E Fogg, FRS Profesor of Botany at Westfield, 1960-1970.

39   Contact with Westfield is still maintained through WCA support of the Friends of the Women's Christian Colleges, Madras.

40   Preserved, along with other material relating to Miss Tseng and I Fang, in Westfield College Archives. See also *Westfield College 1882-1932*, pp 70-75.

41   Letter from Miss Tseng to the Principal, 1971.

42   Contributed to the Temperance journal *Wings*.

The staircase and hall of Old House.

In 1919 the Westfield Council noted as one of the effects of 'the upheaval in society due to the war' an 'extraordinary' increase in the number of students seeking admission to women's colleges. The number applying for places at Westfield continued to rise throughout the 1920s, to reach their peak for the inter-war years in 1931.[1] A contributor to Westfield's Jubilee history pointed to the contrast between the early days, when going to College was 'a great adventure, embarked upon by but a few dauntless pioneers, heedless of opposition or ridicule', and the present, when it was regarded as 'the natural sequel to the secondary school for all with the ability to secure entrance in a highly competitive examination'. Bound up with the growth in demand, as the same writer acknowledged, was another contrast, between the state of affairs when 'it was taken for granted that daughters lived at home and

Miss Chapman in 1932, leading her staff and students to a service to celebrate Westfield's jubilee.

were in some sort provided for', and 'the financial stringencies of the present time', when daughters were expected (and wanted) to make a place for themselves in the world and to be in a position, when necessary, to help their families. An understandable note of nostalgia creeps in as the writer imagines the student of the early 1930s looking back 'with mingled feelings to the more spacious days...when students...knew the thrill of the

pioneer, seeking wisdom rather than posts'.[2] Yet while it may be agreed that some of the spontaneity had gone, there were undoubtedly compensating gains to students who entered the more mature Westfield of the 1920s and 1930s, staffed by experienced teachers and scholars and led by Principals (Miss Phillpotts, 1919-1921, Miss Lodge,* 1921-1931, and Miss Chapman,* 1931-1939) who proved themselves true professionals.

Westfield's academic standing, already considerable, was powerfully reinforced by the appointment of Bertha Phillpotts, a scholar of international repute, as its third Principal. Even a first year student, admittedly one already attracted to the linguistic studies in which Miss Phillpotts had made her mark, could recognise that Westfield had won an exceptional prize: 'All Oxford and Cambridge are raving that we have snapped her up'.[3] Before long, however, the situation was reversed. In 1921, to everyone's deep regret (and not a little private 'raving'), Miss Phillpotts left Westfield College to become Mistress of her own College Girton, a position she had not sought but which out of loyalty, she felt bound to accept. As well as being Westfield's first scholar Principal, Miss Phillpotts was also the first to play a significant part in public life. In 1919 she was appointed to the Consultative Committee of the Board of Education and after leaving Westfield served on two Statutory Commissions for the University of Cambridge, 1923-1927, and for the University of London, 1926-1928. In 1929 she was promoted DBE, having been awarded the OBE in 1919 for her wartime work in Stockholm.

The future Dame Bertha was forty-two when she took up her position at Westfield. She looked young to be a Principal, so thought one student, and 'absolutely charming'.[4] The students were surprised that a scholar of such brilliance could be so 'unbookish' in the telling of her adventures in Iceland in pursuit of her material, and more surprised still to be lured away from their own books by the offer of a prize for the best entry in an examination (made to seem more serious than it really was)

which tested first-hand knowledge of Hampstead Heath. It was characteristic of Miss Phillpotts to wish the students to discover things for themselves, and to venture outside the regular syllabus.

In her first Commemoration Day address (May 1919), Miss Phillpotts was able to announce the enlargement of Westfield's scholarship programme by the offer of two Research Studentships, funded by 'friends of the College'. These were open to women graduates of any university, and since few other colleges were as generous in admitting outsiders to studentships, competition was soon keen. Out of some three dozen awarded between 1919 and 1938, roughly a third went to Westfield graduates, another third to Oxford graduates, and the remainder to graduates from Leeds, Manchester, Queen's University, Belfast, Trinity College, Dublin, Wisconsin, USA, Utrecht,

Two pictures from a memorial album compiled for Miss Phillpotts in 1921 by her students. Top: the staff, including Miss Phillpotts, sitting fourth from left, middle row. Below: the third year students of 1921.

Dame Bertha Phillpotts, Principal 1919-21.

THE REVOLUTION OF 1920

and Marburg. Holders of Studentships (tenable for two years) were given rooms in College and had the opportunity to take a small share in undergraduate teaching, thus gaining experience which in several cases was the preliminary to a distinguished academic career.[5]

At undergraduate level the ending of the war brought a renewed influx of overseas students, not only from countries such as Japan and Holland, which had sent students in the past, but also from India, Switzerland and Iceland, the last in the person of Anna Bjarnadóttir, who in her third year was elected Senior Student. More would have liked to come, but had to be refused on account of the great upsurge in applications from home students.

For the session 1919-1920 the total number of students stood at 110, nearly a third more than the College could accommodate as residents. Extra rooms were contrived by splitting up some double sets and carving living space out of over-large bathrooms,[6] but even so a record number of 26 students had to live either at home or in lodgings. The most acute problem, however, was that posed by the pressure of additional numbers on the Dining Hall and kitchens, and on the Laboratory, still in its original attic. The Council quickly recognised that the only solution was to build. The space next to the Dining Hall formerly occupied by the Conservatory, which had been demolished in Miss de Sélincourt's time, was enclosed to form a 'domestic block', containing new kitchens and an annexe to the Dining Hall, which became known at once, as it has been ever since, as 'the Bay'.[7]
To house the Laboratory the Council acquired a wooden building, 'the Hut', which was planted on waste land near the southern edge of the main site (not far from where 'New Orchard' now stands). News of this development was sent by telegram to Dr Delf in South Africa, where she was on leave of absence, and was the decisive factor in persuading her to return.[8]

These improvements to the buildings, modest in themselves, have historic interest as the

first projects for which the College received support from public funds, in the case of the Laboratory from the University Grants Committee, and for the Dining Hall and kitchens from the Higher Education Committee of the London County Council. To present Westfield's case for support from these two bodies the College could have had no better advocate than Miss Phillpotts, of whom it was said in another connection that 'she never spoke unless she had something to say; or contended unless the matter were worth contending for'.[9]

Especially crucial was the application to the University Grants Committee (UGC), set up in 1919 to advise the Treasury on grants to universities and university colleges. Before Westfield could be accepted onto its list, the Committee had to be satisfied that 'the volume and scope' of the College's work were on a par with those of other institutions in receipt of Treasury grant, and that Westfield had the will and capacity to add to its capital endowment. Since it was rumoured that the Chairman, Sir William McCormick, had 'a wholly wrong idea of Westfield',[10] the students looked forward to the Committee's first, exploratory, visitation in November 1919 as an opportunity to display their erudition. On the day, however, the visitants spurned an invitation to attend lectures and instead closeted themselves for an hour and a half with the Principal, during which time 'roars of laughter echoed from her room'[11] – proving that it was on more than one level that Miss Phillpotts was able 'to meet the most distinguished men on terms of equality'.[12] In February 1920

The 'Hut' (Laboratory) acquired in 1921.

Left: a strip cartoon showing something of the impact Miss Phillpotts' Hampstead Heath examination had on her students.

95

the Council received the welcome news that, notwithstanding the disappointing result of recent efforts to add to the Endowment Fund, Westfield could expect in future to receive an annual grant, fixed initially at £3,000, 'to enable the College authorities to make considerable increases in the salaries of teaching staff and...to facilitate the provision of pensions'. Occasional grants-in-aid would also be forthcoming for scientific equipment and other academic needs; the first beneficiary under this head was the Hut Laboratory, for which a grant covering two-thirds of the costs was received.[13]

Whereas the UGC had the task of dispensing grants with a view to the national interest, the London County Council and other Local Authorities were chiefly concerned to help university institutions which admitted students from their own localities, or seemed likely to produce graduates to teach in local schools. The LCC considered Westfield worthy of support under both headings and from 1920 onwards made the College an annual

grant, initially of £500, as a contribution towards running costs. Prospects were also held out of a larger grant, if the College would undertake to admit annually, for the next 25 years, up to twelve students awarded four-year grants in connection with the London Day Training College.[14]

The London Day Training College had been in existence since 1902 and was run by the LCC in conjunction with the University (to whose sole control it passed in 1932, when it became the London University Institute of Education). The system of awarding grants to intending teachers to cover the three undergraduate years, as well as the postgraduate training year, had the advantage of bringing university education within the reach of many who might otherwise have been excluded; and since students accepting the award were required to give an undertaking, known as 'the Pledge', to teach in a maintained school for a specified number of years, Local Education Authorities were assured of a steady supply of graduate teachers. Students embarking on

From an article published in "The Sphere", July 1922. Below: the students and staff all ate together in the Dining Hall. Miss Phillpotts' portrait hangs on the chimney breast. Right: the noticeboard "conveniently placed outside the dining-room of the new building".

the four year course needed to be fairly robust. In their second and third year they were obliged to journey once a week to the London Day Training College, in Southampton Row, to receive training in a subject, needlework, which as graduates they were not likely to be called upon to teach; and when the time came for Finals, which at this date was October, the LDTC students were already immersed in their professional training, the LDTC year having started in September.

Made anxious by what she had observed of the effects of the extra load on nine LDTC students already at Westfield, Miss Phillpotts warned Professor John Adams, Principal of the LDTC, that she would be reluctant 'to recommend girls who are not very strong to indenture themselves under the present system', and with backing from Miss Tuke, Principal of Bedford College, and from the Association of Headmistresses, she secured a concession which allowed students the option of starting the training year in January, when Finals were safely behind them.[15] But although ultimately victorious, Miss Phillpotts had at first found the LDTC not at all co-operative, which had a bearing on the decision of the Westfield Council to limit its commitment to take a fixed quota of LDTC scholars to a period of approximately five years, even though it was known that in return for a more permanent arrangement the LCC was prepared to make a substantial grant (£5,000) for the erection of light construction lecture rooms and a common room. It seems that, while willing to co-operate with the LCC in efforts 'to secure University education for girls in the London area and for those entering the teaching profession', the Council was reluctant to see Westfield too closely identified with a scheme calculated to attract a high proportion of non-resident students in whose selection, if the past attitude of the LDTC authorities was anything to go by, the College might soon cease to have the last word.[16] The reduced time scale was arrived at by amicable agreement on both sides, the LCC undertaking to double its annual grant over the next few years as a contribution to the rebuilding of the kitchens, during which

time the College committed itself to receive a quota of LDTC scholars, so long as they were admitted in the normal way.[17] The annual grant from the LCC in fact continued at the same level (£1,000) until 1930, when the system of grant to individual schools, whether from the UGC or Local Authorities, came to an end and was replaced by the payment of block grants to the Court of the University.

Miss Phillpotts was Principal to less than a complete generation of students; yet for those who knew her in that capacity, as one of them recalls, 'Dame Bertha was Westfield'.[18] Although it is reported that Dame Bertha herself 'frequently doubted her power to interest and uplift',[19] all accounts agree that her talks at the Sunday evening 'Function', which she made a fortnightly event, did not fail to find their mark. Stories, the basis of the Icelandic literature she knew and loved, conveyed her message as effectively as the more overtly didactic approach which had come naturally to her predecessors, and were made the more memorable by the zest with which she told them. For all her unlikenesses to previous Principals, her friends at Westfield recognised in Dame Bertha someone who had been happy there, and 'in harmony with its spirit'.[20]

The vacancy created by the departure of Miss Phillpotts in 1921 was filled by the appointment, this time with no delay, of Eleanor Constance Lodge, Tutor in History and Vice-Principal of Lady Margaret Hall, Oxford, and a 'College woman to her fingertips.' Since Miss Lodge, like her successor Dorothy Chapman, remained in office to the retiring age, the College was spared the experience of further unexpected upheavals and settled into a period of stability which lasted until the much greater upheavals attendant on the outbreak of World War Two in 1939. Throughout Miss Lodge's and Miss Chapman's time the Council had as Chairman one of the leading political figures of the day, Sir Thomas Inskip.* Although almost continuously in office — from 1936-1939 as Minister of Co-Ordination of Defence, previously as Solicitor-General and Attorney-General and finally, with the title Lord Caldecote, as Lord Chancellor, he was present more often than not at Council meetings and was 'never too busy to attend to every detail of its business'. Inskip became Chairman in January 1921. A short time before, the Council had appointed as Secretary the redoubtable Evelyn Colpoys Gedge* whose responsibilities, following a re-arrangement of the work of the Council's officers, covered a larger share of financial administration than had fallen to her pre-decessors. Miss Gedge, a Girton Classicist who liked to say that she had been appointed to the Westfield post on the strength of her ex-perience as Treasurer of the Girton Games Club, was an indispensable third, along with the Chairman and the Principal, at interviews with representatives of the University and other public bodies. Miss Lodge declared: 'If she was there, I never felt the least anxiety as to whether everything could be satisfactorily answered...She had all the finance at her finger ends.'[21]

The decade of Miss Lodge's principalship coincided with the introduction, following an Act of Parliament passed in 1926, of revised statutes for the University.[22] Under the new consitution Westfield's status as a School of the University was reaffirmed, the Principal being accorded a seat on the Senate and on the newly formed Collegiate Council. The great constitutional event of Miss Chapman's time was the grant by the King in Council in 1933 of a Charter of Incorporation to 'the Governors of Westfield College, a School of the University of London'. The stated objects of the College as set out in the Charter were the same as in the now superseded Trust Deed, notwithstanding an attempt by the Board of Principal Teachers to secure 'the removal or modification' of the limitations imposed by the old Clause 4 (under which the religious teaching was to be 'strictly Protestant'...).[23] The grant of the charter was well-timed, since it came at the end of a year of celebrations to mark the College's Jubilee. Also set in train during the Jubilee year was the College's application for a Coat of Arms, although the details were not finally settled with the Col-lege of Arms before January 1934. The ele-ments of the design include a gold cross,

taken over from the arms of the University, an open book to stand for learning, and punning references to some of the founders: a left hand (also signifying integrity) for Miss Maynard ('main') and a brown bear's paw ('bruin') to do double duty for Miss Dudin Brown and Mrs Alexander Brown, major benefactors.[24]

The main concern of those who directed College policy in the 1920s and 1930s was to ensure that the character of Westfield remain-ed both collegiate and residential. Miss Lodge's conviction that 'a College is and should be something much more than a hostel' was based on the assumption, valid enough at the

Miss E C Lodge (D Litt), Principal 1921-1931.

time, that in a College the academic staff would also be resident. She continues: 'That something comes, I feel sure, from the meeting of young and old; the possibility of experience coming to the help of immaturity; the encouragement a more advanced scholar can give to a learner.'[25] The view from the students' side was not very different. 'Perhaps one of the most valuable things that Westfield gave us was the actual day to day contact with so many members of the academic staff', writes a graduate of 1921, who continues: 'I wonder sometimes how they could have endured sharing those dinner conversations with us, especially when their minds must often have been far above the ordinary interests of the average undergraduate...yet they did find things about which to talk to us...and I am certain that they came to know far more about us than we ever realised. Nowadays (1978) it is difficult to remember how shy and inhibited some of us were sixty years ago'.[26] No wonder that Caroline Skeel once placed 'a fund of good stories' high on the list of qualifications for the career of university teacher![27]

There was agreement at Westfield that the virtues of residence were most operative in a College which was both compact and small. At the time the new University statutes were being drafted there was a real danger that Westfield, just because it was so minute, would be excluded from the Schools eligible for direct representation on the Senate and the Collegiate Council [28] and so find itself reduced, in Miss Lodge's words, 'to a non-University college'. Seizing the opportunity to present Westfield's case to the Commissioners appointed to draw up the new Statutes, Miss

Below: Sir Thomas Inskip in 1936 on the day he became Defence Minister. He was Chairman of the Council from 1921-1945.
Right: Miss EC Gedge, Secretary of the Council 1920-1948.

NOVEMBER 29, 1957

PORTRAITS OF PERSONALITIES
Evelyn Gedge, Village Evangelist

MISS GEDGE would be horrified at receiving publicity, if she could not think that in some way the Village Evangelists, for which she is Correspondent, would benefit. V. E. is the orchestra, and E. G. only the instrument. But she is an essential instrument —the organizing genius, in fact. She is an old Pauline and a graduate of Girton, who became secretary of Westfield College. But she was drawn into Village Evangelism by Bishop Carey and Brother Edward, to become one of the mainstays of a movement which numbers some hundreds of priests and lay people, and conducts over two hundred missions a year. The work of Correspondent involves the relating of offers of service to the requests for missions, and Miss Gedge has her own inimitable style of conducting this part of the business with epistolary gaiety, and her own unfathomable system of using different colours of paper ("I enclose a pink ..."). Also, the work can only be done by a personal visit to the priest of the parish contemplating a mission. As a result, no car knows its way so well to remote parsonage houses over the length and breadth of England as does the grey Ford which the VEs presented to Miss Gedge as a token of their affection ("My essential four wheels"). No car has stood so long outside halls where diocesan conferences, deanery meetings and church councils have been discussing evangelism. There have been times when its occupant, owner of a pair of brown eyes, alert and merry, and wearer of an evangelist's dress, has found herself stranded with nowhere to lay her head—nowhere except the car, that is. She has then spent the night in the car and gone on unperturbed in the morning. The English countryside must be full of her friends; and they are not friends soon forgotten, for among her gifts is a singular memory for people. Nor do they forget the happy evangelist who came to the village.

Maynard Wing (left) and Chapman Wing in 1929.

Lodge and Sir Thomas Inskip argued that Westfield had as good an academic record as that of much larger Schools; and that in providing residence it met a clear demand. They referred to the value of residential colleges as a means of equalising opportunities for girls living in remote areas, and claimed in addition that employers (by which they must have meant Headmistresses, still the largest users of the services of Westfield graduates) preferred women who had been educated in residential colleges. Their advocacy, assisted it may be by the fortuitous presence on the Statutory Commission of Bertha Phillpotts, carried the day, with the result that in May, 1929, Miss Lodge had the well-earned satisfaction of becoming the first Principal of Westfield to take her place on the Senate of the University.[29]

Westfield's determination to keep student numbers within bounds was not so rigid as to rule out all ideas of physical expansion. In 1927 a new wing, named for Lady Chapman, had been added. Its prime purpose was to contain the regular overflow of students re-

quired to live at home or with 'hostesses' approved by the College, but it also provided sets of rooms for additional staff, (the students had bed-sitters), two lecture rooms, and a badly needed second library.[30] The placing of Chapman wing at a right angle to Maynard and facing Dudin Brown showed that it was the ultimate intention of the Council to complete the quadrangle. They hoped the fourth side would be formed by a Great Hall, but this project had to be postponed in favour of another residential and teaching block, Orchard,[31] erected as a detached building on a site close to the College's boundary with the Croftway and well away from the putative quadrangle. The completion of Orchard in 1935 increased the provision of residential places to 150, the number the Council had fixed on as the desirable maximum, and at last made it possible to accommodate the Botany Department in laboratories worthy of the name. These were on the top floor and were supplemented by a greenhouse built on the flat roof, the rest of which was laid out as a roof-garden. Verner Rees,[32] the architect of Orchard, was also responsible for improvements to the Dining

Hall, amongst them the introduction of a shallow dais for the High Table, which in consequence became elevated in fact as well as name.[33]

The decade of physical expansion which had started with the erection of the Chapman wing was rounded off in 1937 with the acquisition of two houses, Nos 15 and 17 Kidderpore Avenue, on the side of the road away from the main site and adjacent to Sélincourt Hall. Named Phillpotts and Lodge in honour of the most recent past Principals, the houses were used mainly by staff; they supplied, amongst other things, urgently needed bases for three non-resident Heads of Department. The gardens were some compensation for the loss of the much-loved orchard across the road, and under the care of successive official and unofficial gardeners became an increasing delight.

The cost of the additions to the stock of College buildings between 1927 and 1937 amounted in total to about £65 000,[34] of which only a very small proportion was borne by outright grants from public funds.[35] The residential accommodation was eventually expected to pay for itself, out of the extra income it engendered. In the meantime the money for building was found from loans, both internal and external, new benefactions, and the modest accumulation of capital in the Endowment Fund. Between 1926 and 1939 the College received several anonymous gifts of £1 000 and upwards; the largest of these, of £6 000, was given specifically for the purchase of Lodge Hall, and in most cases the terms of the benefaction were wide enough to allow the income, if not always the capital, to be applied to the extinction of the building debt.[36] An Appeal launched a year or so after the Jubilee, but in connection with it, brought in another £2 000 in smaller gifts or as loans. While these and other, larger, loans were being paid off there had to be 'much curtailment of desirable expenditure in other directions', but the Council had every reason to feel satisfied with the achievment of a building programme which in less than ten years had increased the residential capacity by a third. In 1935 they passed a resolution ex-

pressing heartfelt appreciation of the work done in this connection by Miss Gedge, whose appointment had been converted two years earlier from a part-time one to full-time, so greatly had the business of the Council increased.[37]

With the competition for entry to women's colleges now so keen, Westfield could afford to be more selective in its admissions, and offer places only to those who were prepared to read for Honours. The statement, 'Students wishing to read for BA Pass...are not as a rule admitted', appears in College regulations for the first time in 1926, but it seems that the policy was already in operation in 1924, when University inspectors ventured to question the exclusion of 'the best of those students who seek a broader basis of culture', only to have their argument turned back on them in the Council's somewhat oracular response: 'It is well,' they declared, 'to secure the advantage of a College course for the best students, that is to say for those fitted to take an Honours degree.'[38] Belief in the superior educational value of the Honours degree was no doubt prevalent among the staff as a whole, but it was held with especial firmness by Miss Lodge, as the following extract from her memoirs makes clear. 'The value of the training and development of mind which may come from the actual Honours work is surprising, even if in the end the candidate is placed with justice in the third class. Pass-work that is merely a sort of advanced school-work has nothing like the same effect, and scarcely seems to me to be worthy of a University'.[39] The situation with regard to the BSc was different, since from 1925 it was possible under University regulations to take a three-subject BSc leading to both Pass and Honours, and for this Westfield was willing to admit students. It goes without saying that room could no longer be found for students not intending to sit for any examinations — the old style General Students[40] — although an exception was sometimes made for overseas applicants, provided they could demonstrate by their performance in a special entrance examination that they had the capacity to benefit from courses already being provided.[41]

Although mildly critical of the concentration on Honours work, the University inspectors who visited the College in 1924 were unstinting in their praise of what it had accomplished: 'The best testimony to the efficiency of the work done by Westfield College is the exceedingly large proportion of its students who obtain first-class Honours in the University Degrees. In June 1924, there were thirty-one candidates who obtained the Degree of BA Honours, two with first-class Honours in History and four in French; four, too, took BSc Honours including two first-classes in Botany.'[42] But they also expressed concern at the very limited choice of courses available, especially in those Honours Schools (Botany, English and French) in which a subsidiary subject had to be taken. So far as Botany students were concerned, the Council's answer was to introduce Chemistry, as the subsidiary subject most wanted by those intending to teach. In 1929, when Chemistry teaching started,[43] the only place at all suitable was the former attic laboratory, then in use as a non-residents' common room, which was reinstated for the purpose; however, in 1935 the Lecturer, Dr Phyllis McKie, was able to transfer her department to the Hut, left vacant by the removal of Botany to the new laboratories in Orchard. German, the subject eventually chosen to enlarge the options on the Arts side, was introduced in 1937, not just as a subsidiary subject but as a full Honours course. To head the new department the Council appointed a distinguished Rilke scholar, Dr Gertrude Craig Houston, who for the first six years ran it singled-handed.

As the College approached and passed its Jubilee, the teachers whose service had begun under Miss Maynard started one by one to disappear from the scene. Miss Richardson retired in 1925, having served successively as Classical Lecturer, Senior Lecturer, and Vice-Principal. Known to postwar generations of students by the affectionate name of 'St Anne', Miss Richardson had come to be so closely identified in people's minds with the spiritual aspirations of Westfield that the building of a chapel was decided on as the most fitting commemoration of her life's work. Secluded

and unostentatious, the Chapel designed by Morley Horder fulfilled Miss Richardson's wish that it should be 'small and simple' and a place 'in which no Christian ministry shall be impossible'.[44] In this same spirit, the ceremony of dedication (11 June 1929) was conducted jointly by a Free Churchman, the Principal of nearby New College, and an Anglican, Archbishop William Temple of York. Temple,

The Chapel.

who gave the address, took as his theme 'The Christian Student'. In it he recalled how 'Anne Wakefield Richardson had lived in the College with a strongly independent mind and a friendly and genial comradeship toward all about her; and how this was accomplished because her inner life was so full of the spirit of reverence.'[45]

Dr Caroline Skeel, creator and sustainer of the History School at Westfield, resigned on grounds of ill health in 1928, only three years after her advancement by the University to a Chair as Westfield's first Professor. At every level Professor Skeel was a superlatively successful teacher. In her Intermediate classes she immediately impressed on schoolgirls drilled in facts 'the greatness of History and the many types of original sources', amongst which physical remains had a high priority. She demonstrated in the astonishingly wide range of courses she taught for Honours that her vision was at once broad enough to encompass world movements and sharp enough to focus on their local, not to say their minutest, manifestations. To postgraduate students, working it might be in fields remote

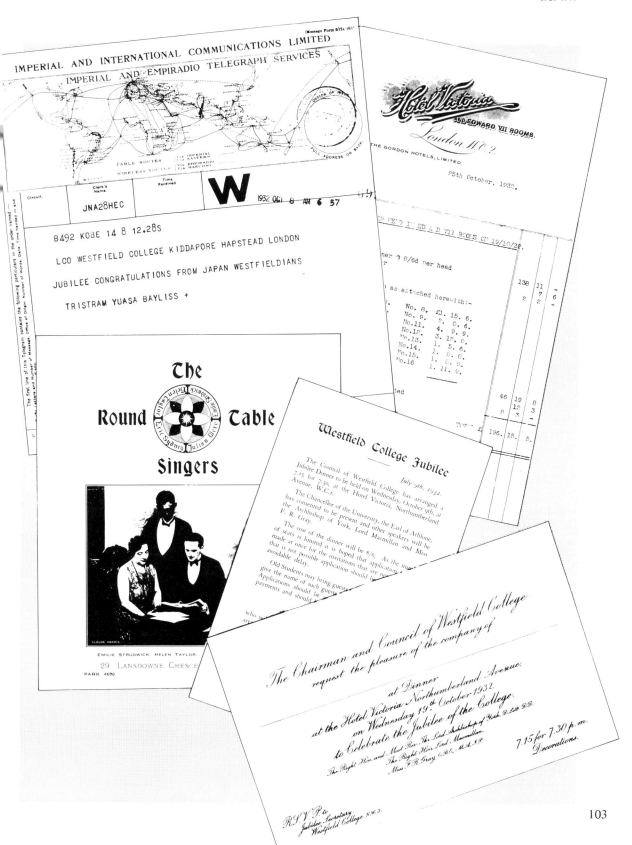

(Message Form S/TA-161)

IMPERIAL AND INTERNATIONAL COMMUNICATIONS LIMITED

IMPERIAL AND EMPIRADIO TELEGRAPH SERVICES

CABLE ROUTES { VIA IMPERIAL / VIA EASTERN }
WIRELESS ROUTES { VIA EMPIRADIO / VIA MARCONI }

FULL ADDRESS ON BACK.

Circuit.	Clerk's Name.	Time Received	W
	JNA28HEC		1932 OCT 8 AM 6 57

B492 KOBE 14 8 12.28s

LCO WESTFIELD COLLEGE KIDDAPORE HAPSTEAD LONDON

JUBILEE CONGRATULATIONS FROM JAPAN WESTFIELDIANS

TRISTRAM YUASA BAYLISS +

Hotel Victoria
AND EDWARD VII ROOMS.
London, W.C.2.

THE GORDON HOTELS, LIMITED.

25th October, 1932.

DINNER HELD IN EDWARD VII ROOMS ON 19/10/32.

Dinner @ 8/6d per head	138	11
	2	7	6
as attached herewith:-		
No. 8. £1. 15. 6.		
No. 9. 2. 0. 6.		
No.11. 4. 9.		
No.12. 3. 12. 0.		
No.13. 1. 5. 6.		
No.14. 1. 8. 8.		
No.15. 1. 0. 9.		
No.16 1. 11. 9.		
	46	19	8
	8	12	3
TOTAL £	196.	15.	5.

The Round Table Singers

EMILIE STRUDWICK. HELEN TAYLOR.

29 LANSDOWNE CRESCE...

PARK 4600

CLAUDE HARRIS

Westfield College Jubilee

July 9th, 1932.

The Council of Westfield College has arranged a Jubilee Dinner to be held on Wednesday, October 9th, at 7.15 for 7.30, at the Hotel Victoria, Northumberland Avenue, W.C.1.

The Chancellor of the University, the Earl of Athlone, has consented to be present and other speakers will be the Archbishop of York, Lord Macmillan and Miss F. R. Gray.

The cost of the dinner will be 8/6. As the number of seats is limited it is hoped that application will be made at once for the invitations that are necessary so that is not possible application should be made without avoidable delay.

Old Students may bring guests ... give the name of such guests ... Applications should be ... payments and should ...

who ...
are ...

The Chairman and Council of Westfield College
request the pleasure of the company of

at Dinner
at the Hotel Victoria, Northumberland Avenue,
on Wednesday 19th October 1932,
to Celebrate the Jubilee of the College.

The Right Hon. and Most Rev. The Lord Archbishop of York D.Litt D.D.
The Right Hon. Lord Macmillan.
Miss F.R. Gray, O.B.E., M.A., J.P.

7.15 for 7.30 p.m.
Decorations.

R.S.V.P. to
Jubilee Secretary,
Westfield College, N.W.3.

Above: Professor CAJ Skeel. Right: Miss LJ Whitby.

from her own, she extended advice which was informed and practical — down to earth advice was a strong suit with her, as when she exhorted examinees to be sure their feet were warm.[46] Two of Professor Skeel's students followed in her footsteps at Westfield. Eveline Martin (Dr EC Martin), appointed Lecturer in 1923 and Reader in Imperial History in 1926, worked alongside her for several years as a colleague. 'What I've seen as your assistant,' she wrote to Professor Skeel at the time of the latter's resignation, 'will remain my ideal of university teaching'.[47] Gladys Thornton (Dr GA Ward), like Dr Martin an Alexander Medallist of the Royal Historical Society, was appointed to the staff in 1927 and remained until shortly after her marriage in 1936. A third pupil of Professor Skeel's, Nora Carus Wilson,* became a luminary of the London School of Economics, where as Senior Lecturer, Reader and finally, from 1953 to 1965, Professor, she probed ever more deeply into the sources and problems in the field of economic history which had first engaged her attention at Westfield.

When Miss LJ Whitby retired in 1931 she vacated the position not only of sole full-time Lecturer in Mathematics but also of unofficial Registrar. With so much on her mind it is no wonder that Miss Whitby often seemed preoccupied: 'Tall, thin, quiet and unassuming... she walked down corridors with her head held down and somewhat to one side, hands clasped together in front'.[48] But neither her abstractedness nor her wraithlike appearance exempted Miss Whitby from the ritual of being 'chaired' down the long passage next to the Hall when one of her students came home with a First. One such student was Gertrude Stanley, (Miss GK Stanley), who on Miss Whitby's retirement was appointed to the Readership in Mathematics newly instituted at Westfield by the University.

The last notable retirement of the interwar years was that of Miss CE Parker, in 1936. 'Composed and learned of countenance', as a student once described her,[49] Miss Parker stood for precisely those values which, to quote Miss Lodge again, made a College 'something more than a hostel'. This meant, amongst other things, that she applied her mind as keenly 'to the detail of ordinary life' as to matters of academic policy: nothing passed muster if it threatened to hinder, rather than to promote, the advancement of learning.[50] Miss Parker's twofold service as Classics Lecturer and, from 1911 to 1933 as Librarian, was

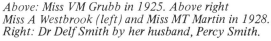
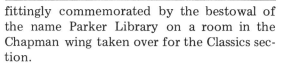

Above: Miss VM Grubb in 1925. Above right Miss A Westbrook (left) and Miss MT Martin in 1928. Right: Dr Delf Smith by her husband, Percy Smith.

fittingly commemorated by the bestowal of the name Parker Library on a room in the Chapman wing taken over for the Classics section.

Dr Delf, still nowhere near retirement, caused something of a sensation in 1928 with her announcement that she was to be married. In a letter to her future husband, the epigraphic artist and book illustrator Percy Smith, Dr Delf described the reaction of the Principal, Miss Lodge, to the news of their engagement. She 'was amused, and excited and friendly and dismayed all in one breath'. wished them every happiness, and implored Dr Delf not to resign, 'I couldn't bear you not to be Head of the Botany Department'.[51] Miss Lodge's wish was granted. From her home in Haverstock Hill, Dr Delf Smith continued to direct the Botany Department as effectively as before. She was aided, again as before, by a succession of her own former students: Dr Violet Grubb, Dr Alison Westbrook, Dr Margaret Martin.[52]

The gratifyingly high proportion of Westfield graduates on the staff, in the early 1930s just under half, was not so great as to run the risk of in-breeding. Dr Gladys Turquet (née Milnes), Reader in French and Head of Department from 1916 to 1934, when she left for a Chair at Bedford, was a graduate of University College, London; she was succeeded by Dr Mysie Robertson, an Edinburgh graduate. Elizabeth Levett, Professor Skeel's successor in the Chair of History, was an Oxford graduate and a distinguished medievalist: she came to Westfield from a Readership at King's. On her all too early death, in 1932, Professor Levett was succeeded by the Reverend Dr Norman Sykes, graduate of Leeds and Oxford, previously Professor of History at University College, Exeter. Bernard EC Davis, appointed Reader in English and Head of Department in 1926,[53] and the first man to join the full-time staff, was an Oxford graduate who had been a Lecturer at the East London (Queen Mary) College. Miss Parker's successor as Head of Classics was George Dyson, previously lecturer at University College, Southampton.[54]

The increased student numbers, and still more the greater specialisation demanded by Honours work, led to a corresponding increase in the number of teachers. Information supplied to the University in 1924 and in 1936 shows a rise from 10.5 to 17, only one new Department (Chemistry) having been created in the interim. Even so, the load borne by individual members of staff remained heavy. Dr JM Jackson, appointed Lecturer in Mathematics in 1937, recalls that he and his two colleagues between them coped with the full syllabus for the Honours degree, and that he personally was responsible for all the applied mathematics. His timetable of 'sixteen lectures a week plus individual tutorials' was probably not untypical.

It was now taken for granted that academic staff would also be engaged in research and that, in view of their shorter vacations by comparison with colleagues in Oxford and Cambridge, they would carry on their independent work in term-time -- a necessity, declared Miss Lodge, 'if anything is to be done'.[55] That a great deal was done can be seen from the lengthening list of staff publications in College *Annual Reports* of the period, which do not lack variety. In 1932, for example,

Bernard Davis published his book on Edmund Spenser, Dr Mary Serjeantson (Reader in English Language) produced, in collaboration with Dr Joan Evans, *English Medieval Lapidaries*, and Dr Violet Grubb contributed a paper on 'Marine algae of Korea and China' to the *Journal of Botany*. Publications in the 1920s and 1930s by historians range in period from the late medieval, with the appearance in 1934 of *English Constitutional Documents 1307-1485*, the joint work of the ex-Principal and Dr GA Thornton (known familiarly to generations of history undergraduates as 'Lodge and Thornton'), to the eighteenth century studies by Professor Sykes, of which one of the best known, *Church and State in the Eighteenth Century*, came out in 1935. Dr EC Martin's *British West African Settlements 1750-1821*, (1926), followed three years later by her edition of the Journal of Nicholas Owen, a slave dealer, confirmed her as an authority in a field known at that time as 'imperial studies'. A similar spread of interest is observable in the publications of the French Department, Dr Turquet specialising in the works of modern writers (Henri Bergson, Paul Valéry), Dr Jessie Crosland, her part-time assistant, in the editing of medieval texts.[56]

The collective role of the academic staff was given a sharper definition when, in 1922, the Council dissolved its Education Committee with the clear intention of looking in future to the Board of Principal Teachers for advice on all academic matters.[57] The meetings of the Board became more frequent and were conducted by Miss Lodge with the expertise to be expected of a constitutional historian well-versed in the traditions of an Oxford College. The status unofficially accorded to these meetings of Heads of Department and other senior staff was given official recognition in the Statutes annexed to the Charter granted in 1933: 'There shall be a body called "the Academic Board" composed of the Principal and such Members of the Teaching Staff as may from time to time be prescribed in the by-laws'. At the same time the Board's elected secretary, who had kept the minutes and dealt with correspondence, was replaced by the Secretary to Council, Miss Gedge, it being argued that the recommendations of the Academic Board were 'of an importance which demands an official link with the Council.'[58] The University inspectors who visited the College in 1936, mindful perhaps that the process of persuading the Westfield Council to involve the academic staff in the government of the College had been initiated by their remote predecessors in 1909 and 1911, expressed their pleasure at finding the 'powers and duties' of the Academic Board 'clearly and satisfactorily defined'. Noting with equal pleasure that the Staff as a whole had the means of expressing their views at General Staff Meetings, from which representations were forwarded to the Academic Board for submission to the Council, the inspectors remarked that the provision for consultation was 'more liberal than in many Colleges', and concluded: 'It is apparent that harmonious relations exist between the Staff

and the Governing Body, there being an atmosphere of friendly co-operation.'

The friendliness prevailing at all levels, frequently commented upon in recollections of this period, was achieved without any sacrifice of formality. Staff did not address students by their first names, or at any rate not until their final year, and until well into the 1920s the students observed a similar convention among themselves, using Christian names only after a form of 'proposal' had been successfully negotiated.[59] Ladylike conduct was still the norm, and authority still desired the students to present themselves to the outside world suitably dressed, which in effect meant equipped with hat and gloves (wisely, no attempt was made to prohibit the bobbed hair and abbreviated skirts which in the 1920s liberated women from the constricting fashions of prewar days).

Less ladylike, in fact positively tomboyish,

An outing to Sutton's Seed Ground in 1925. Sitting, from left to right: A Westbrook. M Martin, Dr Delf, Mr and Mrs Sutton. Miss J Sutton (student at Westfield 1922-26), stands second from right.

were some of the pranks indulged in within
the four walls of the College. Practical jokes
of the 'sand in sugar basins' and 'fireworks in
coal scuttles' variety, prosecution of inter-
departmental feuds by personalised ragging,
general ragging on 'hockey nights', torch-lit
junketings in the gardens at the end of term —
all are indications that in its own way Westfield was as much affected as other universities
and colleges by the ebullience of the postwar
years. Some of the rags took the form of organised entertainments, as when on Guy
Fawkes night the Freshers were given licence
to 'guy' their seniors, the Finalists returning
the compliment at their 'going-down' entertainment in June.[60] Freshers evidently felt
themselves especially down-trodden, as in the
doggerel which represents the life of a Fresher
as one of continual bombardment with ex-
hortations from student officers (JPs, Captain
of the Fire Brigade, Senior student), each
verse ending with the refrain:

'And you always most meek and repect-
ful must be,
For this is the life of a Fresher you see'.

The immediate postwar years saw some
notable additions to the already large number
of student societies. The Dramatic Society,
founded 1919 and welcomed by *Hermes* as
supplying 'a long felt need', boldly chose
Ibsen's *A Doll's House* as one of its first productions and went on to tackle Shaw's
Pygmalion ('Rather well done', noted Miss
Lodge, 'but with too much swearing to please
everyone')[62] and Congreve's *The Way of the
World*. These, like many later productions,
had to be staged in the Dining Hall, but
imaginative use was also made of other
locations, as when Miss K M Lea, Lecturer in English, mounted the miracle play
Everyman in the Chapel[63] and Peele's masque,
The Arraignment of Paris, in the garden (both
in 1935). The Art Club, started in 1920, inevitably found itself pressed into service for the
making of costumes and posters, but its scope
was very much wider and included visits to
galleries and architectural monuments, talks

*Top: J Elliot as Kate Hardcastle and H Forbes as
Marlow in the 1921 Dramatic Society production.
Below: Apollo in 'The Arraignment of Paris', 1935.*

from practising artists (among them Sir Gerald Kelly, RA, who painted the College's portrait of Miss Lodge, and Percy Smith, who spoke on 'Artists and Book Production'), and experiments with photography, lino-cutting, and other media; some of the results found their way into the pages of *Hermes*, which at this period took on an unwontedly lively appearance.

The need for some all-embracing organisation to coordinate student activities had been met as early as 1920 by the establishment of the Westfield College Union Society. With the Principal as Honorary President and the Senior Student as Executive President, the WCUS and its committees assumed responsibility for the allocation of funds to its constituent societies, drawing for the purpose on the pooled subscriptions of students and staff, and in general ordered 'all things with the tyranny of a complete democracy'.[64]

Joan Elliot, almost the first Senior Student to preside over WCUS, was closely involved with the launching in 1921 of the University of London Union (ULU), successor to the Students' Representative Council which had been in abeyance since 1914. Just before it ceased to function, the SRC had made a strong plea to students to assert their identity by wearing academic dress, arguing that 'the more it is worn in the streets of London, the sooner will men realise the existence and size of the University' and that the bond between students would be strengthened.[65] If the reaction of Westfield undergraduates is anything to go by, the plan must have failed to achieve either of these purposes: gowns were donned with enthusiasm for lectures within the precincts of the College, but they did not appeal as outdoor garments. ULU, which unlike SRC had its own base, provided London students with more effective ways of becoming 'mutually acquainted' and of combining, to use the metaphor of its own propagandists, to form 'a good hearty atom'.[66] Westfield students were quickly drawn into the debates, club meetings and socials organised by ULU in its premises in Bloomsbury, so much so that in 1929 Miss Lodge felt obliged to warn the Council that 'the standard of work was in danger of being lowered' by participation in so many activities external to the College.[67]

Miss Lodge was no spoil-sport, and she was

Art Club contributions to Hermes *in the early 1930s.*

"COLLEGE"

as keen as anyone to let it be seen that West-field was an integral part of the University of London, but she was in no doubt that if students were to make the most of 'the precious bit of life' represented by their years at university, work must come first. Accordingly Miss Lodge made it plain that she considered eight hours steady work a day not at all too much to expect, and countered requests for weekend exeats with the question, 'Do you consider five and a half days in a week sufficient to give to your studies?' Since most first year students still had Intermediate subjects to pass, timetables were apt to be full, with classes, seminars and individual tuition as well as the staple diet of lectures: these were apt to proceed at such a cracking pace that, as one student recalled of Miss Barratt's course in comparative Greek and Latin syntax, 'there was never time to blow one's nose!'[69] The amount of 'academic surveillance' exercised may sometimes have appeared oppressive, especially to students who had come up expecting 'only to be taught to learn',[70] but it was not inconsistent with Miss Lodge's ideal of a community of scholars in which the difference between teacher and taught was only one of degree (the pun was surely unintentional), not of object.[71]

Miss Chapman, who succeeded Miss Lodge as Principal in 1931, came to Westfield from Liverpool, where she had combined wardenship of a Women's Hall of Residence with a Special Lectureship in Latin. Perhaps because the numbers reading Classics were small and the College well-stocked with Classics Lecturers, Miss Chapman did not take part in the regular teaching, differing in this from Miss Lodge, who throughout her time as Principal had taken an effective share in the work of the History Department, then the largest of the Arts Schools. However, in the papers she read to the Classical Club[72] Miss Chapman displayed the wide range of her scholarship and culture, and showed her versatility by producing the Dramatic Society in an English version of a play by the Spanish dramatist, Calderon.

Although 'very forceful when she had to be',[73] Miss Chapman is remembered above all for her gentleness: 'her hands were on the reins — but lightly'.[74] Where Miss Lodge had been swift in action and direct in coming to the point, it was Miss Chapman's way 'to move slowly, to take her time', just as she did in the discursive speeches for which she was famous, when she would keep an audience on tenterhooks as, sentence by sentence, she progressed by way of densely constructed clauses and 'agonisingly long pauses' to the word or phrase which formed each beautifully apt conclusion. Although with little past experience of collegiate life, Miss Chapman

Miss Dorothy Chapman, Principal 1931-1939.

seems to have well understood the art of keeping Westfield's academic community, which had its full share of strong personalities, 'in good humour and good spirits'. To the students she could at first appear a little awesome, but her kindly interest converted many into lifelong friends — it is worth remarking that Miss Chapman was the first Principal since Miss Maynard to live to a ripe old age.

The students of the 1930s appear to have been more sophisticated in their outlook and tastes than those of the previous decade, when enthusiasm for team sports had been at its peak. It is true that the Boating Club, (founded in 1908 by Miss Parker and given a fresh impetus by Miss Phillpotts, herself a skilled oarswoman), the Netball Club (started 1921), the Lacrosse Club (started 1928), not to mention the old-established Tennis and Hockey Clubs, all continued to have their faithful adherents and to supply members to University teams, but there were signs that interest was starting to wane in the face of competing attractions. One such was the lure of the Saturday matinée, which was said by the Secretary of the Lacrosse Club,

writing in *Hermes* in 1938, to have accounted for as many 'scratched matches' as the 'much abused weather'. It is only fair to mention, however, that students keen on outdoor pursuits could now join the College Climbing Club, initiated in the early 1930s by Miss Barratt, Lecturer in Classics, and warmly supported by Miss Chapman, a dedicated hill-walker. The school-girlish pranks of the 1920s appear to have died out, along with the practice of referring to staff by nicknames.[75] First-years continued to receive semi-jocular advice from their elders, but in a more cynical vein, as in this *Address to a Fresher* published in *Hermes* in 1936:

> *'I the bitter ghost implore you*
> *you with three whole years before you*
> *Work hard.*
> *Work to make your conversation*
> *Quite a "liberal education..."*
> *Work out plans of future action*
> *To give your conscience satisfaction*
> *While you proceed the primrose path to*
> *find...'*

1936 was also the year when, because no

Left: a news shot of the Boating Club in the 1930s. Below: the pioneers of the early 1920s; (left) the staff 'Dongola' and (right) the students'. A Member recalls: 'We wore blue skirts kept in by an elastic band'.

fresh 'odes' had been sent in, the singing of College Songs was omitted at the annual Banquet, the Students' Union having resolved that 'no past odes be sung'.[76]

These shifts in attitude, which to a large extent reflected the temper of the times, did not signify that students had ceased to appreciate the distinctive character of Westfield. 'Often and often', writes one who came up in 1934, 'I think back on those glimpses of eternal truths that it was our lot to experience at Westfield and am devoutly thankful I was privileged to share a life which combined faith, learning and friendship'.[77] The Chapel provided a more dignified setting for Morning Prayers than the workaday surroundings of a lecture room, and Miss Chapman's reading of lessons and prayers of her own choosing is remembered as the 'personification of sincerity and faith'. Divinity Lectures were still provided, but as short courses in the Michaelmas and Lent terms, the Lecturers being chosen by a committee of students from a list prepared by the Principal. Attendance at the Lectures, as at Prayers, was still generally expected of all students (as it was, tacitly, of Resident Staff), but there was now a clause in the College regulations, first inserted in 1918, which excused students 'debarred by conscientious objections'.[78] The fortnightly Function, its name irreverently contracted by students of the 1920s to 'Princ's Func', had long since been voluntary but continued to draw appreciative listeners, even if there were some who preferred to escape from College to spend the afternoon in the National Gallery, at a concert, or 'simply wandering about London'. By this time there were two student religious societies, a branch of LIFCU (the London Inter-Faculty Christian Union) having established itself alongside the SCM.[79] Both played their part in upholding Westfield's traditional interest in missionary concerns. In LIFCU the emphasis tended to be on foreign missions, in SCM on the application of Christian principles to current social and international problems,

which in the 1930s provided ample subject matter for the study circles held jointly with a recently revived Political Club.[80]

'The past year', runs the opening paragraph of the Council's report for 1938-1939, 'has been for the whole nation a time of anxiety and unsettlement, in which Westfield College has shared'. When this was written the outbreak of war was still a few months away, but the need to make contingency plans had been brought home by the Sudetenland crisis of the previous autumn (1938), when it had been predicted that in the event of war, 'London would be bombed to bits in the first week'. Hasty measures taken at Westfield during this nervewracking 'dress rehearsal' concentrated on the conversion of the basement of Orchard Wing into an air raid shelter, an operation accomplished by 'the physically tough among the SCR and the gardeners toiling together through hot September afternoons to fill and drag into position a great rampart of sand bags'.[81] Advantage was taken of the breathing space of 'Munich' to enter into negotiations with St Peter's Hall, Oxford, a men's Hall of which Sir Thomas Inskip (by now Lord Caldecote) was a Trustee.[82] By April, 1939, it was settled that if war came, Westfield would move to St Peter's and take the place of its normal occupants. Accordingly, in the early days of September, 1939, the College transferred itself to Oxford, to take up residence 'for the duration'.

By coincidence, the change of scene was accompanied by a change of Principal. For among the 'unsettling' events of the session 1938-1939 had been the impending retirement of Miss Chapman, which from the College's point of view could hardly have come at a more awkward time. Yet just as Bertha Phillpotts had been the ideal Principal to rejuvenate the College at the start of the interwar era, so was Mary Stocks,* a great triumpher over adversity, the right choice (*ipsa dixit* Evelyn Gedge)[83] for the critical years which lay ahead.

Notes & references

1   *Annual Report*, 1919, p 9. In 1922, the first year for which the *Annual Report* gives exact numbers, there were 91 applications for 20 places; in 1931, 149 for 46 places. In the early 1930s this trend was reversed, the lowest point being reached in 1936 (102 applications).

Details given for 1928 and 1929, but lacking for other years, indicate that about 1 in 7 failed to reach the required standard. Each year an unspecified number withdrew, having accepted awards or places elsewhere, usually at Oxford or Cambridge.

English is the subject mentioned most frequently as attracting the best field, both in quantity and quality.

2   *Westfield College 1882-1932*, pp 67-68.

3   HAC Green, in a letter to her family, 7 December 1918.

The complete set of Hilda Green's weekly letters home while a student at Westfield (1918-1921) passed after her death in 1980 into the possession of Royal Holloway College, where she was on the staff of the English Department from 1927 to 1967. I am most grateful to Dr Mary Bradburn, of RHC, for allowing me access to this unique source.

4   Hilda Green, letter dated 4 May 1919.

5   Holders of College Research Studentships 1923-1939 are listed in the *Annual Reports*. The exact standing in College of the Research Students evidently proved hard to define and was usually decided *ad hoc*. Thus in the case of a very new graduate from Somerville (Mary M Lascelles, English scholar, afterwards Fellow and Vice-Principal of Somerville), the Board of Principal Teachers decreed in November 1922 that she should 'have tea once or twice weekly in the Senior Common Room, breakfast at the High Table on Sundays and all other meals with the students'.

6   Household Committee Minutes, 13 June 1919. The majority of students still had two rooms (or a bedroom and a shared sitting room), for which the charge, inclusive of tuition, was now £120 pa (*Annual Report*, 1919). From 1921,

however, residence and tuition fees were charged separately: £90 for residence (£70 for less eligible rooms); tuition fees according to the course – 42 guineas for Intermediate Arts, 38 guineas for the BA, 53 guineas for the Intermediate and Final BSc, *Annual Report*,1920.

7   And not 'The Vestibule', as proposed by the Resident Staff Meeting, October 1921. The conservatory had been demolished following a decision of the Council in March 1914.

8   Dr Delf's leave of absence had started in 1919, when she accepted a temporary appointment as Senior Lecturer in Botany at the University of Cape Town, during which time her work at Westfield was done by Dr MC Rayner, of Reading. In 1921 Dr Delf was offered a permanent position at a Medical Research Hospital in Johannesburg which would have enabled her to continue with work of the kind she had done at the Lister Institute during the war. The choice she had to make was a difficult one: 'On the last day before I had to give a firm reply, a long cable arrived from Miss Phillpotts saying that a hut laboratory had been erected in the garden …A grant had been received…on the understanding that I should be returning and the College Council would feel badly let down if I did not. So I had to refuse a job which was not only higher in salary and status but seemed to be more directly useful in the human sense than trying to introduce an element of Science into a predominantly Arts College'. EM Delf, 'Botany at Westfield 1906-1948'. Unpublished memoir, Westfield College Archives.

9   Said of her by a fellow member of the Statutory Commission for the University of Cambridge and quoted by the Mistress of Girton, Miss HM Wodehouse, in an address given in Girton College Chapel on the Sunday following Dame Bertha's death in January 1932. *Girton Review*, Easter Term 1932, p 4.

10   Miss Richardson claims this in a letter to Dr Caroline Skeel 6 November 1918, when the College had just been told that the Board of Education Committee, chaired by McCormick, which was the predecessor of UGC, might not consider Westfield eligible for grant even when the prospective amendment to the Trust Deed had been effected.

11   Hilda Green, letter dated 23 November 1919.

12   Quoted from the obituary tribute to Dame Bertha by Anna Bjarnadóttir (Saemundsson), *Hermes*, 1932.

13   *Annual Report*, 1920, pp 9-10; *ibid*, 1921 p 12. By the time direct funding from the UGC came to an end in 1930 (see n 22 below) the recurrent grant had more than doubled and stood at £6 750. With its help Lecturers' and Readers' salaries could be raised to the recommended levels, but the Council were unable for some time to come to contemplate appointments on the professorial scale, which in their opinion was pitched too high for smaller colleges.

In 1920 the College entered the Federated Superannuation Scheme for Universities (FSSU), and so met the stipulation in regard to pensions.

14   Council Minutes February-October 1920, *passim*. For the London Day Training College, see *Studies and Impressions*, issued 1952 by the University of London Institute of Education.

15   The progress of the campaign for the 'January option' conducted by Miss Phillpotts can be followed in correspondence preserved in the Westfield College Archives (11 October 1920-9 May 1921). In 1924, with the transfer of degree examinations to June, the problem of overlap disappeared.

16   The Council also thought 30% of the annual intake too high a proportion.

17   Students holding LDTC scholarships (from 1932 Institute of Education scholarships) continued to come to Westfield. The weekly 'half-day training' requirement appears to have lapsed, but 'the Pledge' was not abolished until 1951.

18   Quoted in the memoir 'Our Teachers' compiled by MG Clark (Westfield 1918-1921) in commemoration of the 'Diamond Jubilee' of her contemporaries, 1978.

19   *Westfield College 1882-1932*, p 43.

20   A Bjarndóttir, *Hermes*, 1932.

21   EC Lodge, *Terms and Vacations*, (published posthumously), p 202.

22   The Act of 1926 was the outcome of resumed discussion of the Report of the Royal Commission on University Education in London ('Haldane'), published 1913, which had in effect recommended the reconstitution of the University on a unitary basis. The new constitution which emerged after 1926, and which was based on the recommendations of a Departmental Committee of the Board of Education, represented a rejection of Haldane's proposals in favour of a federative structure in which certain Schools were represented on the Senate and on a new body, the Collegiate Council. However, on the ground that it was 'fundimentally inconsistent with the idea of a self-governing University ... not to have sufficient resources and authority to initiate and pursue a policy of well-balanced development and to prevent wasteful duplication and competition', a University body, the Court, was set up to receive and redistribute the grants from the UGC and Local Authorities which had hitherto been paid direct to individual Schools. See H Hale Bellot, *The University of London*, 1969, pp 37 ff.

23   Letter from Dr PV McKie, Secretary of the Board of Principal Teachers, to Miss Gedge, Secretary to Council, 15 December 1932.

24   Correspondence with Chester Herald, 24 January 1933-23 January 1934, Westfield College Archives; Minutes of the Academic Board, 30 May 1933 (refers to 'university design'); description in *Hermes*, 1934.

Miss Maynard claimed kinship with the family of Viscount Maynard of Long Easton, Essex, whose arms included 'three sinister hands couped at the wrist'.

25   EC Lodge, *Terms and Vacations*, p 235.

26   'Our Teachers' (see n 18 , above).

27   In a talk she gave at Notting Hill High School, (which she had attended as a girl), c 1925.

28   As would have been the case had the scheme recommended by the Report of the Departmental Committee, referred to in n 22 above, been implemented as it stood.

29   For Miss Lodge's retrospective account of the proceedings which led to Westfield becoming 'one of the eight Colleges forming the central part of the University' see *Terms and Vacations*, pp 201-202.

A typewritten copy of the 'Summary of Evidence' given to the Statutory Commissioners is preserved in Westfield College Archives.

30   The Chapman wing was formally opened on Commemoration Day, 1927, when Sir Frederick Kenyon, Director and Chief Librarian of the British Museum, gave the address.

31   Opened summer 1935 by HRH Princess Alice, Countess of Athlone, whose husband, the Earl of Athlone, was Chancellor of the University from 1932 to 1955.

The Council's intentions with regard to the Orchard building (which was begun in April

1934) and a future 'Great Hall' are set out in the *Annual Report* for 1933-34 and in the minutes of an ad hoc Building Committee, 27 June 1933 and 28 June 1934.

32 Verner Rees, designer of the London School of Hygiene and Tropical Medicine in Gower Street, continued as consultant architect to the Westfield Council until well into the 1950s.

33 The work done to enlarge the Dining Hall, the adjacent Bay, and the areas above, was in fact quite substantial; externally it resulted in the continuous facade as seen today.

34 In round figures: Chapman wing, £25 000; Orchard £21 200; Dining Hall etc, £9 000; house purchases, £10 000.

35 For the Orchard Laboratory the College received, via the Court, £4 000 from the LCC's annual capital grant to the University. The position regarding grant for the Library is less clear-cut, but it seems that part of a non-recurrent grant of £1 700 mentioned in the *Annual Report* for 1930-31 was intended to go towards the extinction of the building debt on the Library.

36 The anonymity of the donor of £100 in 1926 remains impenetrable. The later gifts — £1 000 in 1930, £2 000 (towards building debt) in 1932-33, £5 000 in 1935 (for scholarships, but with power to vary at the Council's discretion), £1 000 annually 1936-38 — are known to have come from Professor Skeel. Scholarship funds were further augmented in 1935 by a benefaction of £3 300 from the Leverhulme Trustees, and in 1936 by a legacy of £2 000 from Miss Maynard.

37 Council Minutes 22 October 1935 and 23 May 1933.

38 'Report of Inspectors of Research, Teaching and Equipment', issued February 1925, paragraph 7 (i); for Council's reply, see undated draft, Westfield College Archive. The inspectors, Professor Oliver Elton of Liverpool and Professor J G Robertson of University College, London, visited the College 15 December 1924: 'they were kind but non-committal', noted Miss Lodge in the Principal's Log Book.

39 EC Lodge, *Terms and Vacations*, p 234.

40 Since 1917 these had been provided with a College-based two-year course leading to a 'Diploma in Citizenship'. When the scheme came to an end in 1923 a total of nine students had been awarded the diploma.

41 Council Minutes 24 May and 28 June 1932.

42 For an overall picture of degree results see the Table in Appendix III.

43 Initially Chemistry was taught only for the Intermediate, Biochemistry being offered as the new subsidiary subject for Honours BSc; but when the latter was withdrawn by the University in 1931, Chemistry took its place. From 1932 Chemistry was also taught at Westfield as one of the three subjects for the newly introduced General Honours BSc. Council Minutes, 24 November 1931 and 26 January 1932.

44 *Hermes*, 1926, p 2.
    P Morley Horder had recently designed the East Quadrangle at Somerville College, Oxford: Enid Huws Jones, *Margery Fry*, 1966, pp 150-152. The cost of the Westfield Chapel, just over £5 000, was met largely from donations: Finance Committee Minutes, 8 February, 1929.

45 *Hermes*, 1929.

46 The profound impression Professor Skeel made as a teacher is clear from the tributes which appeared in *Hermes*, November 1925, in celebration of her professorship, and from the host of letters she received on that occasion and on her retirement.

47 Letter dated 19 November 1928, preserved like those mentioned n 46, in the Caroline Skeel Papers, Westfield College.

48 As remembered by Mrs F R Lyle (Hoyte, 1906).

49 Hilda Green.

50 See the obituary tribute by Dr EC Martin, *Hermes*, 1956. In 1931 Miss Parker was appointed to the office of Vice-Principal, left vacant since the retirement of Miss Richardson in 1925.

51 Letter preserved Delf Smith Papers, Westfield College.

52 Dr VM Grubb: Lecturer 1923-1925, and after an interval in the Far East, from 1932 to 1937, when she left to succeed Miss M E Popham as Headmistress of Westonbirt.
    Dr M A Westbrook (Mrs Wilson): Demonstrator and Assistant Lecturer 1927-1931.
    Dr M T Martin: Demonstrator and Assistant Lecturer 1930-1935, Lecturer 1935-1941.

53 Among the candidates interviewed was Helen Waddell, not yet famous as the author of *The Wandering Scholars* (first published April 1927): see Monica Blackett, *The Mark of the Maker. A portrait of Helen Waddell*, 1973, p67.
    Mr Davis married in 1933 one of his first Westfield students, Elisabeth Landon; the wedding took place in St Luke's and was followed by a reception in the College garden.

54 GW Dyson, MA Cambridge; appointed Lecturer in Classics 1929, Head of Department 1936-1948. An authority on Roman history, his lectures on Tacticus were especially remembered as 'a never-forgotten inspiration'.

55 See *Terms and Vacations*, p207. Miss Lodge, while regretting that as Principal she had so little consecutive free time, nevertheless continued to write and publish.

56 Thus the chanson de geste *Guibert d'Andrenas, 1923, and Raoul de Cambrai*, Old French feudal epic, 1926. Mrs Crosland was a much-valued member of staff from 1921-1947 and on the death of Dr M Robertson in 1943 acted briefly as Head of Department. Her daughter, the pianist Eve Crosland, read History at Westfield 1941-1944.

57 Council Minutes, 10 March 1922. It was resolved that the Board 'should make representations to the Council on all academic matters and the management of the College generally,' No use appears to have been made of the power to co-opt members of the Council to assist in the Board's deliberations.

58 Letter from Miss Gedge inserted Minutes of the Academic Board, 13 June 1933.

59 Known as 'propping'. Mentioned several times by Hilda Green, the custom was still kept up in the late 1920s. It is mocked at gently in a verse monologue 'The Proposal', author and date of composition unknown.

60 Reminiscences contributed by Mrs A Carter (Le Mesurier, Westfield 1927-1930), *Hermes*, 1967. Mrs Carter's description is fully borne out by the detailed accounts of student life relayed to her family by Hilda Green.

61 Verses 'To the Freshers of Westfield' composed by E Tansey (Westfield 1916-1919).
    Chores expected of Freshers included rolling the tennis courts before breakfast and carrying chairs for their elders to sit on. *Hermes*, November 1925.

62 Principal's Log Book, Lent Term 1924.

63 Sir Thomas Inskip, an Evangelical of the old school, reportedly did not approve.

64 *Westfield College 1882-1932*, p63. WCUS operated alongside two existing institutions, themselves fairly recent innovations, which provided a forum for general discussion: the College Meeting, attended by Principal, Staff and Students; and the Student's Meeting. Minutes of all three survive from their inception.

65 *Hermes*, October 1914, report by Westfield's SRC representative Gladys Burlton. The Principal, Miss de Sélincourt, willingly gave her consent to the wearing of gowns but did not wish it to be obligatory.

66 *Hermes*, March 1922, pp4 and 19. Miss J Elliot, whose involvement with ULU is there described, was subsequently Head Mistress of Queen Anne's School, Caversham.

67 Council Minutes, 13 December 1929.

68 Obituary tributes, *Hermes*, 1936; EM Delf Smith, 'Reminiscences of Westfield College'.

69 M Kelsey (Pantcheva, Westfield 1934-1937), writing in *Hermes*, 1967.

70 A Carter, *ibid*.

71 It was probably at Miss Lodge's prompting that in 1926 the Arts lecturers agreed to follow the example of the students in wearing gowns to lectures. Minutes of the General Staff Meeting.

72 For example, on 'The birth of the comic spirit', and Cicero as a provincial governor'. *Hermes*, 1933 and 1936.

73 As recalled in 1976 by Professor Rosalind MT Hill, who joined Westfield as Lecturer in History in 1937, in a talk to the College History Society.

74 Quoted from the address given at Miss Chapman's memorial service, 1967, by Miss Kathleen M Lea, Vice-Principal of Lady Margaret Hall, Oxford, and from 1927 to 1936 Lecturer in English at Westfield. Miss Chapman's personality is further illumined by the farewell tributes printed in *Hermes*, 1939, and the recollections contributed by M Kelsey to *Hermes*, 1967.

75 Thus, in the 1920s, 'Skeelie', 'Pookie' (Miss Parker, whose initials CEP were held to have

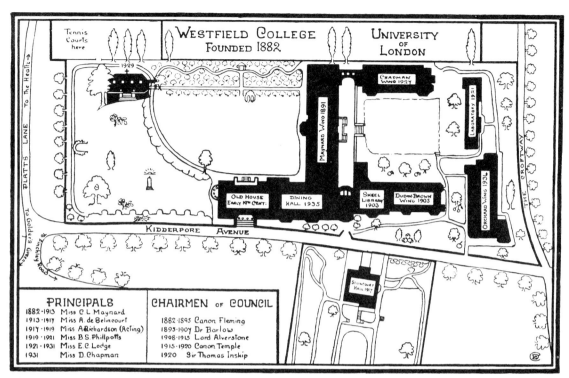

Plan of Westfield College in its Jubilee year, 1932.

the arcane meaning 'Can Elucidate Pindar'), 'Crassus', for Miss Whitby, after M Licinius Crassus, a Roman plutocrat of the first century BC who had his own fire brigade.

76 Note by Miss Chapman in Principal's Log Book, Easter Term, 1936.

77 M Kelsey, *loc cit*.

78 The 'conscience clause' was necessary to demonstrate to the public bodies about to be given representation on the Council that Westfield was open to all-comers who qualified for admission on academic grounds. So where in 1913 a Hindu applicant had been told she could not be admitted 'because every resident student must profess Christianity', in May 1918, a Jewish candidate was declared eligible to sit for the Scholarship Examination, although it was known that she would not be prepared to attend Prayers. Council Minutes, 30 April 1913 and 10 May 1918.

79 SCM is mentioned in *Hermes* for the first time after a long silence in 1938; LIFCU makes its first appearance in the same issue. It can be taken that the absence of reports of their activities did not signify lack of support for student religious societies.

80 *Hermes* reports in 1933 the formation of a Political Club from 'the remnants of the old Conservative and Socialist Clubs' (not otherwise mentioned). The only other society to concern itself with public affairs was the College branch of the League of Nations Union, established 1920.

81 R M T Hill, *loc cit* n 73.

82 Eric H F Smith, *St Peter's. The Founding of an Oxford College*, 1978, p 234.

83 In conversation with the author, 1972.

CHAPTER **6** 'A TIME OF WAR & A TIME OF PEACE'

1939 ~ 1962

Anyone with time for such reflections must have found it ironic that Westfield's removal from London in 1939 should coincide with the inauguration of the first London graduate to become its Principal. As a student at the London School of Economics, Mary Danver Stocks, then Mary Brinton, had specialised in economic and social history, in which she obtained First Class Honours in 1913. Married in December of that year to John L Stocks, philosophy don at Oxford, Mary Stocks thereafter combined wifehood and maternity with professional and public work

A Westfield student at St Peter's Hall Oxford, where the College moved for the duration of the war.

of various kinds, all of it inspired by her 'faith in education and social reform' as the means of bettering the human condition. Manchester, to which the family moved when John Stocks became professor of philosophy there in 1924, provided ample opportunity for his wife to observe at first hand, and seek to remedy, 'the many deplorable gaps in the existing welfare services'; and for both it cemented ties of friendship dating back to Oxford days with William Temple, then Bishop of Manchester. After the sudden death of John Stocks in 1937, only a few months after he had taken office as Vice-Chancellor of Liverpool University, Mary Stocks found full-time employment as general secretary of the London Council of Social Service. But congenial as this was, the invitation to become Principal of Westfield, extended to her by the Council on the warm recommendation of William Temple, was one she felt unable to refuse: 'It was a more responsible job and .... a great unlooked-

for honour. And did it not take me back to the university world in which I had so long sojourned with John Stocks?'.[1] As it happened, residence in a women's college was an aspect of university life she had not yet encountered, a lack which the Council, in announcing her appointment, did not gloss over. Her breadth of experience, as they recognised, was an asset and likely to 'widen the students' outlook on life' without detrimental effect on College traditions which they were confident Mrs Stocks would maintain.[2]

Mrs Stock's introduction to the students, on the first day of term in October 1939, necessarily broke with tradition: 'It was she who welcomed us to a strange abode, not we who received her into well-known places'.[3] To the second and third year students the arrangements at St Peter's might well appear strange: staircases in place of corridors, benches in the Dining Hall, 'gentlemen's wardrobes' in the bedrooms, a draughty porter's lodge instead of the cosy Bay as the collecting point for letters. Not surprisingly, some sighed 'for the comforts we were blessed with in Hampstead'.[4] The only real drawback, however was shortage of space. St Peter's[5] normally accommodated 90 undergraduates. Westfield had 150, and this meant that many had to share while others (35 in 1941-2, when numbers reached their wartime peak) found themselves in lodgings. Lecture rooms were so scarce that an enclosure, known as the Pen, had to contrived at the top of a staircase for the Classics department; History lectures were given in the back pews of the unheated church of St Peter-le-Bailey. The iron ration of 3500 books transported from Hampstead was too large to be ingested by the St Peter's Library (which had been inspected by Westfield's librarian, Miss Eileen Mackenzie, in April 1939 and deemed too theological for Westfield's needs);[6] books for which there was no shelf room overflowed into passages or even remained in their packing cases. Meetings of the Academic Board, as remembered by Professor Rosalind Hill,[7] took place in the Principal's room: five members could sit on the bed — dubbed by Professor Sykes 'the saints' everlasting rest' — and anyone without a chair sat on the floor.

There was naturally another side to the picture. For an academic community, exile to Oxford could not be construed a hardship, and Westfield was doubly blessed in having the ready-made setting of St Peter's in which to maintain its corporate life. The tribute paid by the Westfield College Council (*Annual Report* 1940-1941) to the forbearance of the St Peter's Bursar and Tutors in face of 'the occupation of their premises by an alien college' was certainly well-deserved. In the absence through illness of the Master, Dr Christopher Chavasse, who had personally conducted the negotiations with Westfield, no one at St Peter's knew precisely what had been agreed. Although the resultant misunderstandings[8] took a little time to resolve, the general tenor of relations was much more in keeping with the spirit of Westfield's parting gift to St Peter's, a handsome silver loving cup copied from a Dublin original of 1717, which the Master and Fellows kindly lent for display in the historical exhibition mounted at Westfield in 1982 to commemorate the College's centenary.

Contact between undergraduates of the two colleges was necessarily slight, the St Peter's men (who did not disappear on the outbreak of war with the immediacy or completeness Dr Chavasse had anticipated) having

Westfield College at St Peter's in 1942. Mrs Stocks is seated in the 4th row from the front, 9th from right.

been decanted to make way for the Westfield women.[9] But the closeness of St Peter's, in New Inn Hall Street, to the centre of Oxford meant that there could be considerably more involvement than in Hampstead with undergraduate activity in general: *Hermes* reported in 1942 that five university societies had Westfield presidents. The assimilation became so complete that a student who came up in 1943 'had to explain to Oxford freshmen that Westfield was not an Oxford College'.[10] The mistake was understandable, the host University having been generous enough to meet an 'unprecedented situation by according to Westfield an unprecedented status'.[11] One effect of this was that Westfield undergraduates were subject to proctors' regulations and had to accustom themselves to bicycling after dark in their treacherously long London gowns. Brushes with the University authorities appear to have been few — 'the only trouble I had with the proctors', writes the student just quoted, 'was when I attempted to open the OU Liberal Club's summer term with a mixed punting party at dawn on May morning'.

The academic benefits of Westfield's 'unprecedented status' were manifold: right of entry to Oxford libraries, entitlement to attend Oxford lectures, access to the Botanic Garden and the use of the University's Botanical Laboratories. In return, members of Westfield staff contributed lectures to the Oxford programme and addressed undergraduate societies, Mrs Stocks in particular being in great demand.

The war, which was the reason for Westfield's presence in Oxford, was never far from people's minds: 'although by no means in the civilian front line, we were naturally involved through our families and friends in the forces and more vulnerable areas'. Direct involvement in the form of call-up for national service affected chiefly the entrants of 1941 and 1942, some 65 of whom departed for the services or for civilian war work. About half of these completed their degree course in two years, no easy feat in face of the University of London's insistence that the full quota of Intermediate passes must still be obtained. Students whose courses were interrupted by call-up were given the opportunity, accepted by the majority, to return after the war. In consequence of a government decision to allow women students intending to teach to stay for the full course, the third year remained in being, although cut by nearly half. The shortfall in numbers was made up by larger intakes, the age limit of eighteen being slightly relaxed to allow under age students two years before call-up at nineteen and a half.

Warwork of a scientific kind claimed two lecturers in the Mathematics Department, Dr John Jackson,[12] who departed on secondment for the Admiralty early in 1941, and Dr Olga Taussky-Todd,[13] who left in 1943 to work on aerodynamics for the Ministry of Aircraft Production. Mrs Stocks, without ceasing to be an energetic full-time Principal, served on two important government committees which enquired, respectively, into conditions

St Peter's Hall, Oxford (below and right).

*Extracts from the minute book of Westfield
College Union Society Meetings 1940-1945.*

16

The Honorary President announced that College had been fined £5 on two counts for black-out offences and added that next time the fine would be increased. It was therefore the duty of every student to black-out with the greatest care.

Thefts of money had been committed [in] Porter's Lodge and staircase II during the [recess]. From the Non-Resident Cloakroom a hockey stick and some biscuits had disappeared. There was evidence that a missing cake [had] been consumed on the spot. The Honorary President cautioned students to keep valuables locked up as far as possible, reminding [them] to bear in mind the fact that all Colleges were alike. She said that any light [on] the recent occurrence would be welcomed.

H. Ske[...]

20

She apologised for this momentary inadvertance and said that should anyone express strong feelings about the matter she would give a donation to the Red Cross out of her own pocket.

The Secretary then gave her report. The College Dance was held on Dec 14th. 1940. 62 tickets were sold, 15 of which had been bought by St. Hugh's College who were unable to hold their own dance. They had enjoyed the evening very much and had expressed gratitude for being allowed to join. The Dance as a whole had been a great success.
... due to the Bursars for catering
... who had
... Secretary
... any
... the one to
thanked [...]
done to

56

1) The N.U.S. Secretary said that the Arts Faculty Commission was intending to hold a conference at Bangor in July. The Science Faculty Commission would hold a conference at Reading July 28-29. Details of both would be available nearer the time.

2) An appeal for Books had been issued by the N.U.S. Books on standard subjects were urgently needed for British Prisoners of war who wished to continue their studies, and books in various languages were also required for Prisoners and aliens in this country. Educational books for children between 14-16 in all languages were needed and Fiction or books of any kind for shelters in the London Area. Any offers of Books or Money would be gladly received by the N.U.S. Secretary or the Under Secretary. Books intended for British Prisoners should have all marks erased.
Reports of the Cambridge Conference were available and could be [...]
Under Secretary
then

100

An extraordinary College Meeting was held on Wednesday, 11th. Feb. at 1.45 p.m. in lecture Room I.

The President asked that, if possible, extraordinary College Meetings should be avoided in future as it led to considerable extra work.

The reading of the Minutes was postponed until next College Meeting.

The President read Miss Odom's proposal re the election of a committee to centralize the war-work already being done in College and to provide more.

a) N.U.S. The N.U.S. secretary stated that at the N.U.S. Congress recently held in Birmingham, a resolution had been passed that war work should be provided for women equal to that done by men in the S.T.C., and that compulsion should be applied where possible. The reason for compulsion was to make for ease in organization.

The N.U.S. secretary asked that those members of College who set up the committee should take it upon themselves to volunteer to do the work provided.

b) W.A.A.F. Training Corps. Miss Franklin proposed

102

should form a W.A.A.F. T[...]
Scottish Universities ha[...]
be recognised by the
[...] of this sort would b[...]
commission or for
As a result of enquiries
at a W.A.A.F. instruct[...]
available in Oxford. Sh[...]
College in this venture
[...]
[...]titution of the Committee
suggested membership
approval of the meeting
third year representativ[...]
second year represent[...]
first year represent[...]
S. C.R. member[...]
followed
President ga[...]
Oxford women[...]
[...]ical excessive a[...]
pointed at
during the [...]

104

from war work was freely granted to oppressed honours students.

Miss Dyson supported the election of a committee as she had found war work difficult to obtain unless through an organisation. She did not approve of compulsion.

Miss M. James protested against the introduction of compulsion.

Miss Franklin thought that compulsion should not be necessary. War work was a public obligation and we have social as well as academic functions to fulfill.

Miss Morton announced the following interesting forms of war-work that needed to be done.
1) Organisation of a knitting party
2) Collecting, darning, and delivering soldiers socks.
3) Entertaining convalescent soldiers.
4) Challenging soldiers to a debate.

Miss Gordon Brown stated that some forms of war work (e.g. knitting) could be combined with academic work.

Miss A. Bennett felt that compulsion was [...] not democratic and in all probability not legal. She thought that six hours a week extra reading by each student would be more beneficial than six hours of the type of war-work that other colleges were doing.

HERMES

MAGAZINE OF WESTFIELD COLLEGE

UNIVERSITY OF LONDON, AT ST. PETER'S HALL, OXFORD.

WESTFIELD COLLEGE UNION SOCIETY.

EDITORIAL.

THIS year the call for paper economy is even more insistent. *Hermes* appears without covers and with far fewer pages than usual. We have refused photographs and reduced the number of College contributions by half, thinking thereby to maintain *Hermes* as news bearer while restricting his less essential services.

It would be presumptuous to try to assess the gains and losses of our years in Oxford. Yet to us who have never seen our proper home two things are clear. The opportunities offered by a corporate University life, if not always realised, are wide, and we should be both to surrender them to the narrower limits of an entirely intra-College activity. There is much talk of replanning and rebuilding Britain and a rumour that London University might be grouped in its Colleges on the pattern of the older Universities. We would welcome this. We have, however, felt in this very system :—the loss of the College as the centre of interest can mean the loss of responsibility and a community sense, both of which we think to be important in determining individuals' right relation to society, whether in a single unit or the country itself.

May a plea for modern living be inserted here? The ...
us and clearly the individual may obtain ...
achievement from ...

"UNTOUCHED BY WAR."

So long ago! Forgotten until suddenly
Some joke or half-suggestive phrase
Flings wide that tight shut door.
Then knife-sharp memories rip the mind
As merciless as showering shrapnel,
And light afresh in the brain
The lurid fires of that May night when London
burned.
Not afraid then, when death and danger reigned,
But now a terror eats into the soul.
The mind beyond control re-lives
Every worst moment of those murdered years
In a few swift and silent shuddering minutes.
Air still, sky empty of both plane and shell,
A peaceful world outside,
But in imagination worse than war.
No sheltering steel helmet can save now—
Evacuate the mind? Would God one could!
Once fear-defying, quite untouched and calm
Now screams in silence, utterly worn down—
This is a mind "untouched by war"!

A.C.H.

WESTFIELD COLLEGE MAGAZINE.

8

WESTFIELD COLLEGE.

SCHOLARSHIP AND ENTRANCE EXAMINATION 1943.

GENERAL PAPER.

Afternoon 4.30—4.45.

(Candidates are urged to write on both sides of the paper, and in both margins).

1. Under hibernal conditions in a student's room which of the following articles should be used, in view of the National Emergency?

(a) an ample rug ; (b) a hot water bottle (stone) ; (c) a Bunsen burner ; (d) a gas fire turned very low.

2. "Is there honey still for tea?" Consider this hope, and estimate its possible fulfilment :—

(a) in 1914 ;

(b) in 1942.

3. According to your calculations, could Archimedes' principle be demonstrated in a bath 5 inches deep ?

4. "They also serve who only stand and wait." How far does this apply in the following cases ?

(a) On hearing the gas rattle.

(b) On seeing a child (under five) climbing into a static water tank.

5. Estimate the importance to a University career of the following Supplementary Subjects :—

(a) Washing up ; (b) Sweeping up leaves ; (c) Waiting at table ; (d) Dusting on alternate days

6. "The cup that cheers but not inebriates." Develop, with particular reference to treatment for shock.

7. Which would be the safest way for a left-handed student sheltering behind a stone wall (six inches thick) to tackle a phosphorus bomb (type 5 (a)) which has burst on top of her gas-mask?

(N.B. *Right-handed candidates need not attempt this question.*)

8. "Will these hands ne'er be clean?"

Answer this question with reference to the soap ration.

9. With half a cup of milk at your disposal, explain how you would meet two of the following contingencies :—

(a) a coffee party numbering seven ;

(b) a tea party numbering eleven ;

(c) an ink stain.

10. "A garden is a lov'some thing, God wot."

Show how this applies to work on an allotment.

11. What valuable lesson can we learn from Man Friday and/or Little Dorrit?

12. "Tempus fugit." Develop.

C.L.C.C.
B.D.G.

(Candidates are requested to hand this paper in to their local Salvage Depot).

But the magnet for all is the ripping strife
That covers the scene of the tragic strife.
And they try then to learn of the beautiful decorum,
Skilful, theatrical handling of life.

P.M.

VACATION INTERLUDE.

One damp July morning the telephone rang. A distraught Matron at one of the Ministry of Health's hostels for evacuee children, was speaking. Two of her six helpers had gone away; the holidays were imminent—in short, could I possibly come over to fill the gap? I agreed, and that evening I found myself in a melee of tough little cockneys, attempting to undress, bath, and get them into bed. This tumultuous company were to be my companions for six weeks. The Hostel housed sixteen boys between the ages of five and thirteen; the majority being under eight. All these were classed by the authorities as "difficult" or "childless children. We were at work almost non-stop from hard. There were, besides the Matron, two matron, two men, and a cook, who did all the housework, laundry, gardening, and caring for the sixteen children.
8 a.m. to 8.30 p.m. with breaks for meals.

BACKS TO THE LAND.

"Don't sweat, or yer won't last out while night!" We paused thankfully in our slow uninspired efforts to bring one lot of hay to another by means of a two-pronged fork, and were instructed in the technique of the modern agricultural labourer. Our shortcomings alas, were numerous. In the true Westfield style, we had tackled each job with a vigour which horrified our male companions. Before the foreman could make undesirable comparisons, we were rapidly initiated into the three golden rules of farming.

(1) Make each job last until it is too late for the foreman to think of a fresh one.

(2) Leave undone that which someone else might do.

(3) Do nothing at all if it can be managed unnoticed.

... follow this code and were soon on very good terms with the men. Jack, the ... discussing social reform ; (he was, incidentally, ... a week for legitimate ...

"The Pastoral Convention......"

... permission of Mr. Davis, who says he is pleased to realize that he looks so picturesque.

in the three women's services and the policy to be adopted after the war in regard to the recruitment and training of teachers (the 'McNair Committee', set up in 1942). Dr Eveline Martin, the Vice-Principal, spent part of 1944 overseas whilst serving on a government commission to enquire into the provision of Higher Education for West Africa - - 'the right woman in the right job!' as Mrs Stocks remarked. Westfield played a further part in the commission's work by providing, at St Peter's, a tranquil, bomb-free meeting place for the drafting of the final report.[14]

Bombing never deterred the Principal and the staff representatives on Council from journeying to London for meetings, which were held in whatever place — the Royal Courts of Justice, the Jerusalem Chamber of Westminster Abbey, the Principal's Kensington flat — was most convenient for the Chairman, Lord Caldecote, and others with important official duties. Aware of its remoteness in wartime from the working life of the College, the Council assented in January 1944 to a recommendation from the Academic Board which had the effect of achieving a place on the Council for all Heads of Department.[15] This became permanent practice, and was welcomed by Mrs Stocks, astonished on arrival to find the academic staff so 'poorly represented' on Council, as a further step away from what she termed 'the orphan asylum pattern of college government'.[16] Another wartime difficulty, that of maintaining contact with the University and other Schools, gave added importance to the functions of the College's Registrar. This office had been created in 1936 but was not officially linked with the proceedings of the Academic Board until 1940 when, 'after heated discussion', it was agreed that she should in future attend all its meetings.[17]

The prevailing austerity gave the bursarial department (increased from two to three) a hard time, but was accepted by the students more or less as a matter of course. In any case, there were always reserves to fall back on: 'If the meals sometimes failed to satisfy, there were precious food parcels from home, the British Restaurant near the station, two fish and chip shops and the Jam Tart factory at Banbury.'[18] Westfield had arrived at St Peter's complete with its own domestic staff. As vacancies occurred, for reasons of matrimony, call-up or economy, students took over some of the domestic chores, strictly according to rota and with only the minimum of complaint. In 1942 the students decided against the policy, adopted about that time in the Oxford colleges, of setting six hours per week as the norm to be spent on 'warwork'.[19] All the same, local youth clubs, convalescent homes and maternity units, shortstaffed because of the war, received regular help from Westfield students. Among a number of vacation activities, mention should be made of the mutually rewarding work (or play) with children and old people undertaken by small contingents of students at the Maurice Hostel in East London, a connection which lasted well into the 1950s. In the final phases of the war Westfield united in its efforts to collect books and money for despatch by ISS (International Student Service) to students in liberated countries.

With so much work of differing kinds to be done, and with all the distractions offered by an Oxford still miraculously 'alive with plays, poetry and excitement',[20] Westfield might have lost its accustomed facility for self-entertainment. There did indeed come a time, in October 1942, when a halt was called to 'all non-essential activities'. The chief casualties were College societies, already suffering from University competition and in 1944 declared by Hermes to be moribund. But abstinence from informal music making and dramatic productions did not last long, and throughout the war there was scarcely a term in which Mrs Stocks, herself a talented actress and improviser, failed to persuade similarly gifted colleagues to join in providing an entertainment 'calculated to sustain morale and keep cheerfulness afloat'.[21] Another frivolity not dispensed with was the annual College Dance, which despite exposure to hazards not known in Hampstead — 'the Oxford and Cambridge Rugby teams roaming the City in search of mischief',[22] for example — generally passed off without disturbance.

123

On arrival in Oxford the rules governing College closing times and the admission of visitors were brought into line with the slightly more liberal arrangements of the women's colleges *in situ*. Nothing remarkable seems to have come of the signs observed by the Principal in the first term that 'the comparative freedom of Oxford and the presence of the male sex' were 'mounting like strong wine to the heads of some students', and although later on she felt obliged to warn of the 'impropriety of prolonged good nights and the dangers of the US army',[23] the regulations remained unchanged. Policy regarding married students, a problem never posed before, was settled early in the war when it was decided to allow students to marry and remain in residence only in special circumstances, for example a fiance being ordered abroad on active service.[24]

Public Lectures, with the exception of the annual 'Inaugural Lecture', were dropped from the Westfield programme during the war. The College nevertheless had opportunity to hear some distinguished outside speakers: Professor Eileen Power of the London School of Economics, a close friend of the Principal's, who gave the Inaugural Lecture in October 1939, only two months before her untimely death; Margaret Bondfield, whose previous visit back in the 1890s seems to have gone unnoticed, Dorothy L Sayers, who addressed the SCM on 'Religious Drama' and afterwards kept the Principal talking until 4 am. A lecture by Professor Norman Baynes[25] in 1941 under the title 'After reading Hitler's speeches' evidently made a deep impression since it inspired a contributor to *Hermes* to plead fervently for greater emphasis on the study of contemporary issues: 'The cause of the Ancients is daily put before us and clearly the individual may obtain a greater sense of the heights of human thought and achievement from Plato than from Marx and Engels ... Yet as people in society we cannot afford to ignore the contemporary approach. Professor Baynes set a pointer ... which will continue to be valid.'

From 1944 onward the pointer was set firmly toward the better world being planned for the future: 'Beveridge was in our midst at

University College and William Temple held Open Forum at the Oxford Union.'[26]

The beginnings of postwar planning for the universities go back to June 1943, when the Committee of Vice-Chancellors and Principals wrote to the University Grants Committee proposing 'an authoritative review' of the problems, financial and other, likely to confront universities after the war.[27] Drawing attention to 'the many schemes now under discussion for extending the applications of science to the whole field of social and industrial reconstruction', they emphasised the need for greater assistance from government if universities were to discharge 'what is at once their peculiar function and a dominant need of the nation at the present day — the exploration of new fields of knowledge'. Also foreseen was the likelihood that universities would soon be dealing 'not only with a greater number, but also with a greater variety of students'. With the proposed review in mind, the University of London shortly afterwards invited individual Schools to submit statements of their development policies for consideration by the court.

The task of formulating plans for Westfield was given to an ad hoc Postwar Policy Committee set up by the Council in November 1943.[28] Its recommendations, while geared to preserving the prewar pattern of a College in which the great majority of students and a substantial proportion of the staff were expected to be in residence, envisaged a total student population of 200 rather than 150 and a correspondingly enlarged staff, reinforced at the top end by established professorships, or at any rate readerships, in every department. It appears to have been tacitly assumed that the number and nature of Honours courses would remain unchanged.

With so many factors still uncertain, such planning could only be tentative. Certainly, in the winter of 1943-4 no one would have dared to predict that Westfield's Hampstead base would emerge from the war in a state ready to receive its existing students, let alone a larger number. Yet so it was. Apart from the destruction of the roof and top floor of Selincourt by an incendiary bomb in October 1940, the buildings escaped damage. Moreover, the College was exceptionally fortunate in its wartime tenants. In 1939 the self-contained Orchard wing had been let by pre-arrangement to the Tavistock Clinic and was occupied throughout the war by a band of 'discreet and civilised psychiatrists'.[29] The main buildings were at first left untenanted, in the hope that the College might soon return. They were thus still vacant when the heavy bombing of central London started in September 1940, and so could be offered at a moments notice to the YWCA, whose headquarters in Bloomsbury were in the thick of the raids. Nine months later, in May 1941, the greater part of the College was requisitioned by the Admiralty for use as a training depot by the Women's Royal Naval Service (WRNS),[30] a tenancy which lasted until the end of the war and one much preferred by the College authorities to occupation by the Army, 'reputed to be no respecters of interior decoration'. The College Secretary, Miss Gedge, who with Mrs Stocks had skilfully warded off several attempts at military invasion, remained based on London and in occupation of Selincourt Hall which was used for committees and for the Principal's 'At Homes' (a misnomer in the circumstances) to former students — sparsely attended until Mrs Stocks scandalised the sabbatarian sensitivities of the older generation by shifting the day from Saturday, a full working day for many in wartime, to Sunday.[31]

Whatever future increase there might be in the level of support from public funds, it was clear that brand new buildings for the accommodation of additional students could not be expected either immediately or in the foreseeable future; and even if money were to be available from some other source, labour and materials could not be spared, nationally speaking, for non-essential work. It was therefore vital for Westfield to continue its prewar policy of acquiring neighbouring houses, to be used more or less as they stood. Thanks to the depressed state of the property market in wartime London, and thanks also to the careful husbanding of the College's financial resources[32] by Miss Gedge and her assistant, Miss Rosalie M Forster, a former Westfield

student who returned in 1938 on appointment to the newly created position of Finance Officer, a start was made, even before the war had ended, with the purchase in 1944-45 of Nos 19 and 21 Kidderpore Avenue. Named respectively Chapman and Stocks Hall (in the latter case several years after Mrs Stocks retired), these houses — to which No 23, named Richardson Hall, was added a year later — continued the chain already formed by Selincourt, Phillpotts and Lodge Halls. With the purchase in 1947 of the house between Selincourt and the Croftway, Westfield's 'dominance of the hill'[33] was complete; known formerly as The Grange, this house, No 11, was renamed Maurice Shute Hall in memory of the airman son of the previous owners, killed during the war.

The original Maurice Shute Hall (1950s).

The first advances to the Finchley Road likewise belong to this immediate postwar period. Possession of No 302, bought in 1945, was of crucial importance since its backland extended up the hill to include a strip running along the rear of existing College houses, which were thus preserved 'from the danger of being overshadowed at some future date by other people's building enterprises'[34] (it was not foreseen how enterprising the College itself would become). A similar remark was made in regard to the purchase in 1949 of No 322: 'Its garden will form a valuable addition to our own and its acquisition will diminish the threat to Westfield amenities of possible future building operations in the Finchley Road'.[35]

The cost of these various additions, which were intended for teaching as well as residence, was eventually borne by capital grants from the UGC. But although relieved of the major financial burden, the College administration had many difficulties to overcome, ranging from building controls to sitting tenants, before the conversion of the houses to College use was complete. After 1948, when Miss Gedge retired from the office of Secretary, the task continued under the supervision of her successor, Miss Forster, whose unremitting energies and eye for detail were applied with great effect to the rehabilitation and improvement of all College properties, and to much else besides.

'Great hurley burley. Everyone new to everything'. Mrs Stocks's hasty comment in the Principals's Log on the opening of term in October 1945 was certainly true of the students, but so far as the staff were concerned a pardonable exaggeration: only about half were new to Westfield-in-Hampstead and some of these, Beatrice White, for example, appointed Lecturer in English[36] in 1939, al

ready occupied a distinctive place in Westfield's academic community. For those with longer memories, the sight of the Old House, battleship grey on the outside and, like Maynard and Dudin Brown, dingy with black paint within, was mitigated by the good order of the gardens, which had been maintained throughout the war by the curator of the Botanical garden, Dorothy Nash, and the head gardener, AG Johnson. However, as Professor Hill recalled in 1976, the picture across the road was different. 'The whole of the garden

WESTFIELD COLLEGE, UNIVERSITY OF LONDON

The Inaugural Lecture
Session 1945-1946
will be given by

Mrs. J. L. STOCKS, B.Sc. Econ.
Principal of Westfield College

Friday, November 2nd, 1945, at 5.15 p.m.

Subject - "LONDON"
Chair - THE MAYOR OF HAMPSTEAD

Below: Phillpott's Hall in the 1940s or 1950s. Right: Caldecote Hall (No 322 Finchley Road) in 1966.

there was covered with sycamore. Those of us who were tough went out with billhooks and slashed and burned and cleared...Gradually we cut our way back into some semblance of civilisation...We learned dry-stone walling to replace the little stone walls...which is why they are still there.'

The Inaugural Lecture which opened the session 1945-6 was delivered, unusually, by the Principal herself whose subject, 'London', was chosen in conscious celebration of West-field's return to metropolitan life. For students who came up in the later 1940s and after there was unalloyed pleasure in the feeling 'that London was ours', that theatres, concerts, exhibitions, films were 'all there for the asking'.[37] But for the generation which returned to Hampstead from Oxford, accust-

From the 1951 College portrait: Left: Professor Winnington-Ingram and Miss OR Gee (Mrs Anderson). Below, from l to r: Miss Forster, Dr Mary Beare, Mrs Stocks, Dr EC Martin, Miss GK Stanley, Professor Rubinstein, and Miss Irene Glanville.

omed to having such delights, along with extra-collegiate lectures and society meetings, only a short bicycle ride away, the pleasure was mixed; and it was mingled with regrets for the 'prestige and privileges' which membership of their own University did not so obviously provide. Within a year or two, however, the revival of ULU activities helped to reanimate a 'University of London' spirit in its scattered Colleges and in 1947 *Hermes* confidently pronounced the 'myth of Oxford' to be dead.[38]

In one department, the Library, the Oxford period had been marked by a development of permanent significance: the appointment in 1941 of Dorothy Moore, FLA, as Westfield's first professional Librarian.[39] At St Peter's, with only a fraction of the Library under her hand and that most inconveniently disposed, Miss Moore had set to work on the task of re-classifying the collection on the Congress Library system in circumstances which, as someone said, 'must savour of Alice's attempts at a croquet match.' In London, where the books were still housed in two separated buildings, Miss Moore undertook in addition the long overdue task of producing a unified catalogue. But the greatest problem was lack of space. 'Extra library accommodation' was among the desiderata mentioned by the Postwar Policy Committee; in the form of proposals to extend the Lady Chapman building, it continued to hold a high place in the College's priorities, until the flux of time made possible the vastly superior solution of an entirely new, purpose-built Library, realised in 1972. In the

meantime, however, the crucial importance of the Library to the work of the College had been acknowledged by progressive enlargement of the staff, which from 1950 included a qualified Assistant Librarian, and the recognition of the Librarian in 1947 as a Head of Department and a member of the Academic Board.

The most important academic development of the immediate postwar period was the establishment of two new Chairs. In 1946 application was successfully made to the University for a professorship in Romance Philology and Medieval French Literature to which Denis Elcock,[40] still in his thirties, was appointed the following year. Elcock's interest in the comparative study of the romance languages, in which he was already an acknowledged authority, led almost at once to the introduction of subsidiary courses in Spanish and Italian.[41] The second Chair was in Classics, not the subject with the largest number of students but one regarded as of special importance in a College developing strongly on the Arts side. The first holder was Reginald Winnington-Ingram, Reader in Classics at Birkbeck College, who was appointed in 1948.[42] Although the establishment of Chairs in other departments had to be deferred, the standing of German was advanced by the institution of a readership, to which Mary Beare[43] came from Cambridge in 1947. By the end of the 1940s every Honours Department, with one exception, had one or more Appointed Teachers on its strength.

The exception was Botany which in 1948, when Dr Delf Smith retired, was within two years of extinction. The phasing-out of Botany had not figured in the plans of the Postwar Policy Committee. Indeed, as recently as June 1946 the Council had voted at a special meeting to seek recognition for the College as a School in the Faculty of Science, thinking it possible to meet the more comprehensive requirements of a new Botany Honours syllabus, due to take effect in 1948, by the introduction of ancillary Zoology and the reinstatement of Chemistry, which had been allowed to lapse after the departure of Dr P McVie in 1943.[44] The University, however, did not look favourably on this plan and indicated that only 'a complete Faculty', comprising departments offering Honours degrees in Chemistry, Zoology, Physics and Botany, was likely to be acceptable. Expansion on this scale had not been contemplated and was acknowledged by the Council to be impossible in present circumstances, and for some time to come. Since the continuation of existing arrangements, under which the subjects ancillary to Botany 'must necessarily be taken outside the College' was considered academically unsound and in any case impracticable, the Council concluded early in 1947 that it could do no other than accept the advice received from the University, namely to relinquish the teaching of Botany.[45] Writing in the *Annual Report* for 1946-7, Mrs Stocks summed up the feelings of the College as it contemplated the passing of one of Westfield's most cherished departments: 'Its premises and equipment were a matter of pride...and under the dist-

A lament for the passing of Botany (Hermes, 1948).

THE LAY OF THE LAST BOTANIST

The dust lies thick, the labs. are cold,
The students all have left the fold.
The bottles in their blank array
Seem to have known a better day.
The instruments which gave such joy
Are play things for some orphan boy.
The last of all the students we,
Who lived by learning Botany.
For lackaday! the days are fled
When knowledge and true joy were wed,
And now neglected and oppressed,
We watch decay and pray for rest.
No more in gown across the lawn
We carol by the light of dawn ;
No longer counted of the best,
High placed in Hall as welcome guests ;
No longer wander in the bay
And have a friendly word to say.
Old times are changed—old students gone—
And there are none to follow on.
Authorities have dealt the blow
That we the Botanists must go.
So, wandering post-grads, scorned, unowned,
We'll think of Labs. we worked in loaned
To strangers, while to foreign ear
Are told the tales we loved to hear.

A. M. BROADBENT.

inguished leadership of Dr Delf it has produced many generations of good graduates and
much valuable research. The ensuing three
years...required for its extinction will carry
for those who have loved the Department
something of the pain of a lingering death'.[46]
Dr Delf's personal sadness at this painful ending to her life's main work was intensified by
her conviction that it was anachronistic, at a
moment when the whole field of education
was rapidly widening, to offer 'an entirely
one-sided curriculum'.[47] Within ten years of
her retirement she was to have the satisfaction
of seeing her point proved.

On the positive side, the later 1940s saw initiatives in some new directions. In October
1947 two undergraduates from Barnard College, New York, arrived to spend the session
at Westfield, precursors of the many American Junior Year students who have subsequently, and in increasing numbers, come
to add spice and variety to the Westfield scene.
The necessary space was created by the out-
ward movement of Westfield modern language
students, who started at this time to take advantage of the 'intercalary' year abroad permitted under University regulations, helped
financially in some cases from a fund of
which the nucleus was a bequest from a former Head of the French Department, Miss M
Robertson, who had died in 1943. Finally, by
making available a lecture room in one of the
Finchley Road houses (No 302, 'Kidderpore')
to the Workers' Educational Association
(WEA) for evening classes, Westfield began to
take a share, albeit small, in meeting the needs
of part-time students. Since then Westfield
has regularly been the setting of summer
schools, whether organised by the BBC ('English by Radio') or, as in recent years, by the
Open University, and has so become known
to a far greater number than the original band
of WEA students who, on being entertained
to tea one Saturday by the SCR, 'learned with
surprise that the house which they were accustomed to approach in the dark was in fact
the farflung outpost of a large and important
institution...of whose purpose they had been
unaware'.[48]

Other contacts with the wider world were

due in part to the Principal's growing eminence
in it. In retrospect Mrs Stocks wondered
whether she had perhaps kept 'too many irons
in the fire' but confessed that, having the support of a very adequate administrative and
bursarial staff',[49] she found it hard to resist
invitations to serve on, and in some cases to
chair, Government and other committees with
a bearing on one or other of her wide range of
interests. In this way, as the Council grace-
fully acknowledged in its farewell tribute, Mrs
Stocks helped to carry the name of Westfield
into public affairs (her fame as broadcaster
was still to come), just as she was the means
of bringing into the College well-informed
speakers on topical issues to address student
societies. Genuinely interested in hearing the
views of students, Mrs Stocks attended many
of their debates and discussions and on Wednesday evenings was 'at home', sometimes in
company with a guest of her own, to any who
cared to come for talk, coffee and cakes — her
version of the now abandoned Sunday
'Function'.

The prolongation of food rationing and
other shortages into the postwar period made
entertaining difficult. Truly convivial occasions, for example the dinner parties instituted
by Miss Chapman to round off the intellectual feast of a Public Lecture, were reinstated
more quickly than the formal exercise of the
Commemoration Day garden party, not revived until 1949 and after a single repetition, in
1951, dropped completely. Sherry parties,
once unthinkable at Westfield, were now an
accepted mode of hospitality, among the staff
at least, but the temperance tradition still
held good at the Banquet where the health of
the graduates, the only toast now offered,
continued to be drunk in lemonade.

The Divinity Lectures, in abeyance during
the war, were revived in 1946 under the title
Maynard-Chapman Divinity Lectures[50] and
made open to the public. Students, whose attendance although still 'expected' was now in
effect voluntary, were well-represented in the
large and enthusiastic audiences which assembled to follow courses given by such lum-
inaries as the Regius Professor of Divinity at
Oxford, Leonard Hodgson, and the Dean of

Mrs Stocks (left) talking to Nancy, Viscountess Astor, in a special tenth anniversary edition of 'Woman's Hour' in 1956.

St Paul's, Walter Matthews. Morning Prayers, still an integral part of the College day, were conducted by Mrs Stocks along the undenominational lines she believed to be in keeping with Westfield's tradition of corporate worship. Her readings from the Bible were especially impressive and, as Professor Rosalind Hill recalls them,[51] showed 'a depth of knowledge and appropriateness of choice' rare even amongst professional theologians.

Mrs Stocks stands out in the line of Westfield Principals, and of women Principals in general, as a departure from the model then usual. Her qualifications for the post were unorthodox, and there were ways, chiefly sartorial, in which she cheerfully diverged from the conventions observed by her more correct colleagues. Stockings she particularly abhorred, so it was a disappointment to find herself in a minority of one when the SCR voted for their retention, even in wartime, as an essent-

ial part of academic dress.[52] But she did not set out to shock, and while amused to be in charge of a college which 'had the reputation among London students of being ladylike', Mrs Stocks was impressed by the politeness and consideration for others which went with it. True, she had felt on arrival that the students received almost too much consideration, 'I could almost sense a kind of softness — excessive concern for minor ailments, overemphasis on the ordeal of final exams',[53] and this may explain why in her own dealings with the students she came over as 'sympathetic but astringent'. Her constitutional inability to remember names, while it distressed her and may have been interpreted by some students as a mark of indifference, did not stand in the way of 'an unusual and most perceptive understanding' of the students' needs: 'she helped them far more than anyone knew'.[54]

Mrs Stocks was not a professional scholar

and it was thought in some quarters that she undervalued academic excellence. However that may be, there can be no doubt that Mrs Stocks was prepared to spread the net widely in the search for academic promise. She welcomed the postwar influx of grant-aided students as a sign that university education was becoming less of a class privilege, although long afterwards she admitted that during her last year at Westfield she began to wonder whether 'our universities were opening too wide a door to students who, though competent examinees, left school without any serious interest in academic studies'.[55] Her own acute mind, it should be said, played over a wide field and was rarely allowed to be idle.

Mrs Stocks is remembered for a great many qualities: for her 'effervescent sense of fun, her scintillating wit and complete, blessed lack of any pomposity';[57] for the warmth and discernment of her interest in all the people who make up a college community; for her powers of organisation; and for her seemingly light-hearted courage, which during the war infected all around her.

In 1951 Mrs Stocks was succeeded by Kathleen Chesney,* Vice Principal of St Hilda's College, Oxford, a scholar whose great distinction in the field of early French literature was recognised by the award of an Oxford doctorate of letters in 1954. Miss Chesney's appointment added momentum to Westfield's progress as an Arts College, as signalised by the institution in 1954 of an established chair in English, to which Harold Jenkins,[58] the Shakespearean scholar, was translated from his readership at University College, and the reinstatement in 1955 of the chair in History, vacant since the departure of Professor Sykes in 1944 for the Dixie Professorship of Ecclesiastical History in Cambridge. May McKisack, the eminent medievalist from Oxford[59] who was appointed to the professorship, devoted her inaugural lecture to the theme 'History as Education', defending the worth of a subject 'seemingly remote from everyday experience' with arguments, deployed with her characteristic blend of good sense and humane intelligence, which could be extended to the defence of Arts disciplines in

Kathleen Chesney, D Litt, Principal 1951-1962.

general. The newest of these at Westfield, Spanish, was elevated in 1955 to the status of an Honours Department under the direction of John Varey,[60] who was appointed in 1957 to the newly established readership. The building-up of existing departments, assisted by additions to the staff at a junior as well as senior level, was preferred to the introduction of new Arts disciplines, although both philosophy and geography were mentioned at various times as desirable.[61]

Applicants for places were clearly not deterred by the limited range of subjects on offer. Throughout the 1950s candidates for the Scholarship and Entrance Examination were regularly two or three times in excess of the vacancies, a superfluity in part more apparent than real, since the majority applied also to women's colleges elsewhere, but also no doubt a reflection of the larger numbers of young people staying on at school to the age of 17 — twice as many as before the war, according to a UGC report issued in 1958 — and the consequential increase in numbers qualifying for admission to universities, many of whom could now expect support from public

131

funds in the form of LEA and State Scholarships.[62] Westfield's capacity to respond to this rising tide of aspiration was limited in the 1950s by a shortage of residential.places: for it was still the Council's policy to agree to non-residence 'only in exceptional cases', and UGC capital grants were not available, as they would be in the 1960s, for new buildings designed solely for residence. Undergraduate numbers could therefore be increased only gradually as and when neighbouring houses became available, and by dint of pairing up first year students in their spacious former reception rooms and main bedrooms, an arrangement described as having the effect that 'no one was lonely, but a very great deal of time was wasted'.[63] By the end of the decade 1951-1960 the total undergraduate population was still well below three hundred.

Postgraduate numbers, by contrast, showed a noticeable increase, reflecting the expansion of this side of the College's work which had been proceeding steadily since the resumption in 1945 of the award of College research studentships, suspended during the war. When government grants in support of postgraduate research in Arts became more freely available in the early 1950s, the benefit to Westfield's burgeoning research schools was naturally considerable.[64] As might be expected, the titles of postgraduate theses, published from 1949 onwards in the College's *Annual Report*, reflect not only the older established specialisms of medieval literature and ecclesiastical and colonial history but also certain new fields, renaissance studies and comparative linguistics, for example, in which more recently appointed teachers were acknowledged experts. Apart from the common bond that all were working on Arts subjects, the postgraduates had much less cohesion than the undergraduate community and were soon seen to be in need of a College base. This was provided in 1955 when a newly acquired house, No 6 Platt's Lane, was placed at their disposal to serve as a centre for all postgraduates, whether married or single, male[65] or female, Westfield-educated or otherwise, and to provide residence for a few, mostly from overseas.

The Honourable Sylvia Fletcher-Moulton

OBE, who opened the new Hall and after whom it was named, had retired a few years previously from the chairmanship of the Westfield College Council, the only woman so far to have held that office. In her own description 'a working Chairman', Miss Fletcher Moulton had a grasp of affairs made all the more sure by her experience as a barrister, civil servant and administrator.[66] Apart from its strong complement of academics, both internal and external, the Council over which she presided included distinguished representatives of the local Hampstead community: Sidney Arthur Boyd, FRCS, Treasurer of Westfield from 1948 to 1961, was consultant surgeon to the Hampstead General Hospital and several times Mayor; Mrs Henry Brooke (created a Life Peeress in 1964, when she took the title Baroness Brooke of Ystradfellte), long prominent in local affairs, joined the Westfield Council in 1950, the year her husband first became Member of Parliament for Hampstead; and it was a local resident, already a visitor to the College in his pastoral capacity, that the Right Reverend Gerald Ellison, then Bishop Suffragan of Willesden, succeeded by Miss Fletcher-Moulton as Chairman of Council in 1953.

Miss Chesney welcomed Dr Ellison in terms which accurately predicted the benefits his chairmanship would bring, both in her own time and afterwards. 'Already', (she was writing within a few months of his arrival), 'we are benefiting by his wise counsel and by his friendly concern for the good of the members of the College, and we may well trust that under his guidance Westfield will continue to fulfil its founders' intentions of furthering 'true religion and sound learning' '. Herself totally in sympathy with the founders' intentions as here expressed, and the most loyal and obedient of Churchwomen, Miss Chesney's expectation of a harmonious partnership between Principal and Chairman proved amply justified. Notwithstanding his translation to the see of Chester in 1955, Bishop Ellison continued as Chairman until 1967[67] and made a most fitting return as preacher at the service held to commemorate the College's centenary in October 1982.

Writing in the *Annual Report* of the academic year 1952-3, Miss Chesney summed it up as one in which 'a good deal of quiet work was accomplished'. The description could be aptly applied to her own *modus operandi* as Principal. Habitually modest and innately shy, Miss Chesney served the College self-effacingly. Accounts of how she coped with a prolonged influenza epidemic — tending the sick through the night and carrying out her normal round of duties by day, having appeared 'as fresh as paint in Chapel at 8 o'clock'[68] — show that Miss Chesney possessed qualities such as might be found in the head of a religious order. She did indeed care deeply for the Chapel, both as a house of Anglican worship and as a meeting place for sincere Christians of whatever denomination, and took great care to see that everything was done there 'decently and in good order'. The furnishings of the Chapel, liturgical and otherwise, were added to and improved, and services became more frequent;

in the late 1950s, when informal links with the Church of England Chaplaincy to the University of London were established, Sunday celebrations of Holy Communion became a weekly instead of a termly occurrence.[69]

Miss Chesney's dedication to 'sound learning' was exemplified by her evident concern at the constant deferment of plans for the re-accommodation of the Library, by the interest she took in the welfare of the research students, and by her own teaching of her special subject. Only a small minority of Westfield students knew her in the role of tutor, but one who did remembers that she was 'very quiet, very scholarly, very witty'. The aura of Oxford no doubt still clung to Miss Chesney, as it did still more markedly to Professor McKisack, of whom it has been said[70] that she 'always viewed Westfield as another Somerville.' But the atmosphere of Westfield at this date, recollected in 1981 by Professor Win-

Miss Chesney (left) with HM the Queen Mother on the latter's first visit to Westfield as Chancellor of London University, 1957. Behind them, from left to right: Miss Barrratt and Dr Gerald Ellison, Chairman of Council.

nington - Ingram as 'intimate, domestic and hospitable', was sufficiently like that of an Oxford women's college for Miss Chesney to feel perfectly at home, and she found no difficulty in adapting to its customs.

Miss Chesney was not yet Principal when the Westfield College Association celebrated its Jubilee in 1950 and she therefore missed the opportunity to meet the Old Students, representative of generations 'as early as 1890 and as late as 1947', who foregathered in unusually large numbers for the event. But like all her predecessors she made a point of becoming known to former students; and for knowledge of them she was able to turn to the printed *Directory of Old Students* compiled by the Registrar, Miss M B Muriel in 1950, which gives brief particulars of all entrants to the College, apart from those who stayed less than three terms, from the foundation down to 1946. As a parting present to Westfield, Miss Chesney herself produced the *Supplement* which brings the record down to 1960.

Interesting information about the career intentions of new graduates in the 1950s is provided by the classified summaries given at this period in each year's *Annual Report*. As in the past, teaching predominated, accounting in most years for about half, with secretarial training as the closest runner up. The numbers given for the remaining catagories — posts in industry and commerce or in the government service, training for social work, for librarianship or as archivists, postgraduate studies — are much smaller, the order of popularity fluctuating from year to year. At the ultra-modern end of the job scale were the handful of computer trainees, all of them Mathematics graduates; the first to be mentioned graduated in 1954. Marriage, bracketed at the beginning of the decade with 'living at home', was expected by the end of it to be combined with at least part-time employment, usually in teaching.

Missionary work, the category which had been well-filled in the lists compiled with such pride by Miss Maynard, is almost entirely absent. Westfield's traditional link with foreign missions had in fact continued well after Miss Maynard's time, and several graduates of the 1920s and 1930s were still active in the field. Nevertheless, postwar changes of outlook, in the former missionary countries quite as much as among potential missionaries, made it much less likely that even the most committed Westfield students would offer themselves for missionary work of the old style. So when Miss McDougall, on a visit to Westfield in 1947, put the question, 'How can we recruit students for the mission field?', Mrs Stocks could only reply that the prospects were not encouraging.[71] But that is not to say that Westfield graduates had ceased to be adventurous, or that they were deaf to the call from developing countries for 'missionaries' of a secular kind. The contrary is proved by those who went out in the 1940s and 1950s to the Gambia and the Gold Coast, to Nigeria, Kenya, Northern Rhodesia and Uganda, to work as teachers or administrators in universities, schools and education services.

Looking back on the small, single-sex Arts college of the 1950s, a graduate of that era writes: 'We may appear to have lived in an ivory tower ... but we seem to have emerged well able to tackle the demands of a world which has altered radically, and in which women's positions have changed greatly'.[72] Westfield itself was to alter radically over the next twenty years, and began to do so when, by a remarkable reversal of university policy, Westfield's long-standing wish for a Science Faculty was at last fulfilled.

Hopes that Science would eventually return, and on a larger scale, had been expressed by the Academic Board even at the moment of Botany's final demise in 1950, and as an earnest of them the Botanical Laboratories had been left unconverted, all movable equipment being carefully stowed away. Opportunity to bring forward Westfield's case for development on the science side came earlier than might have been expected, in fact in the mid-1950s, when universities were once again under pressure to make an increased provision for science in the interests of enlarging the nation's scientific manpower: women, as a largely untapped source, came in for particular mention, women's colleges being exhorted to tackle the problem at its root by producing

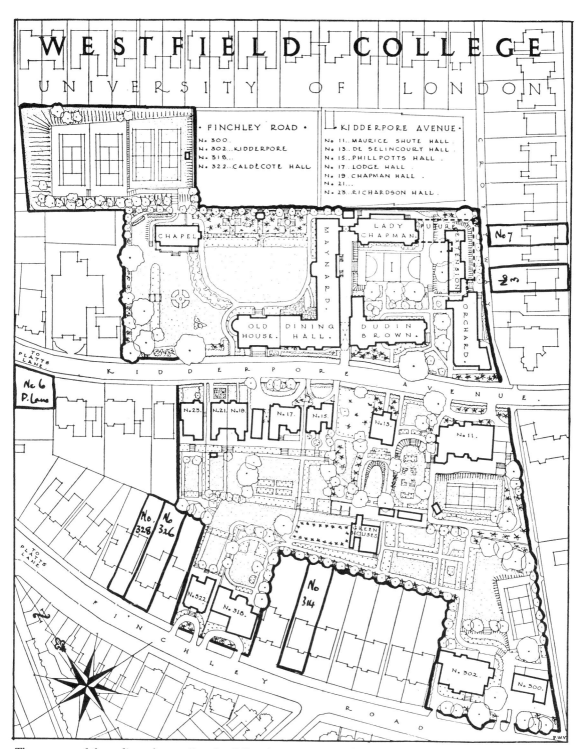

WESTFIELD COLLEGE
UNIVERSITY OF LONDON

· FINCHLEY ROAD ·

Nº 300.
Nº 302..KIDDERPORE
Nº 318..
Nº 322..CALDECOTE HALL

□ KIDDERPORE AVENUE ·

Nº 11..MAURICE SHUTE HALL.
Nº 13..DE SELINCOURT HALL.
Nº 15..PHILLPOTTS HALL.
Nº 17..LODGE HALL.
Nº 19..CHAPMAN HALL.
Nº 21...
Nº 23..RICHARDSON HALL.

CHAPEL

LADY CHAPMAN.

FUTURE EXTENSION

Nº 7

MAYNARD.

OLD HOUSE.

DINING HALL.

DUDIN BROWN.

ORCHARD.

Nº 6 P. Lane

KIDDERPORE AVENUE.

Nº 23. Nº 21. Nº 18.

Nº 17.

Nº 15.

Nº 13.

Nº 11.

TO PLOTS LANE

Nº 328 Nº 326

Nº 322

Nº 318.

Nº 314

GREEN HOUSES

Nº 302.

Nº 300.

PLOTS LANE

FINCHLEY ROAD

P.W.V.

The success of the policy of extending the College's precincts to safeguard future building projects is clearly seen in this beautifully detailed map of the late 1940s.

larger numbers of women science teachers. It was therefore with reasonable confidence of success that the Council, prompted by the Academic Board, included plans for a Science Faculty in the programme submitted to the University Court in 1955 in the hope, not disappointed, of securing an appropriate share of the University's grant allocation from the UGC for the quinquennium 1957-1962.

The Science Faculty as initially proposed was to consist of four departments — Physics, Chemistry, Botany and the existing Mathematics department. Physics and Chemistry would be housed in a new building on the still vacant space between the Lady Chapman and Orchard wings; Botany would reoccupy its former laboratories on the top floor of Orchard, which would also be used for the teaching of Zoology as an ancillary subject. These plans were comprehensively revised following informal consultation with officers of the University, who warned against confining new departments within an 'envelope' allowing no room for expansion -- 'no one can know how Science is going to develop in the next few years' — and who furthermore insisted that Zoology should rank with the rest as a full department. Taking account of these views, and of the space needed for research teams and workshops, Westfield's officers had to agree that the original plan, 'conceived with the object of not being too extravagant', was on the contrary too modest. Encouraged by a broad hint that 'only a sufficiently large scheme' stood a chance of financial support, the Council ruled out the Orchard site and applied to the LCC for planning permission to construct a self-contained science block between Selincourt Hall and the Croftway: a blow to the occupants of Shute Hall, which stood on the site, but an otherwise satisfactory solution.[73]

Though no one at the time could have foreseen it, the grant of planning permission in November 1957 ushered in two decades and more of intensive academic and physical growth. The work immediately in hand was designed to increase undergraduate numbers by two hundred and the staff by nearly a third, with readily foreseeable effect on the already over-stretched living and dining accommodation, not to mention the almost unbearably congested Library. In anticipation of future developments the Council had already set up a Planning Committee (February 1957) under the chairmanship of Sir James Brown, who as Third Church Estates Commissioner had had much to do with architects and planners. In 1958 a Buildings Officer, John B Bate, was added to the administrative staff. Advice on the detailed planning and fitting out of the laboratories was obtained initially from Heads of Department in other Schools and subsequently from Westfield's Professors elect, though, by the time they took office, in October 1960, the main features had already been settled. But when all is said, a large share of what had to be done fell to Miss Chesney, as Principal, and to Miss Forster, the Secre-

Above: press report on the opening of Westfield's Science Building in May 1962.

Opposite, top: Professor W Klyne presents Dr BJ Aylett to her Majesty the Queen.

Middle: Professor GE Fogg conducting the Queen on a tour of the Botany and Biochemistry laboratories.

Bottom: Professor JE Webb supervises students in a zoology experiment.

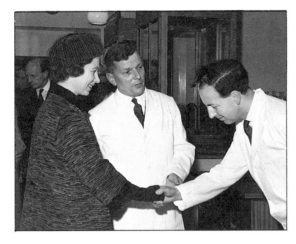

tary to Council, both of whom worked with a will to make the venture a success. Miss Chesney, for example, helped to publicise the 'coming event' of Westfield's Science Faculty by accepting invitations to speak at prize-givings in girl's schools, thereby adding to a volume of work already made heavier by extra committee meetings (the aspect of a Principal's work she least enjoyed) and staff appointment boards.

The first science undergraduates, 57 not counting 14 mathematicians, entered the College in October 1961. The student broadsheet of the day, *Tattler and Layabout*, joined its welcome with hopes that the influx of 'new blood' would 'shake Westfield once and for all from its apathetic rut' and was prepared to overlook the concomitants of 'overcrowded dining halls and smelly lab coats at tea'. To have been 'in at the start', wrote one of the pioneers at the end of the year, 'was a marvellous experience'; and she looked forward to the excitement of seeing the building 'brought more and more to life'. Miss Chesney, retiring that same term, thus left Westfield in a state of transition, but with the intimacy and coherence of its daily life, centred on Old House, still more or less intact. But even as she wrote her last principal's Report, the walls of the new Refectory were rising across the road: a necessary replacement for the Dining Hall, now too small 'to enable the whole College to sit down together' (as was still considered desirable), but a sign that Westfield had finally outgrown the framework which had for so long sustained its corporate life.

The one event that remains to be recorded of Miss Chesney's principalship is the one that made her last term glorious, the opening of the new laboratory block — the Queen's Building — by Her Majesty the Queen on 22 May 1962. Mrs Stocks, it is said, enjoyed social functions and shone at them; Miss Chesney as a rule merely endured them, 'except, perhaps, when she received the Queen at Westfield. She really did enjoy that occasion.'[74]

Notes
&
references

1   Mary Stocks, *My Commonplace Book*, 1970, p 188.

2   *Annual Report*, 1938-9, p 15.

3   *Hermes*, 1939.

4   Ibid.

5   For information about St Peter's Hall I am greatly indebted to Mr E H F Smith who, as a senior member resident in Oxford throughout the war, had much contact with Westfield and its representatives. Mr Smith's diaries, extracts from which he very kindly made available, help to fill out the picture of relations between the two colleges, naturally from the St Peter's point of view.

6   Miss MacKenzie's visit is referred to in Mr Smith's diary.

7   In her talk to the Westfield History Society, 1976.

8   It was not clear, for example, whether the Master's Lodgings had been promised to Westfield. In the event, the private living quarters were retained by St Peter's for the incoming Master, Dr Chavasse having resigned, and Mr Smith gave up his own set of rooms to Mrs Stocks. Having been kept in the dark, senior members of St Peter's were unprepared for the wholesale invasion of their quadrangles by women; it did not help matters when one of their officers heard himself referred to by an innocent visitor as 'the Master of Westfield'.

9   Contact, however, there must have been, since at least one marriage is reported.

10   Mrs A P Monkhouse (Brisbane, Westfield 1943-46), writing in *Hermes*, 1966.

11   *Annual Report*, 1939-40, p 10.

12   Lecturer in Mathematics 1937-1945; subsequently Senior Lecturer in Applied Mathematics, University of Dundee.

13   D Phil Zurich and Vienna. Assistant and then full Lecturer in Mathematics at Westfield 1937-1943; subsequently Professor, California Institute of Technology.

14   *Annual Report*, 1944, p 13. The chairman of the West African Higher Education Commission was the Right Hon Walter Elliot, MP.

15   Those not appointed to the Council in the capacity of representative members were co-opted, under the clause of the Charter stipulating a co-opted membership of 'not less than eighteen nor more than twenty-six'. However, since all but two of the co-opted members were required to be members of the Church of England, care had to be taken to ensure that Heads of Department not so qualified occupied either these places or the two places reserved for the Academic Board, to which no religious test applied.

     The Academic Board's recommendation on this matter, and the Council's agreement, are recorded Council Minutes, November 1943 and January 1944.

16   Mary Stocks, *My Commonplace Book*, p 192. Later in 1944 the Council further agreed to the co-option of a member to represent the Standing Committee of the General Staff Meeting (composed of academic staff not members of the Academic Board), in 1945 to the co-option of a member to represent the newly formed Administrative Staff Meeting. Taken together, these co-options increased the proportion of staff members on Council to nearly a third.

17   As recorded by Mrs Stocks, Principal's Log, February 1940.

     The first Registrar, Kathleen Wooding, was transferred to the office from her previous post as Principal's secretary. At the beginning of the war the two positions were amalgamated, and the practice of making a joint appointment did not cease until 1955. When Miss Wooding joined the WAAF in 1940 she was replaced for the duration of the war by Josephine Fuller, secretary to the Academic Registrar of London University.

18   A P Monkhouse, *Hermes*, 1966.

19   Principal's Log, February 1942.

20   As recalled in 1981 by J M Percy, Westfield 1939-1942.

21   Professor Beatrice M I White, writing in 1981. The entertainment offered ranged from an apocryphal Act VI of *Hamlet* to a ballet of 'College from Dawn to Dusk', presented in this ins-

tance by students. The content of 'an unrehearsed triologue' recited by the Principal, the Vice-Principal and Miss White has gone unrecorded, apart from Mrs Stock's private comment in the Principal's Log, June 1942: 'The result may or may not have been funny but was certainly vulgar.'

22   Principal's Log, November 1942. College dances were first held in the 1920s.

23   Principal's Log, May 1944.

24   Council Minutes and Principal's Log, November 1939.

25   N H Baynes (1877-1961), professor of Byzantine history, University of London 1931-1942 and from 1934 to 1937 University representative on the Westfield College Council; elected Honorary Fellow of Westfield 1939, under powers conferred by the Charter. Professor Baynes was again invited to give an Inaugural Lecture in 1946 when he delivered a paper, *The Thought World of East Rome*, which has had wide circulation.

26   A P Monkhouse, *Hermes*, 1956.

27   A copy of their letter is preserved in the Westfield College Archives.

28   It consisted of the Principal and Vice-Principal and three 'external' members of Council: Professor Lilian Penson, of Bedford College, University representative on Council; Professor W T Gordon, of King's College; and Lady Moberly (wife of Sir Walter Moberly, then Chairman of the UGC). Two Honorary Fellows were subsequently added, Professor Baynes and Miss Eleanor McDougall.

     Minutes of some of the meetings are recorded in a book used by Miss Gedge (who was in attendance) for miscellaneous purposes.

29   Mary Stocks, *My Commonplace Book*, p 198.

30   Under WRNS occupancy the Bay became the fo'c's'le, the Dining Hall the Mess, the Principal's room the Anteroom and the Skeel Library the Ark Royal. *Hermes*, 1942.

31   Principal's Log, September 1943.

32   The rent for St Peter's and the dues payable to Oxford University were to a large extent offset from 1941 onwards by the compensation received from the Admiralty for the use of the Hampstead premises (plus rent from the Tavistock Clinic). The policy of keeping St Peter's well-filled in termtime with students and in vacations with conferences helped both to keep down fees and to achieve a surplus on the residence account. It is nevertheless remarkable that reduction of the building debt could continue throughout the war years, and that money was also set aside for future needs. Among the benefactions received, mention should be made of a bequest from Miss Emily J Skeel in the sum of £12 000 which became free for College use in 1942-3, having previously been subject to a life interest.

33   Miss Chapman, writing as President of the WCA in *Hermes* in 1944, recalls that 'dominance of the hill' was already envisaged when Lodge and Phillpotts were aquired.

34   *Annual Report*, 1945, p 12.

35   Ibid, 1949, p 16.

36   From which she progressed in 1945 to Reader and in 1967 to Professor; retired 1969, elected Honorary Fellow 1976. D Lit London, 1947.

37   Thus Mrs R A Smith (Wincott, Westfield 1951-1954), writing in 1981.

38   The pro-London feeling in this issue is in marked contrast with pinings after Oxford in the two preceding numbers.

39   Miss D M Moore, B A Belfast; previously Assistant Librarian at Dr William's Library and Bedford College. Librarian at Westfield 1941-1975, Honorary Fellow 1978.

40   W D Elcock (1910-1960), a Manchester graduate came to Westfield from a lectureship at Oxford. His book, *The Romance Languages*, was published only a few months before his tragically early death.

41   Spanish, introduced as a subsidiary subject in 1948, was taught initially by Miss Janet H Perry, who had just retired as lecturer at King's College. Italian was introduced at the same level in 1949 and was taught first by J A Cremona and subsequently by Mrs Pamela Waley; unlike Spanish, however, Italian did not progress to the status of a full Honours subject.

42   R P Winnington-Ingram, MA Cantab., Professor of Classics at Westfield 1948-1953; subsequently Professor of Greek Language and Literature at King's College, and from 1964 Director of the Institute of Classical Studies. Retired 1972.

43   Belfast graduate, Ph D Bonn; Fellow of Newn-

ham College Cambridge, 1936-1947 and University Lecturer in German. Reader and Head of Department at Westfield 1947-1964; Honorary Fellow 1979. Dr Beare's speedy appointment in 1948 to the office of Vice-Principal (held for a term of three years) was a tribute to her warm personality and her qualities as 'a good college woman'.

44   To become Principal of St Gabriel's Training College.

45   Council Minutes, January 1947. Correspondence preserved by Dr Delf Smith indicates that the University was guided by observations made by the UGC, which had carried out its first post-war visitation of Westfield in the winter of 1945-6.

46   In 1950 the two remaining members of staff were successful in obtaining positions elsewhere, Dr Mary G Calder as Senior Lecturer at Manchester and Dr Joyce M Lambert as Research Fellow, with a Leverhulme Fellowship, at Newnham.

47   E M Delf Smith, 'Botany at Westfield', pp 38-9. She may have overlooked the continuation of the Mathematics Department, strengthened in 1949 by the establishment of a second readership to which Dr Dan Pedoe, lecturer since 1947, was appointed.

48   *Annual Report*, 1950-1, p 14. Westfield had given an undertaking to the UGC to make Kidderpore (how the house came by this overworked name is not clear) available for local adult education activities.

49   Amongst whom should be mentioned, in addition to Miss Forster, Miss Gwen Chambers, Finance Officer 1948-1980, and at this period also Maintenance Officer; Miss Eileen McCully, a member of the College secretariat from 1949, when she came as Secretary's Assistant, to 1976, when she retired as Deputy College Secretary; Miss Margaret McCall, Domestic Bursar 1949-1961; and the Registrar and Principal's secretary, Miss M B Muriel, 1948-1955.

50   As well as commemorating the concern of Miss Maynard and Lady Chapman to maintain Westfield as a College based on 'Christian principles', this title refers to the two sources from which the Lectures are financed: the Maynard Memorial Fund, collected by Old Students in 1913 to do honour to the Mistress on her retirement; and a legacy from Lady Chapman, who died in 1941. *Annual Report*, 1945, p 13.
        The revival of Divinity Lectures coincided

with a scheme to offer Theology to students as an Intermediate subject, to be taught by the chaplain at the nearby National Society's Training College in Domestic Subjects (Berridge House). The Maynard-Chapman Lectures were at first envisaged as a means of supplementing this tuition, but interest in theology as an examination subject soon petered out, bringing to an end the only 'religious teaching' ever provided at Westfield as part of the normal curriculum.

51   In her obituary tribute to Lady Stocks, *The Times*, 15 July 1975.

52   Principal's Log, 6 May 1940. Mr E H F Smith, of St Peter's, remembers that when Mrs Stocks did wear stockings they were always bright blue.

53   Mary Stocks, *My Commonplace Book*, p 193.

54   Professor Rosalind Hill, *The Times*, loc cit.

55   In 1952-3, for example, 66.5% of London's undergraduates were being supported wholly or in part by grants from public or private funds, compared with 27.3% in 1934-5: see Table 6 of the UGC's report, *University Development 1952-1957*, published 1958, p 24, and Table 7 of the following report (*1957-1962*, published 1964), p 29.

56   *My Commonplace Book*, p 199 f. It is worth remarking that just before she retired as Principal Mrs Stocks had begun a five-year stint as a member of the UGC.

57   Professor Beatrice White, 1981.

58   London graduate (University College), D Litt Rand; after holding the chair at Westfield Professor Jenkins moved in 1967 to the Regius Professorship of Rhetoric and English Literature at Edinburgh, from which he retired in 1971.

59   And more specifically from Somerville College, where she had been successively student, research fellow and tutor. Professor at Westfield 1955-1967; Acting Principal 1965-6; Honorary Fellow 1968.

60   J E Varey, MA PhD Cantab., a specialist in theatre history, came to Westfield as Lecturer in Spanish in 1952 and has been Head of the Department, from 1963 as Professor, since its inception. At the time of going to press he is Acting Principal, prior to taking office as Principal in January 1984.

61   At the students' request, extra-curricular lect-

ures in philosophy were in fact provided for a time (c 1948-1956); there is no trace of a comparable demand for instruction in geography.

62 Between 1952-3 and 1956-7 the percentage of London undergraduates receiving grant-aided support, public or private, increased from 66.5% to 70.4%.

63 Comment made in 1981 by Dr Margaret E Rayner, now Vice-Principal, St Hilda's College Oxford, undergraduate and postgraduate student at Westfield 1947-1953, temporary lecturer in Mathematics 1952-3.

64 The number of postgraduates, in the 1940s between 15 and 20, took a sudden jump from 18 to 31 in 1952-3 and remained for several years close to that level before falling off again at the end of the decade: *Annual Reports.*

65 There was nothing in the Charter to prevent the registration of men as postgraduates, but no advantage of this appears to have been taken until about 1948.

66 Miss Fletcher-Moulton, a Girtonian, joined the Council in 1935 and was Treasurer from 1939 to 1946. She had done important work as regional administrator with the WVS and with UNRRA in Europe, and in 1946 was a Principal in the Ministry of Town and Country Planning. It appears that Miss Fletcher-Moulton was instrumental in introducing the first American Junior Year students to Westfield. Elected Honorary Fellow in 1955 and now first in order of seniority.

67 When he was briefly succeeded by his brother, Randall Ellison, member of Council 1964-1978, and Treasurer 1969-1976. Honorary Fellow 1978.

68 Professor Rosalind Hill, 1976.

69 As can be seen from the Chapel register. The embroidered hassocks which still adorn the Chapel were worked by Old Students and others to Miss Chesney's design; as the College portrait of her by Patrick Phillips reminds us, fine needlework was one of her accomplishments.

70 By Professor C N L Brooke, her successor as Professor of History at Westfield, in his memorial address 27 June 1981.

71 Principal's Log, 4 November 1947.

72 R A Smith (Wincott), writing in 1981.

73 This account of how the scheme finally adopted for Science evolved is based on notes of informal meetings preserved in the College Archives.

Plans for the reaccommodation of students and staff displaced from Shute Hall, by conversion to residence of Orchard's top storey, were immediately put in hand. The name Shute Hall was transferred to No 7 Kidderpore Gardens, purchased 1958-9.

74 Professor Beatrice White, 1981. The foundation stone of the Queen's Building had been laid by Sir John Cockcroft, OM, KCB, CBE, FRS, Master of Churchill College, Cambridge, on 3 May 1960.

CHAPTER 7 WESTFIELD TRANSFORMED

1962~1982

Westfield's unprecedented rate of expansion in the 1960s and 1970s presents a striking contrast with its previous history of sustained but very gradual development. Enlargement, in numbers as well as buildings, was a necessary consequence of the establishment of the Science Faculty since it was agreed that this should not be to the detriment of Arts. The maximum growth initially envisaged was to a total undergraduate population of six hundred, twice the size of the College in the year preceding the first intake of science students in 1961, but by the time this target was achieved in 1966 the number aimed at had again been doubled. Hopes of reaching the new maximum of 1200 by the mid-seventies were dashed by inflation and the reduction from 1973 onwards of government support for growth in universities, which in the mid-1960s had been at an exceptionally high level. Westfield nevertheless entered the 1980s with a student body of well over a thousand, fulfilling a prediction made in her retirement by Miss Maynard when she looked forward, in 1927, to the time 'forty or fifty years hence when our numbers may be counted by the thousand rather than the hundred.'[1]

What Miss Maynard did not foresee was that among that thousand there would be men, who in 1982-3 make up almost half the total number. The first men to be admitted as undergraduates on a regular basis arrived in October 1964; but they had been preceded many years earlier by six Jesuits, who had joined the College in 1939 as a result of the

Dr Bryan Thwaites, Principal, and students (1967).

abnormal conditions then prevailing. How these unlikely recruits came to be received by an all-female (and at one time distinctly anti-Papist) institution is explained by Mary Stocks: 'All were embarked on London arts degrees at University College. When University College arts faculties were evacuated to Aberystwyth, the Jesuits could not follow them because Aberystwyth did not contain a Jesuit House where they could live. Oxford did at Campion Hall. But in Oxford the only London arts degree courses available were at Westfield in St Peter's Hall. Hence their inclusion as Westfield students. I have always hoped that at some future gathering of old Westfieldians I may meet a Cardinal, or even a Pope; but this has not yet happened.'[2] The Jesuits are remembered as having taken a full part in College activities, and their highly creditable examination results were recorded in *Annual Reports* and in *Hermes*.[3] Just after the war the Academic Board put in a plea for the admission of ex-servicemen, 'in view of the present emergency and pressure upon the Colleges',[4] but the idea was not pursued. It was not until October 1956 that the possibility of making Westfield co-educational at all levels began to receive serious attention, the matter having been put by the University at the request of the UGC to all the women's colleges in London.[5] The Westfield Council, taking the view that there was 'still a case for different patterns to enable parents to choose between small and large, mixed and segregated Colleges',[6] was reluctant to make the change. But

142

while not prepared to go the whole way, the Council agreed to consider admitting men to the prospective Science departments until a sufficient number of suitably qualified women became available,[7] and only drew back on being advised that a revision of the Charter might be needed.[8]

When the matter next came before the Council, in November 1962, it took the form of a proposal from the Academic Board to admit men on equal terms with women, that is to say without restriction as to faculty or department, without the imposition of a quota, and as a permanency. On the previous occasion only a very small minority had ventured to express support for the reconstitution of the College on a fully co-educational basis,[9] but in the interim much had happened to bring about a change of attitude. The staff of the Science Faculty, most of them used to working in mixed institutions, could testify from experience that open competition attracted students of the quality deemed essential to the building up of strong research schools. Student opinion, which had at first been divided, had come out in favour as early as December 1960, when it was decided at a Union

meeting that 'as the College was expanding rapidly its unique quality could not be preserved, so men were very welcome.'[10] Lastly, two other women's colleges in London had already made moves in the direction of co-education, Queen Elizabeth by admitting men to its BSc General courses in 1958 and Royal Holloway by seeking enabling powers. The likely effects on the volume and calibre of applications to any remaining single-sex colleges could not be ignored.

The arguments for and against were very fairly set out for the Council in a paper[11] prepared by the Chairman, Dr Gerald Ellison, in which the crucial question of loyalty to the founders' intentions was squarely faced. It was pointed out that the specific purpose for which women's colleges had been founded was now accomplished: 'women have achieved that independence and equality which were being fought for in the nineteenth and early twentieth centuries, and, therefore, so it is asserted, the raison d'être for the women's colleges (which were an element in the struggle) no longer exists.' Second, it was argued that in modern times the founders' intentions to provide for the Higher Education of women would be best served in a college accessible to well-qualified students of either sex. Agreement was swift. On 23 May 1963 the momentous resolution, 'that men students shall be

WESTFIELD COLLEGE

(University of London)

Hampstead N.W.3

ADMISSION
of
MEN UNDERGRADUATES

October 1965

Left: the brochure inviting male applications to Westfield. Below: a Fresher's Squash (1981).

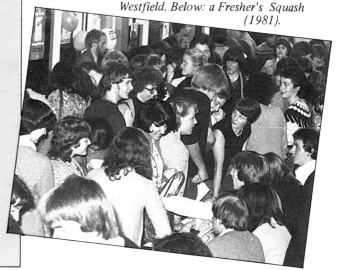

admitted to the College and the necessary powers for the amendment of the Charter ... be sought', was moved from the Chair and carried without opposition. Amendment of the Charter proved easier than had at one time been feared. A Special Statute deleting from the Charter all references to women was passed by the Council, submitted to the Privy Council, and approved by the Queen on 12 May 1964. Although notice was short, twenty-one male undergraduates joined the College in the following October. For the next year over a hundred men were admitted, including the first dozen or so to be accepted by Arts departments.

At the beginning of the academic year 1962-1963 Miss Chesney had been succeeded as Principal by Mrs Pamela Matthews,* an economist with wide experience of public affairs. Mrs Matthews thus arrived at a time when major new policies were in course of implementation or about to be introduced. The Science Faculty, although already in being, was suffering from teething troubles connected with deficiencies in buildings and equipment. The decision to admit men to the College, taken during Mrs Matthew's first year in office, posed as an immediate problem the question of accommodation and, since it was not intended that men students should occupy places which might otherwise be filled by women, made it imperative to review College policy in regard to eventual student numbers and to plan accordingly. In May 1963 the Council agreed to seek the University's approval for an increase in student numbers from the existing target of 600 to 1200. Their request could not have been made at a more propitious moment. For by this time it was an open secret that the Committee on Higher Education (the Robbins Committee), appointed by the Prime Minister, Harold Macmillan, in 1961, was about to issue a Report recommending large-scale expansion of Higher Education. The University was therefore able to consider Westfield's proposals, which it quickly endorsed in principle,[12] in the context of its overall contribution to the 'national crash programme' for which, as expected, government funds were made available following the

Mrs Pamela Matthews (centre), Principal 1962-1965

presentation of the Report of the Robbins Committee to Parliament in October of the same year.

Thus encouraged, Westfield felt free to embark on the formulation of a comprehensive development plan, for which purpose the Council set up a Planning Committee on a permanent basis. In March 1964, Sir Hugh Casson, of Casson, Conder and Partners, was appointed planning consultant and thus began the long association of himself and his firm with the College. In the report he submitted to the Council in October 1964[13] Sir Hugh set out 'in broad terms the principles, physical and conceptual, for the long term future of the College'; emphasising that the plan was intended as 'a guide rather than a blue print'. He indicated a number of areas in which further policy decisions were required, for example the desired proportion between residential and academic accommodation, the question of security — an exceptionally pressing one at this time, because of the number of small houses, some of them isolated, being used as residences in place of larger halls demolished

Berridge House.

to make way for the Queen's Building and the Refectory — and the provision to be made for the College's proliferating administrative departments.

The more immediate matter of making suitable residential provision for male undergraduates was solved with the purchase in 1964, following protracted negotiations with other interested parties, of the greater part of Berridge House. These premises had been the home since 1908 of the National Training College for Teachers of Domestic Subjects and were being vacated because of that College's transfer to another part of London.[14] Capacious enough to house about eighty students and, although on the far side of the Finchley Road, within a short walking distance of Westfield's main site, Berridge House has been an invaluable addition to the College's stock of properties and its acquisition, in face of considerable difficulties, was something of a triumph for Mrs Matthews.[15] A roughly equivalent number of residential places for women was added with the completion the following year, 1965, of the New Orchard building, which at last filled the gap left vacant between the original Orchard building and Lady Chapman.

Plans and properties did not of course occupy the whole of the Principal's attention. Mrs Matthews applied herself equally to problems connected with the day-to-day running of the College. Amongst other things, the administrative structure was revised with a view to defining spheres of responsibility more

clearly, additional maintenance staff were engaged as a partial remedy for the physical difficulties being experienced by the Science departments, and the workings of the residential system were subjected to a thorough scrutiny. Mrs Matthews, who cared deeply about the students and their welfare, had a number of reasons for feeling concern about the quality of their life as residents: the proportion of senior staff willing or able to live in College and take charge of Halls was rapidly declining;[16] security, as already mentioned, was a perpetual worry (as it still is today); and, with larger numbers, the intimacy and protectiveness of the shared collegiate life was less easy to sustain and possibly held a decreasing appeal for a number of students, a few of whom had begun to question quite openly the College's right to monitor their comings and goings.[17] An Ad Hoc Committee on Residence (it has had many successors) was set up by Council, at the Principal's request, soon after her arrival.[18] Several of its recommendations have since become standard practice: for example, the provision of properly equipped living quarters for resident staff, the use of postgraduates as assistant wardens, patrolling of the grounds by security staff at night. However, the greater part of the Ad Hoc Committee's time was given to the revision of College regulations, with an eye to making them 'relevant to present day conditions' and in the hope that 'more reasonable regulations' would be 'more faithfully observed'.[19]

The three years, 1962-1965, during which Mrs Matthews was Principal happened to be especially momentous ones for Westfield, marking as they did its passage from the old order, predominantly female and predominantly Arts, to a new order under which this twofold imbalance was to be redressed. In this transitory period, which was not without its traumas, Mrs Matthews did much by her concern for the students and her regard for College traditions to prevent too abrupt a break in continuity; and, looking to the future, she set Westfield on a course for the 'post-Robbins' era of development.

If the first half of the 1960s was a turning point in the history of Westfield, it was equally so in the modern history of British universities at large. The success of the nation's secondary schools since the war in giving their older pupils both a taste for higher education and the requisite qualifications had not been matched, until the early 1960s, by a comparable effort to provide additional places. In 1962, any financial deterrents to would-be students were to a very large extent removed by the Education Act of that year,[20] which made it obligatory for Local Education Authorities to award grants to all students with two A level passes who were accepted for degree courses. On the basis of estimates drawn up with these provisions in mind, the Robbins Committee, which reported in October 1963, recommended a programme of expansion on a scale that would enable the percentage of the relevant age-group entering degree courses to be raised from about eight per cent, the proportion in 1962-63, to about seventeen per cent by 1980.[21] In an unprecedently prompt response, the Government accepted the Robbins targets (up to 1973) and announced that funds would be made available through the UGC to meet the estimated cost. As plans for expansion proceeded, however, it quickly became clear that, as beneficiaries of a greatly increased national investment in higher education, universities would henceforth come under more intensive public scrutiny, and that they would be exposed as never before to adverse movements in the economy and to shifts in government policy. The effects of such constraints were already beginning to become apparent when Dr Bryan Thwaites,* Professor of Theoretical Mechanics at the University of Southampton, became Principal of Westfield in October 1966.

Internationally distinguished for his research in fluid dynamics and Director since 1961 of the School Mathematics Project (of which he was co-founder), Bryan Thwaites was already well-known to be a man of ideas and a successful innovator. Eager to see Westfield in the forefront of academic advance, he campaigned successfully to establish Computer Studies as part of the College's programme, not omitting to secure computing facilities on a commensurate scale. Less to be expected, perhaps, was

the readiness of Westfield's first male Principal to interest himself in the College's past record, which he signified by his concern to build up a College Archive and his enthusiastic support for this centenary history, and again by his willingness to identify with its former members, demonstrated from the outset by his regular attendance at Westfield College Association meetings and his assurances to old students, made anxious by news of his appointment, that his intentions were unsubversive. The Council's action in explicitly opening the post of Principal to men as well as women in fact attracted little, if any, overt criticism (though it might well have done only a few years earlier), and there was no reason why it should. By this time half the staff, including the College Secretary,[22] and a quarter of the undergraduates were male; and having ended discrimination at the undergraduate level, it would have been inconsistent to deny equality of opportunity to men at the top. Yet when all is said, the break in the long succession of women Principals unquestionably marked the end of an era, as did the retirement in the same decade of Miss Gertrude ('GK') Stan-

Dr Bryan Thwaites, Principal 1966-1983.

ley,[23] Professor Gladys Dickinson,[24] Dr Mary Beare,[25] Miss Christina Barratt,[26] Dr Eileen Mackenzie,[27] Professor Beatrice White[28] and Professor May McKisack,[29] who as teachers and pastors had exemplified in their individual ways all that was 'best and most influential in the women's colleges of former generations.'[30]

Above left: Miss 'GK' Stanley, Left: Dr Eileen Mackenzie.

Residence, which contributed so much to that ethos, was among the characteristics of Westfield most prized by Dr Thwaites, and is one he has made great efforts to preserve. Early on he proposed the 'two-thirds' formula, whereby students should always be assured of residence for two years out of their three. Implementation of this policy at a time when numbers were expanding was not without its problems since support for residence from public funds, which had been available for the Berridge House and New Orchard projects, could no longer be counted on. It therefore gave the Principal particular pleasure to be able to announce, in his Report for 1967-8, that £300 000 had been given by an anonymous donor, 'whose identity is shrouded in impenetrable mystery', for a hall of residence to house about two hundred students (at that date about a quarter of the College). To this munificent gift was subsequently added a further £70 000 from the same source and another £50 000 from the Wolfson Foundation. The new building, whose name 'Kidderpore Hall' perpetuates the original name of Old House, was ready for occupation in 1972. As different as can be from its erstwhile namesake, Kidderpore Hall dominates the junction of Platts Lane and Kidderpore Avenue and from the outside appears to be all of a piece. Inside, however, the Hall is divided into four 'houses', Temple and Ellison for men, Stocks and Chesney for women; a fifth area, Wolfson, contains a refectory and common rooms, it being the donor's wish that the entire complex should form a self-contained unit. In 1981 the same anonymous donor, whose gifts to London colleges, always for residential purposes, have totalled over ten million pounds, favoured Westfield with a second benefaction of £250 000, for a hall to be reserved for women. Her Majesty Queen Elizabeth the Queen Mother graciously gave permission for this latest addition to be named The Queen Mother's Hall, in simultaneous commemoration of her eightieth birthday and of her twenty-five years as Chancellor of London University, and with equal grace came in Dec-

147

*Left: The Library,
built among the gardens between
Finchley Road and Kidderpore Avenue. Above: Queen Mother's Hall.*

ember 1982 to open the Hall in person, thereby bringing the College's centenary year to a satisfying conclusion.

It was already evident in the early 1960s that as the College expanded it would need more and better accommodation for teaching and research. Once the Queen's Building was completed, plans were put in hand for a corresponding Arts block, to be linked eventually with a new library. The first of these stages was assigned a place in the University's capital programme for 1967-68, but by the time the starting date was almost in sight it had begun to seem doubtful whether the money allocated would produce a building commensurate with the Faculty's existing, let alone its future, needs. This was the position when Dr Thwaites became Principal in 1966. Convinced that a whole library, for which the University was prepared to make additional funds available, was preferable to a half-completed Arts block, Dr Thwaites persuaded the Council to change their order of priorities. The resultant building, one of the most impressive modern libraries in the University and named like the first Westfield library after Caroline Skeel, was completed in 1971. Compared with the cramped and scattered premises just vacated, the spaciousness of the multi-storey Library may have looked at first over-generous, but the recent proliferation of modern aids to learning — tape, film, slides, and the equipment to produce them — has ensured that no vacuum remains. Room has also been found for a number of manuscript collections,[31] but pride of place continues to be given to the printed word and to the collection begun and cherished by Caroline Skeel, whose portrait hangs in the entrance hall.

The Queen's Building was twice enlarged during the 1960s, in 1966 by the addition of one and a half floors to the Zoology wing and in 1969 by a full-scale extension to the main block. The Science departments also benefited from the College's aquisition of Berridge House, which apart from its value as a hall of residence also yielded space for additional laboratories, among them the Hillfield Hut, which was in occupation well before the conversion of the main premises.

The quinquennium 1967-1972 turned out to be the last during which major grant-aided projects could be undertaken,[32] with the result that plans for an Arts block had to be shelved. This was less of a blow than might appear, for as residence became concentrated in fewer and larger units, smaller houses were freed for use as departmental bases. Considerable shuffling and reshuffling had to take place in order to assemble staff of the same department under one, or at any rate adjacent roofs, and it was not until the mid-seventies that the operation was finally completed. As a setting for the academic and social life of departments not geared to practical work, the intimacy and individuality of former private houses have come to seem preferable, in the eyes of many, to the uniform impersonality of a modern, purpose-built Arts block.

The developments of the last twenty years have emphasised the supreme importance to Westfield of the 'island site', that is to say the area bounded on its four sides by Croftway, Finchley Road, Platts Lane and Kidderpore Avenue, which has provided space for four large-scale new buildings (Queen's Building and its additions, the Refectory, the Caroline Skeel Library and Kidderpore Hall)[33] and yet remains uncluttered. The unified treatment of the central expanse was made possible by the College's success over the years in acquiring, with one remaining exception, all the houses on the perimeter, whose combined gardens make their own contribution to the refreshingly open prospect. The College's original site on the opposite side of Kidderpore Avenue has also had its share of new buildings: New Orchard, and most recently the Queen Mothers' Hall, placed alongside St Luke's and backing onto the Chapel lawn. The grounds on this site are still recognisably descended from the 'lawns and gardens ... disposed with much taste and planted with shrubs, evergreens, and exotica in abundance' boasted of when the original Kidderpore Hall was put up for sale in 1855 after the death of its first owner (see Appendix IV). For this satisfactory state of affairs, and for the care of the grounds in general, the College is indebted to the expert and imaginative direction of Dr GJ Cunnell, Garden Steward since 1964.

Two additions to the residential and other accommodation made over the last twenty years lie outside Westfield's established territory, in both cases on the far side of the Finchley Road: Berridge House, already mentioned, and Carus-Wilson Hall. The latter, which is reserved for postgraduates, occupies what was formerly New College but is now, under the name of Parsifal College, the London centre of operations for the Open University.

The pattern of communal living at Westfield has naturally altered in consequence of the changes, physical and other, of the past two decades. Mealtimes are an obvious example. Where once there was only the Dining Hall where the whole College sat down together, there is now a multiplicity of eating

places, ranging from the main Refectory to the Bay (in its latest metamorphosis as a lunch bar), not to mention the modest self-catering facilities to be found in halls of residence and departmental common rooms. High Table, provided for the main Refectory (completed 1964) but not in its Wolfson counterpart, built less than ten years later, has fallen out of use for reasons as much financial as social. Even the Banquet — no longer known by that name — has become a less formal occasion.

Underlying these and other alterations to Westfield's way of life is the fact that a greater proportion of those who share in it, students as well as staff, are non-resident. Residence, while available to students for two years out of their three and warmly encouraged, is not nowadays a condition for admission, nor are students out of residence required to live at home or in lodgings found by the College. Students who opt for residence are expected, reasonably enough, 'to abide by the residence rules which the College lays down for the happiness and well-being of its members', but their situation is quite unlike that described by a student from the last all-female generation who recalls: 'We were conscious that we had a reputation of being a rather cloistered breed, flourishing under close supervision in the rarified air of Hampstead (or breaking out and kicking over the traces altogether).'[34] This is not at all to say that Westfield's reputation for taking care of its students has ceased to be valid — quite the reverse. For all students, resident and non-resident, there is a great array of persons 'ready, willing and able' (to quote from the *Students' Handbook*) to give help and advice. These include, as before, the Principal, the Registrar, Heads of Departments and Hall Wardens, and some that are more recent additions to the strength. The position of Senior Tutor was created in 1967 when Mr A Deyermond, Lecturer (and now Professor) in the Spanish Department and a Senior Treasurer of the Students' Union, was appointed to the post.[35] In the same year it was considered that Westfield had reached the stage of requiring the services of a regular Chaplain. The first to fill the office was the Reverend Richard Harries (now Dean of King's College, London), who combined it with a curacy at Hampstead parish church;[36] his successor, the Reverend Michael Porteus, shared the 'cure' of Westfield with that of Bedford College, an arrangement which has continued. In addition to conducting services, the Chaplain co-ordinates the religious activities of all denominations; and, together with his visiting Free Church and Roman Catholic colleagues, he is accessible to everyone. 'whether or not they go to Chapel or participate in the Christian community.' Proper provision for students falling ill or otherwise in need of medical advice had been achieved a little earlier, with the conversion in 1964 of part of Selincourt as a Sick Bay (now called the Health Unit).

Members of the Westfield College Union Society were warned by their President in 1962 — almost the last year of an all-female undergraduate membership, as it turned out — that 'the Union should and must change from a group of girls preoccupied with laundry ... to a body of students whose concerns are of general student interest as well as specifically Westfield's.'[37] Reports of subsequent meetings show that domestic issues such as 'the quality of food, extensions for parties, wearing trousers under gowns' continued to hold the floor, but at the same time the proceedings became noticeably more businesslike. The introduction in 1963 of the present system of 'Hustings' gave more point to the annual ritual of electing student officers, which had previously generated less excitement in the pages of *Tattler and Layabout* than speculation as to the whereabouts of Westfield's lost mascot, a wooden penguin named Honeysuckle.[38] Outside Westfield, support was given to NUS campaigns and to the annual ULU carnival in aid of charity, forerunner of the now familiar Westfield Rag Week. As WCUS activity increased, the need began to be felt for an amenity described vaguely in 1963 as 'a focal point'.[39] The place suggested was the JCR attached to the new Refectory, which did indeed become 'a focal point' when it was converted a few years later into the College Bar.[40] By this time WCUS had elected its first

male President, Roger Mayhew,[41] setting thereby a trend largely followed ever since but not, appropriately enough, in the College's centenary year, when by a happy chance the choice fell on a woman, Kate Standen.

The clubs and societies affiliated to WCUS have increased in number and variety, as might be expected from the number of new interests needing to be represented. Societies formed within the Science departments sprang up alongside the older subject societies, clubs for 'Men's Hockey' and 'Men's Cricket' (as they were at first described), and later for Rugby, made their appearance.[42] Very few sporting clubs, however, are now single-sex; the rest — Golf, Sailing, Sub Aqua, Martial Arts, to name only some of the more recent additions — welcome members of both sexes, and the same applies to clubs and societies in general. The Dramatic Society, which in 1982 claimed to be the largest and most active in College, has perhaps gained more than most from the admission of men, not only through no longer having to import male actors (all-female productions had already died out in the 1940s), but also as a main beneficiary of yet another facility that came with Berridge House, a hall properly equipped for stage performances. The emergence of societies linked with specific religions or cultures, Jewish,

Student life at Westfield in the 1980s. Left: a student's room in Kidderpore Hall. Below: the College Bar. Above right: Talent contest winners — 'Vicious Rumours' dance group. Right: Athletic pursuits.

Chinese, Islamic, testifies to the growing diversity of Westfield's student population and, since these clubs are not exclusive, to the desire to build bridges. Socialising, indeed, figures predominantly in the programmes of most College societies, the serious no less than the frivolous; so do excursions into the outside world, for example by groups such as the Bethnal Green Playgroup, which continue Westfield's tradition of social concern.

Never merely the sum of its affiliated societies, WCUS has nevertheless added substantially to its functions and responsibilities over the past twenty years. Backed by a grant running into tens of thousands, the Union is now able to offer an information service, provide regular entertainments, produce an annual *Students' Handbook* and the twice-termly *WC*, the latest in the line of student broadsheets, and run a shop with a sizeable yearly turnover. The College's practice of granting a

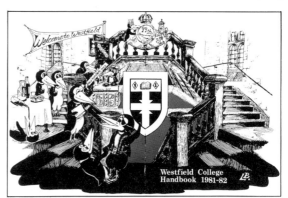

Top: Student protest at fee increases in 1973.
Above: Union society handbook employing the
penguin motif (see Honeysuckle, next page).

year's 'semi-sabbatical leave' to senior student officers dates back to the start of the 1970s and at first applied only to the President: the Treasurer and Vice President have since been added. WCUS also has a small permanent staff.

The WCUS office, first mentioned in 1947 when it was described as 'tiny', has lately moved into space below the Refectory which became available when the entire block was reorganised in 1980, and it is hoped at some future date to convert the whole of this area for student use.

The student protest movement which disturbed the peace of universities in the late 1960s also made its impact on Westfield, although in a fairly muted form. For a brief moment, as the Principal recounted in his Report for 1968-69, 'the relationship between the Union Executive and the College authorities slipped rapidly through the gears into over-drive and an exhilarating ride was enjoyed by all those of us who were competing for the driving seat'. But as he went on to say, 'the majority of our students were not even on the same motorway, let alone in the same car.' One casualty, seemingly minor but indicative of a dismissive attitude towards academic paraphernalia, was the undergraduate gown, which about this time, and without becoming an issue, 'softly and silently vanished away.'[43] That the movement had a constructive side was seen when a new WCUS Executive presented the case for the representation of students, as 'active participants in the educative process', on Council and its committees. The generally responsible attitude of Westfield students, as compared with the more violent methods employed elsewhere, no doubt played its part in overcoming some initial obstacles and objections. The decision to admit two students to Council was taken in December 1970 and immediately put into effect, legitimate use being made of the provisions in the existing Charter regulating the appointment of co-opted members.

Although serviceable enough on this occasion, the Charter and Statutes of 1933 by now had an antiquated air, especially noticeable in the formulation of its religious provisions, which reflected the strictly Evangelical loyalties of the founders. Work on revision of the Charter and Statutes began, on the Principal's initiative, in 1969 when an Ad-Hoc committee[44] was set up to study 'certain fundamental issues'. The College as a whole, including its past members as represented by the WCA, was given opportunity to comment on the committee's findings and the product of these consultations, cast into appropriate form, was carried forward into a petition for a Supplemental Charter, which received the Royal Assent on 15 September 1976. The document preserves from the original Charter

Above: A Christmas Lunch stunt for Rag Week, 1982. Right: adoption of Union Mascot 'Honeysuckle' at London Zoo, 1955.

its provisions for the incorporation of the College as a legal entity but is otherwise an almost complete replacement. Amongst the Objects of the College, as set out in the Supplemental Charter, the intention 'to carry on the work of the College in accordance with Christian principles' is reaffirmed, but not the original Charter's insistence on strict conformity with the principles of the Reformation, which was considered to be inappropriate 'in the context of the modern striving after Christian reconciliation'.[45] Under the Supplemental Charter and Statutes it has ceased to be necessary for the Principal or any other member of the Council to be Anglican, and co-opted membership is now reserved for 'external members',[46] with a mandatory preponderance of four in their favour. The Statute concerning the Academic Board is more explicit than its predecessor and includes a specific requirement that the Council 'shall seek the Board's advice on all the subjects of greatest importance to the College's primary functions — teaching and research'. A completely new Statute gives formal recognition to the Westfield College Union Society and provides for its regulation by the Council through by-laws.[47]

The one reference in the Supplemental Charter to a specific Christian denomination occurs in the article safeguarding the provision 'of facilities for regular worship in accordance with the doctrines of the Church of England'. The Chapel (not mentioned in the original Charter) continues to be well-used, and in a manner consistent with the present usages of the Church of England as prescribed in the Revised Canons of c 1970. Equally in keeping with the spirit of the Supplemental Charter is the adoption of the article, 5c, which redefines Westfield's religious and moral objects, as one of the principal objectives of the ecumenically based Joint Christian Council, first set up in 1965. Read in full, the article requires that 'the work of the College shall be carried out in accordance with Christian principles in a spirit of tolerance, freedom of opinion and community service'. Within this wider context, the activities of the JCC — worship, prayer, bible study, discussion of the

faith in its bearing on moral and social issues — diverge remarkably little from those of the past, from which it can be seen that 'what lay at the heart of the College's foundation' remains a living force, unaided now by any element of compulsion and without detriment to the pluralistic character of a community which, under another article of the Supplemental Charter, eschews any form of 'political, racial, social or religious discrimination.'

A feature of the Supplemental Charter and Statutes not so far mentioned is the recognition it accords to the Faculties as distinct entities and the inclusion of their representatives, the Deans, among the *ex officio* members of Council. The two Faculties of Arts and Science were constituted on a formal basis in 1965 with Professor JE Varey and Professor GE Fogg, FRS, as their respective Deans. The introduction in 1966 of a new scheme for the BSc degree, which freed Colleges from the obligation to adhere to a common University syllabus, presented the Science Faculty with the welcome opportunity to experiment with new courses, several of which cut across the old subject boundaries, and to offer students programmes of study tailored to their particular interests. This new degree structure, based on Course Units and internally examined, was not adopted for the BA degree, which is still taught and examined on the basis of a university-wide syllabus. But the Arts Faculty has not stood still. In the late 1960s the Westfield Classics Department was instrumental in setting up the Combined Studies BA degree in Two Subjects which the Faculty as a whole has since done much to promote, with the result that more than twenty Combined Studies options are now on offer to Westfield students.

Not withstanding these developments, the academic life of the College continues to be focussed on the departments, perhaps to an even greater extent than in the past. As both administrative and teaching units, the departments perforce operate on a scale undreamed of even twenty years ago, when Professor McKisack 'ran the History Department from a small portable typewriter on her table in Fletcher-Moulton Hall, with no office, no

files, and no permanent secretary.'[48] Fears that increased numbers might lead to a lessening of personal contact between teachers and taught have been effectively countered by the adoption of less formal modes of teaching and by allocating students to members of staff who act as their personal tutors.[49] Teaching methods and syllabus content were naturally matters of great concern to the student generation whose heightened awareness of themselves as 'participants in the educative process' came to a head in the late 1960s and Heads of Department responded by making arrangements for students to be represented in discussions germane to their legitimate interests. It was no doubt necessary at this stage to bring in formal procedures for consultation, but as a means of convincing students of their teachers' credentials and good faith they have been of secondary importance compared with the manner in which departments succeed in translating their aims — academic, pastoral and social — into practice.

It is not possible to give here more than a token account[50] of what has been achieved at

Westfield since 1960 in teaching and research. The summaries that follow are intended merely as an indication of the main interests represented in each department and of the lines of enquiry pursued by particular groups and individuals, named and unnamed. As will be seen, over the past twenty years Westfield has added substantially to its professoriate. This has come about partly through the creation of further established Chairs and partly through conferments of title; the same applies to Readerships, and without the limitation on senior posts imposed by the University Grants Committee from 1970 onwards the number in both cases might well have been larger. It has also to be borne in mind that staff numbers in general, although much higher than at any time in Westfield's previous history, reached their peak in the early 1970s and thereafter slowly declined while student numbers continued to grow or remain constant.

The order in which the departments are listed below is of significance only in so far as it groups together Departments belonging to the same Faculty.

Mathematics

The opening of the Science Faculty in 1960 was made the occasion for the institution of Westfield's first Chair in Mathematics, to which Dr EH Sondheimer, previously Reader at Queen Mary College and distinguished for his contributions to the electron theory of metals, was appointed, becoming at the same time Head of Department. Expansion was quick to follow, in its early stages thus pre-dating the Robbins Report and the admission of men, and continued into the early 1970s. In recent years the Department has become heavily involved in teaching Mathematics to students reading for degrees involving Computer Science options. The new freedom in the design of undergraduate courses conferred by the Course Unit system has been used to introduce a variety of mathematical options in 'non-traditional' areas of the subject, where modern mathemetical techniques have found many fresh applications in helping to further current technological advances. Examples are Coding Theory, Theory of Designs, Control Theory, Linear Programming and Operational Research. Several courses in Statistics, emphasising modern aspects, have also been introduced, and the old-fashioned courses in Mechanics have been superseded by courses on Dynamical Systems and Differential Equations. For several years a first-year course was given on historical aspects of Mathematics; this, like the opportunity now open to BSc students to include an Arts subject in their degree studies, gave mathematicians a rare chance to practise skills in the writing of essays.

The research interests of the Department cover a wide spectrum. Professor SJ Taylor, internationally recognised for his work in Analysis and Probability Theory, left to go to Liverpool University in 1975, but his particular field continues to be cultivated by Dr NH Bingham; other analysts in the Department work on Measure Theory, Functional Analysis, Analytic Number Theory and Dynamical Systems. Professors DR Hughes and FC Piper have built up an internationally recognised research school in Algebra; in recent years Professor Piper has developed interests in Cryptography and Cipher Systems and through these has established a valuable industrial link with the electronics firm of Racal-Comsec which employs several Westfield graduates. The most senior, Henry Beker, has been appointed to a Visiting Professorship in the Department. The Applied Mathematics group is led by Professor J W Essam, who has made for himself an international reputation for his work on Critical Phenomena and Percolation Theory.

At the postgraduate level the Department has in recent years been able to maintain a healthy intake of research students and research visitors, and there are frequent seminars.

Computer Science

The Department of Computer Science, when it was formed in 1971, met a growing demand for the subject among applicants for admission and provided the College with facilities for research and development. Dr PE Osmon, previously a Lecturer in the Physics Department and already part-time Director of Computing, became Head of the Department and has remained so ever since. At first Computer Science was offered only as a component of a joint honours degree, but since 1975 it has also been available as a subject for single honours. With an annual undergraduate intake of sixty and an academic, technical and programming staff in excess of twenty, Computer Science is now one of the College's largest departments.

The initially small staff was soon augmented by the migration to Westfield of four members of the University's Institute of Computer Science when it was dispersed in 1973. In consequence the teaching base was extended. Furthermore, it was by this means that Westfield acquired its first multi-access computer system, MOSAICS, devised by Mr A Fairbourn, which remained in use for teaching courses on Operating Systems until superseded by microcomputers in 1981. Taken as a single subject, Computer Science covers all aspects of the design and use of computer systems. Provision is also made, however, for students wishing to combine Computer Science with another discipline, and equally for those seeking to apply computer techniques to another main field of study, whose needs can be met by a single programming course. The subject is developing so rapidly that several new courses have been introduced even within the short lifetime of the Department. Examples are Computer Science and Electronics (or, as an alternative, 'with' Electronics), taught in conjunction with Physics, which tackles the 'hardware-software interface', and Microcomputers and Applications. Postgraduate research in progress or completed includes work on data flow languages, microcomputer systems, protection problems and the mathematical properties of programs.

Physicists and mathematicians, who were among the first to seek access to computers for research purposes, were provided with 'on line' facilities in 1969 through a data link with the University's central computer, in those days a large DC 6600. If the capacities of computers have since multiplied, so have the potential users and their demands. The Prime P 750 installed at Westfield in 1981 can support up to fifty interactive terminals and represents a significant enlargement of the local facilities; through it College users also have access to a range of computers connected with METRONET, the University network. Westfield's Computer Unit, which works in collaboration with the CS Department, provides computing services for all departments, administrative as well as academic, and plays an important advisory role. One of its programmers specialises in the applications of computing to Arts subjects; another member of its staff, whose specific concern is with microcomputers, supervised and encouraged the introduction of word processing systems now in use in various parts of the College.

Physics
The Physics Department opened for degree courses in the (still uncompleted) Queen's Building in October 1961 after a preparatory year during which Professor EH Bellamy, Head of Department and Mr P Heaver, Chief Technician, worked to make ready the laboratory and workshop and laid the foundations for subsequent research and teaching.

Both have remained at their posts, enabling a consistent and stable policy to be maintained. Nineteen students, chosen from a markedly competitive field, were admitted, ten for the BSc Special Degree and nine for the BSc General.

The pattern of undergraduate teaching has undergone many changes over the years, some almost imperceptible, some challengingly abrupt. The introduction of the Course Unit system removed much of the rigidity from degree programmes but also led to an increase in the range of specialised topics. The departmental repertoire has been gradually extended to include, for example, astrophysics, metereology, radiation physics and earth sciences, together with other contributions to environmental studies. Following technological trends, electronics and computing techniques have come to occupy a much more prominent position in the teaching of Physics.

Two main research interests were very quickly established. Experimental high energy physics, Professor Bellamy's own field, has involved using the machine facilities at the Rutherford Laboratory (Didcot) and at the giant European complex, CERN, at Geneva. Work in solid state physics, directed by Professor B Donovan (appointed to a Chair in 1966) was at first solely of a theoretical nature, being concerned with magneto-optical phenomena in semi-conductors; later the scope was broadened to include an experimental research programme in infra-red spectroscopy. In recent years Dr TJ Parker has successfully exploited the technique of diversive Fourier transform spectrometry.

In 1967, following sustained progress in the high energy experiments, it became desirable to add a theoretical elementary particle group. Dr E Leader, appointed Professor of Theoretical Physics, quickly assembled such a group, which has been a highly active and cosmopolitan feature of the Department.

Even at its peak size, attained about the end of the first decade, the Department was small in relation to the total volume of its reresearch in particle physics. Substantial support in terms of funds and research posts was received from the Science Research Council but because of national policy changes it was unfortunately necessary to discontinue the work on bubble chamber analysis led by Dr PV March, appointed as the Department's fourth Professor in 1971.

Chemistry

Professor W Klyne, head of the Department from 1960 until shortly before his untimely death in 1977, was appointed to Westfield from the London Postgraduate Medical School, and it is surely no coincidence that the subsequent research activities of the Department of which he was the founder-member have to a large extent been connected with Chemistry's contribution to human health and welfare.

Professor Klyne brought with him the Steroid Reference Collection he had begun in 1954. Greatly expanded, and now with Professor DN Kirk as its Curator, the Collection is internationally recognised as a unique centre for the storage and distribution of steroidal materials. Additions to it have came from three main sources: gifts from the personal collections of individual scientists, notably that of Professor Ewart Jones, formerly Waynflete Professor of Chemistry at Oxford; donations of bulk supplies from industrial laboratories; and synthesis in the Department's own laboratories. Contact with users of the Collection has lately led to close collaboration between the team directed by Professor Kirk and workers in medical and biochemical fields where there is particular need for contributions in steroid chemistry. Projects in which other members of the Department are involved similarly attract outside support in recognition of their value as a service to the scientific community at large. Early work with optical rotary dispersion and circular dichroism by Professor Klyne and Dr Molly Scopes led in 1966 to the provision of a London-wide service in these chiroptical techniques; with SRC support this has since become national. On the inorganic side, Professor BJ Aylett has recieved grants from the British Steel Corporation in connection with his work in the chemistry of metals which has led in the environmental field to investigations of air-

borne pollution. Aspects of chemical pollution, studied in particular by Dr DC Ayres, have also been investigated in collaboration with industrial and government scientists.

Over the years the undergraduate teaching has developed the subject's interdisciplinary potential without neglecting the basic training essential to the future professional chemist. Chemical education figures in its own right among the interests of members of the Department: Dr Anne Walton, for example, has worked on the development of molecular models as teaching aids and Dr JJ Throssell [51] on the History of Science. As new programmes, especially in Environmental Science, were added to the Faculty's repertoire in the 1970s it became necessary to re-equip some of the Department's laboratories in order to provide teaching in biological chemistry for classes of a hundred and more students: a very different scene from the one encountered by the original staff members who welcomed the nine pioneering Chemistry students in 1961 to laboratories still gleaming (but not for long) with unsullied elegance.

Botany and Biochemistry

The appointment of Professor GE Fogg, a distinguished algologist, as Professor of Botany in 1960 ensured that the revived Department would build upon the traditions of its predecessor. Supported by a small group of postgraduates who came with him from University College, Professor Fogg at once established algal physiology as a main area of research activity; in 1965 his outstanding contribution to knowledge in this field was recognised by his election as a Fellow of the Royal Society. When Professor Fogg moved in 1971 to the Chair of Marine Biology at the University College of North Wales (Bangor), he was succeeded at Westfield by Professor PJ Peterson from the Applied Biochemistry Group, DSIR, New Zealand, who rapidly established a school of biogeochemical research. Supported by several government agencies and industrial concerns, this group has since carried out important investigations in various parts of the British Isles and other parts of the world including North America, Africa and Malaysia.

In common with other Science Departments, Botany welcomed the introduction of the BSc Course Unit System in 1966. Following the College's decision in 1964 to increase the intake of biology students, additions to the staff had by 1966 greatly extended the range of departmental specialities, and extra laboratory space had been created at Berridge House and on the main site, making it possible, amongst other things, to house large items of specialised equipment. In 1973, to reflect more accurately the main interests of the Department, its name was altered to include Biochemistry. Thereafter, as well as developing Joint Programmes in Biochemistry, the Botany Department contributed strongly to the Environmental Science Programme (introduced 1975).

Dr EM Delf Smith, founder of botanical studies at Westfield, happily lived long enough to see them not only resumed but making progress and branching out in new directions. In 1973 past and present members of the Department joined in celebrating her ninetieth birthday, and she was always eager to hear from her successors of new advances. The 'lost' decade of the 1950s, while it could never be redeemed, thus did not bring about a total break in continuity.

Zoology

Zoology as a full-scale department was incorporated into the plans for the Science Faculty at a later stage than the other main disciplines, which accounts for the fact that the Zoology wing projects as an afterthought from the side of the main Queen's Building. Professor JE Webb was appointed in 1960 from the University College, Ibadan, Nigeria, (now the University of Ibadan) as the first Professor and Head of Department and remained so until he retired in 1980. The Department was planned for an estimated annual intake of five students, but this was immediately exceeded and grew rapidly to reach a combined intake into Zoology and Botany of about sixty undergraduates. More staff were appointed and the research interests of the Department accordingly diversified to cover many fields of zoological interest.

Among early appointments were Dr J Griffith, who became responsible for palaeontology and vertebrate studies, Dr JA Wallwork, whose speciality is soil ecology, particularly in deserts, and Dr JA Riegel, responsible for studies in invertebrate physiology. All three remained to give the Department long service.

Professor Webb's own line of research was concerned with the ecology and distribution of amphioxus, involving the physical properties of benthic sediments. Early on in the establishment of the Department he appointed Dr Minnie Courtney as his research assistant; later she became a member of the teaching staff and has been responsible for the development of Marine Zoology. In 1964 the Department was joined by Dr J Green, who came at first as Reader and then was given a personal Chair (he is now Head of Department). This led to the development of teaching and research in freshwater ecology (in a long-term co-operation with the Botany Department) and, together with Dr Courtney's Marine course, to the establishment of the College's unique degree programme in Marine and Freshwater Biology.

The Unit which houses Westfield's two electron microscopes was designed by Dr PF Newell, and much of his research on molluscs has been related to the application of electron microscopy.

As befits a department headed for twenty years by a repatriate from the University of Ibadan, many links have been forged with overseas universities, particularly in Africa. Research expeditions have been undertaken not only in various parts of Africa, ranging from Sierra Leone, Ghana and Nigeria across to Kenya and down to South Africa, but also in Australia, Brazil, Canada, Greenland, Iceland, Indonesia, Mexico and the USA, to name only some of the areas whose spread illustrates the wide geographical range of research interests in the Department. This overseas work feeds back into the teaching giving it an authentic quality that can only be gained from practical experience in the field.

Collaborative ventures with the Botany and Biochemistry Department, particularly in Marine and Freshwater Biology, pointed the way towards the merging of the two departments in 1982 as a School of Biological Sciences, the span of which covers 'the various divisions of the biological world from the micro-organisms up to the higher plants and animals' and whose approach draws on a variety of disciplines which cross the traditional organismal boundaries.

In the modern history of the Arts disciplines at Westfield there has been nothing to compare with 'the big bang' which brought the Science Faculty into existence in 1960, not even the admission of men as undergraduates, which at first had less impact on Arts than on Science. In the Science Faculty it took only five years for men to establish the slight numerical ascendancy they have since maintained. The Arts departments, well-supplied by able women candidates from schools in the habit of recommending Westfield as third choice after Oxford and Cambridge, were in no hurry to admit male applicants who did not appear to be strong competitors,[5] and women have in fact continued to be in the majority on the Arts side, in some departments markedly so. In line with the College's general expansion, all Arts departments have expanded their range of activity and by so doing attracted to Westfield scholars in fields previously underrepresented or absent. Two new subjects, History of Art and Drama, have been added to the repertoire.

Classics

When Professor DM Jones, previously Reader at Birkbeck College and specialist in philology, was appointed Head of Department in 1953 it was still possible to assume that candidates for admission would already be proficient enough in one or both of the classical languages to follow the traditional degree course. In the 1960s, however, it became increasingly apparent that an alternative type of course was needed to bring the study of the ancient world within the reach of students who, 'either by choice or necessity', lacked the linguistic equipment which could be de-

manded of their predecessors. The broader curriculum which emerged from revisions of the syllabus for the London BA in Classics, Greek, and Latin gave opportunity for Westfield's team of classicists (never larger than five) to develop other aspects of Greek and Roman civilisation while still encouraging study of the classical languages. History and literature were already well catered for in the Department, which had been joined in 1963 by Dr Jenny A Hall, whose interest in satire has produced a study on Lucian, published in 1981. In 1967 a gap on the side of classical archaeology and art history was filled by the appointment of Dr MAR Colledge, an authority on the arts of Rome and its eastern neighbours, the Parthians. Interest in drama was already strong in the early 1960s, when open air productions of Greek and Latin plays were presented, and Combined Studies degrees in Greek or Latin with Drama have been greeted at Westfield with enthusiasm. Also popular is the recently established BA degree in Classical Studies, which is so constructed that papers from it may be taken, with or without language study, as part of the programme for the BSc.

The retirement in 1980 of Professor Jones and Dr Irene Glanville (Mrs DM Jones) deprived the Department at a stroke of its two senior members. In terms of student numbers, they left on a rising tide of success: the intake for their last session, which was also the first when applicants were admitted to read for the new Classical Studies degree, was one of the largest ever recorded. But since this was also a time of staff reductions, the remaining members of the Department, now headed by Dr Colledge, have been happy to collaborate with the Departments of Greek and Latin at Bedford College, an arrangement which exemplifies in more developed form an already well-established trend towards intercollegiate teaching.

French

In 1960 French was already a large department by Westfield standards and in the following two decades its student membership more than doubled. Since 1976 it has been very happily housed on its own in 316 Finchley Road, with agreeable teaching rooms and a much appreciated student common-room.

The teaching of French has been modernized in many ways but Westfield has not departed from the 'traditional' conception of French Studies held by the University at large, in which the emphasis is on the history of the language and the literature. Historical linguistic studies have been forwarded by successive occupants of the Department's established Chair in Romance Philology, Professor RC Johnston (1961-1974), who worked on Anglo-Norman and Rumanian, and Professor J Marshall (retired 1982) who specialised in Provençal. Dr IR Short, Secretary to the Anglo-Norman Society, and Dr Renée Curtis, editor of Tristan texts, have also made important contributions in their respective fields.

Shifts of emphasis have nevertheless occurred. In the University as a whole, Romance Philology is no longer an obligatory subject of study for all undergraduates reading French, and a much greater choice is allowed between the various elements of an ever-widening syllabus. Since the Second World War, particularly, the study of literature and the history of ideas during the modern period from the eighteenth century to the present day has been more willingly recognised as an exacting discipline, in no need of a 'stiffening' from philology. The new parity between philology and literary/philosophical studies received endorsement when Dr JG Weightman, whose interests centred on problems of literary translation and literary theory, was appointed Reader in 1963 and then to a personal Chair. Among other staff members who deal with more modern periods mention should also be made of Dr Margaret Mein, an expert in the literature of the nineteenth and twentieth centuries and in Proustian studies in particular.

Since 1972 the French Department has shared with other modern languages an audio-visual centre in the library building where students regularly practice the spoken language and attend film shows. Also since that date, there have been every year three visiting *lecteurs* or *lectrices*, who represent exchanges at the postgraduate level between Westfield and the Universities of Grenoble and Nanterre. For some time now it has also been the rule that all undergraduates should spend the third year in France or in some other French speaking environment.

German

The institution of an established Chair in German in 1964 was a sign, belated it is true, of the Department's coming of age. The two successive occupants of the Chair, Dr SS Prawer, who departed in 1969 for the Taylor Professorship of German Language and Literature at Oxford, and Dr CB Bock, came to Westfield conscious of the debt the Department owed to Dr Mary Beare, who 'nursed it like a tender plant',[53] and whose warm and sustained interest in its growth and flowering continues to this day. In Dr Beare's time the scholarly interests of the staff tended to be concentrated on the earlier phases of German language and literature. Her own main field was the sixteenth century; her colleagues were medievalists — Mrs Hanna Connell (1947-1949), co-author of an Old High German grammar, Dr PF Ganz, who had already made a name for himself as an editor of medieval German texts when he left in 1960 to become Reader in Germanic Philology (and subsequently Professor) at Oxford, and Dr Marianne Wynn, specialist in courtly literature who came in 1954. The appointment in 1960 of Miss Marie-Luise Waldeck, specialist in eighteenth century literature and thought, brought the Department closer to the goal, finally achieved in the mid-1960s, of being able to cover most aspects of the Honours syllabus, not excluding the post-1945 period, from its own resources. This did not mean that the Department became more inward-looking. Collaboration with colleagues in other Colleges, once a necessity, continued through choice and members of staff have contributed significantly to the postgraduate activities of the Institute of Germanic Studies of which Professor Bock was for eight years Honorary Director, before becoming Dean of the University Faculty of Arts in 1980.

The Priebsch Prize, awarded by the Uni-

161

versity for the best Final BA paper in medieval German literature has been won three times
by Westfield students (in 1956, 1963 and
1964) and the Bithell Prize, recently instituted
for modern literature, has also come to Westfield. Students' awareness of contemporary
issues is sharpened by contact with Language
Assistants, drawn from the Federal Republic
and either Austria or Switzerland, who have
been coming on a regular basis since 1960;
awards of foreign bursaries to Westfield graduates in German have helped to keep the
traffic flowing in the reverse direction.

Spanish

From its small beginnings in the 1950s Westfield's Spanish Department is now so flourishing that it is one of the largest and most highly regarded in Britain. The original staff of
two, Dr JE Varey[54] and his medievalist colleague Mr AD Deyermond,[55] have both become Professors; subsequent recruits to the
staff include two of the Department's own
graduates, Dr Pamela Waley and Dr Verity
Smith (Wright) and these are by no means the
only examples of former students who have
been appointed to university posts, either in
Britain or abroad.

The Department has comprehensive research interests and in three fields is an internationally recognised centre: medieval literature, theatre history, and most recently
dialectology. The Medieval Spanish Research
Seminar, begun in 1967 as a forum for Westfield postgraduates, has become a regular
meeting-place for London-based visiting scholars: the more advanced undergraduates also
participate. Professor Varey's research group
on the history of the theatre, and the series of
books he has published with his former pupil,
Norman Shergold, now Professor at Cardiff,
have been major factors in Westfield's rise as
an interdisciplinary centre of drama study.
Varey's work is widely recognized as a new
and fruitful approach to the history of the
Spanish theatre; in 1980 he became the first
non-Spaniard to receive from the Mayor of
Madrid the title 'Hijo ilustre de Madrid'. The
Department's work in dialectology, begun on

the initiative of Dr RJ Penny who in 1966
assumed responsibility for the teaching in
historical linguistics, attracts postgraduates
from several countries and the group now includes a flourishing section concerned with
Spanish-American dialect study.

Both teaching and research have been enriched by a succession of language assistants,
several of whom have won distinction as
scholars or teachers. The character of the
undergraduate teaching, which at first followed the usual mid-1950s Westfield pattern of
formal lectures, frequent individual tutorials
and prose and translation classes, has long
since been modified to allow more time for
conversation classes and language laboratory
work (Dr Penny was the first Director of the
College's Audio-Visual Unit), and the students'
written work has become more experimental.
In 1964 the Department was chosen by the
Nuffield Foundation as one of a dozen Arts
departments (and the only representative of
Spanish) to be included in a nationwide study
of innovatory methods in university
teaching. The curriculum has also been made
more flexible and close collaboration among
the University's departments of Spanish allows
students an impressive array of Special Subjects and Options for BA and MA degrees.
First year students have the possibility of
spending the summer term at the University
of Córdoba in Andalusia in company with
staff and students from other London departments and many students return to Spain for
their third year.

English

English studies at Westfield have developed
since 1960 along lines similar to those followed by other Arts departments. Increased student numbers made it possible to appoint
additional staff and hence to teach more of
the syllabus, special subjects included, at
Westfield. This build-up began in the
latter part of Professor Jenkins's time as Head
of Department and gathered momentum
under his successor, Professor WA Armstrong
(1967-1974). When alterations to the syllabus
by the University's Board of Studies opened

up a wider range of options, the Department's keeness to innovate was shown by the introduction of American Literature. At the same time, the Department's traditional interest in the English language, its history and its cognates, has been kept alive through the teaching of Old English and Icelandic for which Dr CG Harlow has been largely responsible. The 'core syllabus', composed of papers 'representing a coherent sequence of literary history' which 'must include work on Chaucer and his contemporaries and on Shakespeare and Renaissance literature' is almost identical with that prescribed in literature for the earliest Honours Students; today it is taught to a student body numbering over a hundred, and in addition the Department is heavily involved in teaching for the Combined Studies degree.

Expansion on the postgraduate side has been marked not only by an increase in numbers, which began in the late 1960s, but also by the range of subjects in which supervision can be provided: medieval literature, the eighteenth century (in which the two current Professors, John Chalker and Peter Dixon, are active), more modern periods and aspects of English language. Members of staff keep up a long-established Westfield tradition by contributing regularly to specialist sections of the *Year's Work in English Studies*, published by the English Association, of which J Redmond has for several years been general editor. Former postgraduates are to be found in university posts in Europe, in Israel, in Egypt, in Canada, in Australia, as well as in this country. A former undergraduate, Mrs Elizabeth Maslen (Thomas), who returned to join the staff after taking the Oxford Diploma in Comparative Philology, is also well-known as a poet. Creative writing, while not a part of the syllabus, is among the activities promoted by the College's English Society.

Drama

In 1976, when the University added Drama to the subjects available as part of the BA degree in Combined Studies, Westfield was the first School to take advantage of the scheme, and was exceptionally well-equiped to do so. In its literary, historical and theoretical as-

pects, drama already figured prominently in many undergraduate courses and the research interests of the staff, especially in the English and Spanish Departments, tended in that direction. Equally important, Westfield was favourably placed in terms of location to collaborate with the Central School of Speech and Drama at Swiss Cottage, to which approaches had already been made by Professor Armstrong before he left to occupy a Chair at Birkbeck College in 1974. The contacts he established were further developed by another member of the English Department, Mr Redmond, who since 1976 has been Westfield's Director of Drama. Under the more formal arrangements entered into in 1976, Westfield students taking Drama enjoy the privileges of belonging to the Central School and are taught by staff of both institutions. This has made it possible to offer a wide range of practical work, in film and television as well as stagecraft. The course is demanding but has proved immensely popular, attracting hosts of applicants: in the first year 350 for the English/Drama combination alone, of whom twelve were admitted. Drama combines just as happily with French, German, Spanish, and with classical subjects — as Dr Glanville demonstrated when she took charge of Drama during Mr Redmond's temporary absence in 1979-80. Extra-curricular drama productions continue as before, benefiting no doubt from the presence in the student body of 'semiprofessionals'; in recent years the Drama Society has won awards at the National Student Drama Festival and contributed original plays to the Edinburgh Fringe.

History and History of Art

The London University School of History has since its beginnings been to a major extent an inter-collegiate one. As a result, Westfield's History Department has been as much influenced by changes emanating from this source as it has been by changes in college. The internal changes which were transforming the College as a whole in the 1960s began to operate on the History Department not in 1961 or in 1964 but in 1967-8, a session which saw advances on three fronts. First, the Department acquired its own base in 25 Kidderpore Avenue; second, the first men students were admitted and formed a sizeable proportion of the intake; third, the creation of a History of Art sub-department was in prospect for the following year and this held out the promise that increase in numbers would be accompanied by growth through diversification.

These changes were given distinctive shape by the new Head of Department, Professor CNL Brooke,[56] supported by long serving members, Professor Rosalind Hill,[57] Professor N Rubinstein,[58] Olive Anderson,[59] and more recent arrivals, Dr LOJ Boynton (1965) and Dr JQC Mackrell (1970); the result was a close-knit community of staff and students, with a strong consciousness of a shared life. From 1972, however, following the introduction of new regulations for the BA degree in History, the Department became less self-contained. The ending of the 'common core' syllabus allowed the intercollegiate element to be further increased and new courses were developed on a lavish scale. Today some 170 papers are open to History undergraduates, who can benefit *inter alia* from the teaching provided at specialist institutions such as the Schools of Slavonic and East European Studies and of Oriental and African Studies.

These increased comings and goings led inevitably to some changes in academic and social habits, but there has been no breach of continuity. The practice of studying together the physical remains of the past in *situ*, begun by Caroline Skeel and revived in the 1930s by Rosalind Hill, took a new turn when Christopher Brooke began the series of field residential courses which took place annually from 1969 to 1982; the scholarly outings organised by Brenda Bolton (who joined the Department in 1975) continue to bring together for the same purpose staff and students, residents and non-residents, historians and Art historians. There has been consistency too, broadly speaking, in the concentration of research interests on particular periods and geographical areas. Professor HR Loyn, who came from Cardiff to succeed Professor Brooke as Head of Department in 1977, continues a line of eminent medievalists under whom the Depart-

ment's traditional expertise in medieval scholarship could hardly fail to prosper. Italian historical studies, established on the high ground of the Renaissance by Professor Rubinstein, continue to develop. French History, Dr Mackrell's speciality, has been taught since 1975 as an element in a course leading to Joint Honours in French and History. Mrs Olive Anderson's teaching and research in modern British history and political ideas are distinguished by their method and originality, as they have been ever since she joined the Department in 1950.

The successful integration of History of Art with History, which came about initially through the enthusiasm of Professor Rubinstein, is due to several factors: a fortunate conjuncture of personalities, the intersection of research interests, the high proportion of shared content in the teaching and a common passion for monuments and museums. As a subject, however, History of Art also has a life of its own. Within a few years of its inception as part of the joint honours degree History /History of Art it became possible to offer History of Art in combination with certain other subjects, and since 1978 it has also been taught for single honours ('with an element of History'). None of this could have been achieved without the willing collaboration of the History of Art Department at University College, with whom all but a few courses are shared. Westfield's specialists, though small in numbers, make a full contribution. They have included Mr N Stratford (now Keeper of Medieval and Later Antiquities, British Museum) and Mr NJ Morgan (now Director of the Christian Art Index at Princeton University) in the medieval area; Dr D Freedberg (now at the Courtauld Institute) and Miss Caroline Elam in the Renaissance; and Mr D Bindman, active in the field of English Art, the first staff member to be appointed and now a Reader. Much of the teaching has taken place in museums, and perhaps for this reason a high proportion of former students are now in positions of responsibility in the National Museums in London and elsewhere; as examples may be cited the Hon Jane Roberts, Keeper of the Queen's Drawings at Windsor Castle and Michael Collins, Assistant Keeper in the Department of Medieval and Later Antiquities at the British Museum.

The picture of Westfield's recent intellectual and cultural life would not be complete without reference to the many ways in which it has been enriched and unified by activities which fall outside the regular academic programme. Under the heading of discourse, they have ranged from the traditional format of the Public Lecture — as professors multiplied, so did Inaugural Lectures — to the more informal lunch-time lectures and early evening Library symposia, both of which began in 1976, organised in the former case by Professor Leader of the Physics Department and in the latter by Miss VM Bonnell, Lecturer in English.[61] The talks, many of them illustrated, discussions, and poetry readings provided under these auspices deploy talents both external and internal. On the creative side, the range

has recently been extended by the Visiting Artists programme arranged by Dr Jeremy Adler of the German Department (himself well known as an exponent of Concrete Poetry). In the early 1970s the month of June was annually enlivened, for local residents as well as College members, by a glittering series of Summer Festivals (supported by grants from the Arts Council and the London Borough of Camden), and 1974 was made uniquely memorable by the Science Carnival, 'Wes-Pop', mounted for the general public by Professor Leader. Not a year has passed without musical offerings, contributed both by professional musicians and by Westfield's choral, chamber music and orchestral groups, which form and re-form according to the talent available; and music of one kind or another pervaded many of the College's centenary celebrations. Appreciative audiences were treated in turn to a lecture-recital on the harpsichord by Mr John Henry, Visiting Senior Research Fellow, a recorder concert, the inaugural recital by Mr

Carlo Curley on the Chapel's new pipe organ,[62] a music and dance revue under the title *Westfield Revisited*, an evening of Victorian Music Hall, a scintillating production by the University of London Opera Group with Westfield participation of Gilbert and Sullivan's comic opera, *Princess Ida* (1884, a take-off of the 'strong-minded' academic women of the day) and to round everything off, a virtuoso performance by the Principal on piano, harpsichord, organ, disc and tape illustrative of his personal 'Pilgrim's Progress' along the road of Johann Sebastian Bach.

Principal for longer than anyone save Miss Maynard, Bryan Thwaites has filled the role with unequalled zest, never deterred by the deflection or frustration of his laudable aspirations for the College and always with an eye on the wider educational scene. Few, if any, of his predecessors have been faced with prob-

lems as numerous, as complex and as much bedevilled by uncertainty as those on which he and his colleagues, academic and administrative, have sought to guide the Council, latterly under the chairmanship first of Sir Peter Parker (1968-1976)[63] and most recently of Sir Harry Melville FRS.[64] Much additional officers' and committee business has been generated by government legislation relating to terms and conditions of employment, health and safety regulations and so on, which affect all employers. But above all the Governing Body has had to interpret the implications for Westfield of trends in government policy towards universities and plan suitable courses of action, difficult enough even in the heady days of the 1960s, when expansion was encouraged but not always backed by commensurate resources, but harder still under the threat of enforced contraction which has

HRH Princess Anne with Dr Thwaites (left) and Dr Janet Sondheimer, at the opening of an exhibition of the College's history to mark the Centenary celebrations of 1982.

been looming since the late 1970s. Severe economies in staffing, equipment and library books have had to be made in response to successive reductions in the real value of the annual block grant received from the UGC through the University Court; and in view of mounting pressure within the University to reorganise and rationalise London's academic resources, it seems likely that further adjustments, involving co-operation with other Schools, will follow.

Present-day prudence in the husbanding of past benefactions[63] has ensured that Westfield is not totally without financial reserves. Efforts to add to these are proceeding through the Westfield College Development Trust, set up on the Principal's initiative in 1979 under the chairmanship of the Right Honourable the Lord Scarman, whose aim is to attract 'the independent financial support necessary to maintain the excellences of the College at a standard well above that which Government funding by itself is likely to allow in future'. As one of its activities, the Trust has launched a Centenary Appeal, organised by a committee headed by Sir Peter Parker. Other means of self-help are constantly being explored such as the recent extension to the College's well-established arrangements for the reception of Junior Year students from the United States.

In October 1982, although reckoning himself a centenarian in the academic profession ('if terms count rather than years'), the Principal could still admit to feelings of excitement and anticipation at the approach of a new academic year, 'of pleasure at the prospect of meeting another generation of students with their own peculiarities and attractions, and of stimulation by plans to be fulfilled. It is a time, too, which is inextricably associated with the onset of autumn ... and yet nearly always the days are brilliant with sunshine and freshness.' Several days made brilliant by royalty (if not always by sunshine) stand out from Dr Thwaites's time as Principal. Her Majesty Queen Elizabeth the Queen Mother honoured Westfield with her presence on three occasions, in 1972, 1979 and 1982. Her Majesty's successor as Chancellor of London University, Her Royal Highness the Princess Anne, graciously timed her first visit to Westfield to fall not only in the College's centenary year but in the exact month, October 1982, of the hundredth birthday. For most of its history Westfield had had no honorific office of its own, but in 1977 this situation was remedied when Her Royal Highness the Duchess of Gloucester was pleased to accept the Council's invitation to become the College's first Patron. The Patron's keen interest in Westfield and her familiarity with the work of a modern university have been demonstrated by all her visits, most conspicuously when she came in 1981 to inaugurate the new computer, and both are encapsulated in her message of encouragement to the College as it entered its centenary year, part of which reads as follows:

Above: HRH the Duchess of Gloucester, Patron of the College.

'It gives me great pleasure to have this opportunity of greeting all present and past members of the College as it moves towards the hundredth anniversary of its

foundation.

When those distinguished scholars, dedicated to the education of women and to the pursuit of high ideals, took their first few students in 1882 they could scarcely have imagined how the College would develop in scope and technology on its present lovely site, and yet retain the friendliness of a small and largely residential community.'[66]

Westfield graduates of the past two decades appear to have brought to an end, at least for the time being, the predominance of school-teaching as the profession claiming the majority, although it still attracts the largest number of those who embark on vocational training. The most recent statistics[67] show that of those graduates who obtained direct employment, well over half were recruits to industry and commerce and just under a quarter entered the public service in one of its branches — the Civil Service, Local Government, the armed forces. About one-tenth of each year's graduates still managed to launch themselves, despite the current scarcity of grants, on postgraduate research or other forms of advanced study. The graduates of the later 1960s, among them the first science graduates, are naturally by now well-established in their careers, many of them in senior positions; a fair proportion of graduates from both faculties are at work in universities, museums, libraries, research institutes and other places actively concerned with the advancement and diffusion of learning.

What Westfield has meant, and still means, to these and all its graduates, only they can say. Among older members, some may still regret that the all-female 'Castle Adamant' is now no more; others, and one hopes there were not too many, found its protectiveness unwelcome and rejoiced when the doors were flung open. Adamantine resolution, however, is a quality not to be despised. It was needed by those who struggled to secure higher educ-

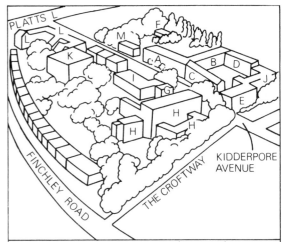

Key to aerial photograph (opposite):

A Old House	H Queen's Building
B Maynard	I Refectory
C Dudin Brown	J New Orchard
D Lady Chapman	K Library
E Old Orchard	L Kidderpore Hall
F Chapel	M Queen Mother's
G Selincourt	Hall.

ation for women and it may well be needed again, this time to defend university education at large. The features of Westfield most cherished by its students — and on this all generations are agreed — are its intimate scale, its setting and location, and the sense of belonging to a friendly community. Westfield's work as a place of learning and research has not in the past been noticeably hindered by these attributes; many would say that they have on the contrary enhanced its effectiveness, not least in the formation of mature men and women, able to be of service to the world. Attempts to sum up the aims of a College, indeed of any institution, run into the twin dangers of banality and vagueness, which is perhaps why Latin mottos, arrestingly succinct, were once resorted to for the purpose. Latinity is now out of fashion, so the custom is not likely to be revived. All the same, there was merit in the motto chosen for Westfield by the students in the 1920s, and its aspiration still stands: *Ut Prosim.*

The shape of the College precinct in the early 1980s (see outline key map on opposite page).
Despite large-scale building works in the last two decades, the College grounds can be seen to have retained
much of their original character. The Queen Mother's Hall, as yet unbuilt in this aerial view, is shown opposite.

Notes
&
references

1 Westfield College Association, President's Newsletter for April 1927.
   Commenting on proposals for the Chapel, Miss Maynard said she would prefer it to be a temporary structure, leaving the permanent design 'to the care of our students 40 or 50 years hence when our numbers may be counted by the 1000 rather than the 100'.

2 MD Stocks, *My Common Place Book*, 1970, pp 194-5.

3 *Hermes* (1943) loyally recorded their ordinations, listing them by a pardonable confusion under the heading 'St Peter's'.

4 Academic Board Minutes, 13 May 1946. Special arrangements had already been made for the admission of ex-service women (as non-residents) without requiring them to sit for the College Entrance Examination, 'if their qualifications on paper seemed reasonable and they passed the University Entrance Examination'. Academic Board Minutes, 27 November 1945.

5 Council Minutes, 24 October 1956.

6 Council Minutes, 28 November 1956.

7 *Ibid*. At the next meeting, 27 February 1957, an unnamed member wished it to be put on record that 'some members ... were sympathetic to the idea of reconstituting the College on a more co-educational basis'.

8 Council Minutes, 23 October 1957. The University had been prepared to promote the passage through Parliament of an Enabling Act which would permit all the women's colleges to admit men as undergraduates, 'if and when they so desired', but because Bedford College was unwilling the scheme was dropped.

9 See n 7 above. Harold Jenkins, Professor of English 1954-1967, was among this small minority: 'I well remember the occasion when ... the possibility of men students was raised at Council and the sense of shock all round when I had the temerity to speak in favour ... What I said was that when Westfield was founded as a women's college in 1882 it was in the van of progressive education. If it wished to be still in the van it must go co-educational. This has been proved right.' Reminiscences contributed 1982.

10 *Tattler and Layabout*, Christmas edition 1960. Before coming to its decision the meeting heard 'some strong argument for and against'.

11 Council Minutes, 27 February 1963, Appendix 3.

12 As reported to Council, 23 October 1963.

13 Presented to a Special Meeting of the Council 28 October 1964. At the Council's regular meeting that afternoon Messrs Casson, Conder and Partners were appointed Architects to the College.

14 The move to join up with St Katherine's College, Tottenham, was made in accordance with a national programme for bringing specialist and general teacher training closer together. In 1964 the two colleges became The College of All Saints. See Graham Handley, *The College of All Saints*, 1978.

15 For a number of reasons, among them a national standstill on grant-aided building work, Berridge House could not be made ready for residential occupation until 1967. Before that date men undergraduates were accommodated in Finchley Road houses.

16 Anxiety on this score was not new. Just after the war the Standing Committee of the General Staff Meeting (Minutes, 4 December 1946) expressed the view that the existing number of resident staff was too small to ensure 'the best traditions of resident life for the students' and asked Council to bear in mind 'the strain of an increasingly wide area of residence' and the restrictions this imposed on the freedom of staff to be away for a night or at weekends. In the early 1960s 'the area of residence' had become greatly extended, staff accommodation in the smaller houses was less good than in the demolished halls, and a far higher proportion of the staff, women as well as men, were married. Early in 1965 Mrs Matthews, normally resident, was herself obliged to move out to enable urgent repairs to be done to Old House.

17 Letter signed 'EF', *Tattler and Layabout*, June 1962: 'At least fifty per cent of people in college must be twenty-one years of age [the then age of majority] and we are supposed to be of above average intelligence. Why, then, as a matter of principle should we be told what time we are to be in at night ... and how many nights

we may spend away from college? Why should we not have our own keys and keys to our rooms? I feel quite strongly that if treated with respect and as responsible individuals, many people would not abuse such liberty. College should, ideally, have no authority over us except in academic and administrative matters.'

18 Council Minutes, 28 November 1962. The Chairman was Miss KA Walpole, WCA representative on Council and until 1961 Headmistress of Wycombe Abbey.

19 Council Minutes, 27 February 1963; the text of the full Report forms Appendix 2 of these Minutes. In the matter of exeats and college closing times, the revised Regulations went a considerable way towards meeting the complaints which prompted the letter referred to in n 17 above.

20 The terms of the Act were based on recommendations put forward by a Ministry of Education Committee on Grants to Students set up in 1958 under the chairmanship of Sir Colin Anderson, which reported in 1960.
   The co-ordinating procedure for admissions devised by the Universities' Central Council on Admissions (UCCA) came into full operation in the autumn of 1963, when Westfield 'somewhat reluctantly' joined the scheme, giving up its Entrance Examination which was held for the last time in December 1962. Examinations for the award of scholarships continued (but only in respect of four of the Arts departments) until 1965. Since then scholarships and exhibitions have been awarded to students at the end of their first or second year on the basis of meritorious performance to date.

21 *Higher Education. Report of the Committee appointed by the Prime Minister under the Chairmanship of Lord Robbins 1961-1963*, Cmnd 2154, p 66 (paragraph 171). The provision postulated for 1980/81 was more than two and a half times greater than the number of students in higher education in 1962/3 — 560 000 compared with 216 000. *Ibid*, Table 30 (p 69).

22 Mr RC Parkin, who became College Secretary in January 1966, was briefly preceded in that office by Mr WL Bell, who resigned in September 1965 on his appointment as Head of the Caribbean Division, Ministry of Overseas Development.

23 Reader in Mathematics 1931-1964 and until 1960 Head of Department. Student at Westfield 1916-1919 and by general agreement the most outstanding of Westfield's early mathematics

graduates, Miss Stanley 'was not a wildly ambitious person. She loved her subject. She loved her College, and she had a rare gift for imparting knowledge which made her an outstanding teacher. Her contentment with her life at Westfield made for a feeling of serenity and security within the department, and indeed within the College generally.' (Memorial tribute from one of 'GK's former students, Marjorie E Peacock, June 1974). An evaluation of Miss Stanley's mathematical work has recently appeared: *Bulletin of the London Mathematical Society*, XIV (November 1982), p 554.

24 Reader in French, and afterwards Professor by conferment of title, 1944-1963 and until 1947 Head of Department; died in 1964. 'A serious scholar and effective teacher, she was also an exuberant and entertaining colleague'. (*Annual Report* 1964).

25 See Chapter VI, n 43.

26 Lecturer in Classics 1930-1969 and twice Acting Head of Department; from 1949 to 1964 Garden Steward; died February 1983. Miss Barratt, an Oxford classicist of the utmost distinction and a notable Greek scholar, devoted almost her entire working life to Westfield. (For an appreciation of Miss Barratt, see *Hermes Newsletter*, 1983).

27 Student at Westfield 1932-1935; Assistant Librarian and then Lecturer in English 1934-1969; Vice-Principal 1956-1961.

28 See Chapter VI, n 36. Professor White was Vice Principal 1956-1961.

29 See Chapter VI, n 59.

30 Said by Professor CNL Brooke of Professor McKisack (in his memorial address, June 1981) but generally applicable in this context. Mention should likewise here be made of Dr Eveline Martin, who retired at the end of the previous decade and died in 1960. As said earlier, in Chapter 3, Dr EC Martin (entered Westfield as an undergraduate 1912) was one of Caroline Skeel's students. After service with the Scottish Women's Hospital in France in the latter part of the war and a brief period on the staff of the East London College (now Queen Mary College), she returned to Westfield in 1923 where she remained, from 1932 as Reader and between 1944 and 1955 as head of the History Department, for the rest of her active life (apart from a year, 1953-54, as Visiting Professor, University College, Ibadan, Nigeria). From 1936-1945 she was Vice-Principal. In her teach-

ing of History Eveline Martin inspired her students 'to attempt the difficult and to be dissatisfied with the second-rate ... Her gritty Northern Ireland plain speaking might chasten suspected insincerity, laziness or – what she greatly disliked – indifference, but genuine blunders evoked sympathetic help.' Eveline Martin's capacity for enjoyment, her affection for the young, her distinctive personality – fiery, stubborn, witty – all imprinted themselves strongly on the College which had helped to form her and which she in turn greatly enriched. For a fuller appreciation, see the memorial tribute by KM Freke (Westfield 1921-1924), *Hermes*, 1961.

31 For example: the late nineteenth century correspondence of members of the Lyttelton family, presented to the College by Lady Tweedsmuir and Mrs Grenfell in 1944; and among smaller holdings, papers and letters from William Temple to John L Stocks (dating from the early years of their acquaintance).

In the early 1970s the important John Lane Archive, owned by the Allen Foundation Trust, was deposited at Westfield in the care of its archivist, Dr MP Rhodes, of the English Department.

32 Grants from the University Court have nevertheless been obtained for several 'minor' works: in 1973 for the modernisation of Maynard and Dudin Brown wings; in 1976 for the reorganisation of 'Bay House' to provide an administrative suite, in course of which the present main entrance was created; and in 1980 a very substantial grant to remodel Finchley Road houses for Computer Science and its attendant hardware.

33 The architect of the Queen's Building and the Refectory was Mr Alan Mitchell, ARIBA; the later buildings are the work of Casson, Conder and partners.

34 Susan Cameron (1961-1964); Reminiscences contributed January 1982.

35 Tutors, one for and of each sex, were introduced on an experimental basis in 1964. It was decided in 1967 that one Tutor was preferable and Mr Deyermond, already Tutor to men students, was appointed with the title Senior Tutor. The office of Senior Treasurer of WCUS was instituted under Mrs Matthews, who brought to an end the practice whereby the Principal was the Unions's Honorary President; since 1967 the offices of Senior Treasurer and Senior Tutor have always been held in combination.

Successive Senior Tutors were fortunate in

being able to rely on the wisdom and unrivalled knowledge of students and their ways possessed by the Registrar, Miss Joan Sims (retired 1982), rightly regarded by generations of students (and by staff) as 'the first port of call in many storms.'

36 It should be mentioned that he was preceded by the Reverend WCA Povey, Vicar of All Saints', Childs Hill, who from 1964-1966 kindly added Westfield to his parochial cares.

37 *Tattler and Layabout*, October 1962. Students of this generation were especially sensitive to the impression made by Westfield on the outside world and were piqued to find that, while Westfield was changing rapidly, 'in the University, Westfield's public image has changed little. One hears far too often the same expressions of mild interest, politeness, or merry quips about girls' boarding schools, convent restrictions and so on ... the fault must be in the lack of positive effort to present Westfield to ULU as an up and coming college – and not merely a women's college.' *Ibid*, June 1962.

38 The original 'Honeysuckle' was a flesh and blood penguin in the London Zoo, adopted by WCUS in 1956 under a nationwide scheme launched by the Zoo in one of its financial crises; upkeep of Honeysuckle cost WCUS £1 a week. On her death in 1958, Honeysuckle was replaced as Westfield's mascot by a wooden effigy, kept in between kidnappings (by students from other colleges, needless to say) in the Bay. Versions of Honeysuckle are still to be seen about the College, for example on the stonework of the Queen's Building, and the penguin motif continues to enliven the covers of WCUS publications.

39 *Tattler and Layabout*, December 1963.

40 The Council agreed to the students' request for a Licensed Bar for the JCR at its meeting on 3 December 1963 but arrangements were not completed until 1966.

41 BSc Special Zoology, 1967. After training as an administrator, Mr Mayhew returned in that capacity to Westfield and remained on the staff until 1973.

42 In 1968, when there were 'enough men to make Rugger, Soccer and Cricket teams feasible', the College acquired its present sports ground at Colindale as an addition to the facilities at or near the main site.

43 There had, however, been some argument about

gowns amongst the students in the early 1960s, culminating in 1962 in a ruling that gowns would not in future be worn at Union meetings: *Tattler and Layabout*, October 1962. Gowns make their last appearance in the photographic record in the Freshers' group, 1967; this, too, was the last of its kind.

44 Composed of the Vice-Chairman of Council, Professor EM Carus-Wilson, Professor EH Sondheimer, Professor CNL Brooke and the Principal.

45 Principal's Report for 1969-70, *Annual Report*, p 16.

46 Student members of Council, of whom there is provision for three, therefore ceased to be co-opted members; they now figure under the heading 'Representative Members'. Students also sit on most of the Council committees.

47 The foregoing summary of the main provisions of the Supplemental Charter and Statutes is based on a Memorandum drawn up by the College Secretary and circulated in December 1976.

48 CNL Brooke, Memorial Address, June 1981.

49 A plea for personal tutors had appeared in *Tattler and Layabout* as early as 1961.

50 I am greatly indebted to members of individual departments for supplying the material on which these accounts are based; since not everyone interpreted my request for information in the same way, there is inevitably some variety of emphasis. I would like in particular to thank: Mrs Olive Anderson, Professor BJ Aylett, Professor EH Bellamy, Dr D Bindman, Professor CV Bock, Dr MAM Colledge, Dr GJ Cunnell, Dr Renée Curtis, Professor AD Deyermond, Professor B Donovan, Dr CG Harlow, Professor EH Sondheimer, Miss Marie Luise Waldeck, Professor JE Webb, Professor J Weightman and Dr Marianne Wynn.

51 Following his ordination to Anglican orders in 1975, Dr Throssell took on extra duties as Assistant to the Chaplain.

52 In fairness it should be recorded that two men students, one in English and one in French, have since achieved the supreme distinction of securing the best Finals results in the entire University.

53 Quoted from Professor Bock's Inaugural Lecture (*A Tower of Ivory?*, 1970).

54 See Chapter VI, n 60.

55 For four years, starting 1977, Professor Deyermond taught for one semester each year at Princeton University, USA, where he was given the task of rebuilding medieval Spanish studies. Strong links with universities in the USA have also been forged by and through other members of the Department, in particular Dr Dorothy Sherman Severin, who was appointed in 1969; in 1982, through her election to the Gilmour Chair at Liverpool University, Dr Severin became the first woman Professor of Spanish in this country.

56 Appointed Professor and Head of Department in 1967, having been Professor of Medieval History at Liverpool University since 1956. Left Westfield in 1977 on election to the Dixie Professorship of Ecclesiastical History at Cambridge. Professor Brooke's publications whilst he was at Westfield included a volume on *London 800-1216* (1975) produced in conjunction with Gillian Keir.

57 Appointed Lecturer in History at Westfield in 1937, Reader in 1955 and to a personal Chair in 1971. Professor RMT Hill's observations of College life over that long period have been frequently quoted in this history. Although she retired in 1977, Professor Hill — one of 'nature's pastors' as well as a notable medieval scholar — happily still teaches in the Department.

58 Appointed Lecturer 1945, Reader 1962 and to a personal Chair in 1966; retired 1978. Trained (first in Berlin and then in Florence) in the continental traditions of historical scholarship, Professor Rubinstein developed undergraduate and postgraduate teaching within a European framework and built up Westfield's present reputation as an interdisciplinary centre of Renaissance studies. Himself a 'daily practical exponent of Renaissance humanism', Professor Rubinstein has not ceased in retirement to shed his benign influence over the Department of which, like Professor Hill, he is an Honorary Research Fellow.

59 First appointed to the staff (as Miss OR Gee) in 1950 and since 1969 Reader.

60 First appointed in 1967; since 1977 Reader in the History of Art.

61 Dr Peter Revell, College Librarian from 1975 until his sadly premature death in January 1983, took over the organisation of the Library Symposia from Miss Bonnell in 1981.

62 Built by Mr Matthew Copley. The chamber organ it replaced was given to Westfield in 1945 by Eleanora Carus-Wilson and came from her family home where it was installed by her grandparents, Colonel and Mrs Petrie, at some time in the 1860s or 1870s, possibly even earlier; this organ is now in a seventeenth century church at Kolhorn in Holland.

63 At the time he was elected Chairman of the Westfield Council, Peter Parker (knighted 1978) was Chairman of Brooker Engineering and Industrial Holdings and a member of the Court of the University; in 1975 he was elected Chairman for a second term but resigned on his appointment as Chairman of British Rail in 1976.

64 Principal of Queen Mary College 1967-1976.

65 It should be mentioned that following Dr Caroline Skeel's death in 1951 the College received a legacy amounting to £50 000 – the last and largest of many benefactions from this source.

66 Printed *Annual Report*, 1980-81.

67 To be found in the *Reports* of the University of London Careers Advisory Service.

68 *Ut Prosim* is referred to as the College motto, 'chosen by past and present students', by Miss AW Richardson in her unpublished 'Notes on the History of Westfield College ...' c 1927. It appears on a students' badge of the same era, an example of which was presented to the College Archives c 1980 by Mrs Gregory (MF Culverhouse, Westfield 1923-26) and figures on contemporaneous Banquet programmes. That *Ut Prosim* survived well into the 1930s is shown by items included in an album compiled in her student days by Miss SM Weston (Westfield 1931-34), lent to the College for the centenary exhibition. See further CM Firth, *Constance Louisa Maynard* (1949), p 250, where there is also reference to the motto which preceded *Ut Prosim*.

APPENDIX I

Biographical Index

The following particulars relating to persons marked * in the text do not pretend to be exhaustive; for example, no reference is made to their publications.

It should be noted that not all the Cambridge women listed claimed the titular degree granted retrospectively by the Senate of Cambridge University in 1921 to all duly qualified members of women's colleges.

Abbreviations: DNB – *Dictionary of National Biography*. GCR – *Girton College Register 1869-1946* (ed KT Butler and HI McMorran, 1948).

BARLOW, WILLIAM HAGGER (1833-1908), MA, BD Cantab, DD Oxon.

Member of Westfield College Council 1882-1908, Chairman from 1894; resigned in protest at admission of a Unitarian as a student.

Principal from 1875 to 1882 of the Church Missionary Society Training College, Islington, having served previously in parishes in Bristol and Oxford. Vicar of St James, Clapham, 1882-7 and of Islington 1887-1901. Dean of Peterborough 1901-08.

His daughter, Margaret EW Barlow, was a student at Westfield 1894-6 but then transferred to Girton. His son, CAM Barlow, MA, LL D, MP (afterwards Sir Montague Barlow, Chairman of Sotheby's 1909-28), was a member of Westfield College Council 1908-17.

DNB

BROWN, SARAH BENEDICT (née BROWN) (1819-1902), MRS ALEXANDER BROWN.

First Treasurer of Westfield College (May 1882-January 1884) and member of Council from 1882 until her death.

Described by Dr Barlow as 'second only to Miss Dudin Brown in her munificence', she purchased in 1892-4 the land on the south side of the College on which the Dudin Brown and Orchard extensions were later built and gave generously to building and scholarship funds. An impressive oil portrait of her (artist unknown) hangs in the entrance hall of Old House.

Like Miss Dudin Brown, she contributed substantially to the endowment and building of St Luke's church, Kidderpore Avenue, where there is a plaque in her memory.

Mrs Brown, although long resident in England, appears to have been a native of New York where her father, James Brown (married as his first wife Louisa Kirkland Benedict) was a prominent banker and highly regarded philanthropist (see article on him in A Johnson, *Dictionary of American Biography*, 1929). Sarah Benedict Brown married her first cousin, Alexander Brown, of Bielby, Yorks, (died 1849), son of Sir William Brown; for the latter's extensive interests on both sides of the Atlantic see article on him in *DNB*. Mrs Brown's twofold connection with this wealthy British-American family emerges from biographical information given about her son, Sir Alexander Brown MP, in M Stenton and S Lees, *Who's Who of British Members of Parliament*, ii. 1886-1918 (1978).

CARUS-WILSON, ELEANORA MARY (1897-1977), BA, MA London, FBA.

Daughter of Professor Charles Ashley Carus-Wilson, Consulting Engineer, and Mary LG Petrie, BA London; for the important part played by the latter and her father, Lt-Colonel Martin Petrie, in the foundation and early days of Westfield see above Chapters 1 and 2.

Educated St Paul's Girls' School and Westfield College (Scholar); BA Hons History. Assistant Mistress, St Elphin's School, Darley Dale, 1922 and at Putney County Secondary School, 1924-5. For several years thereafter visiting teacher at Hayes Court School, Kent, while engaged simultaneously in research, MA (with Distinction) 1926. Leverhulme Research Fellow 1936-8. Head of Branch, Ministry of Food, 1940-45. Lecturer, London School of Economics 1945, Reader in Economic History 1948, Professor 1953-68. Honorary Fellow of LSE 1969. Ford's Lecturer in English History, University of Oxford, 1964. President, Council of the Economic History Society and of the Society for Medieval Archaeology, 1966-9.

Member of Westfield College Council (representing WCA) 1937-40 and Vice-Chairman 1967-77. Old Students' editor of *Hermes* 1929-40; editor and part-author of *Westfield College 1882-1932*. President of WCA 1974-77.

Her great-niece, Alison Carus (Mrs L Ducane) graduated from Westfield in 1976 with a BA in History/History of Art.

CHAPMAN, DOROTHY (1878-1967), MA St Andrews.

Principal of Westfield College 1931-1939. Member of Council 1939-60. Honorary Fellow 1960.

Educated at schools in Scotland and University of St Andrews; Classical Hons, Cl I. Postgraduate work at University College, London. Warden of Women Students, University College of North Wales, Bangor, 1909-11 and at the University of Liverpool, 1911-31. Special Lecturer in Latin, University of Liverpool, 1911-31. Twice President of the British Federation of University Women.

President WCA 1942-45.

CHAPMAN, GEORGIANA CHARLOTTE CLIVE (née BAYLEY) (1855-1941), LADY CHAPMAN.

Secretary to Westfield College Council 1884-86. Member of Council 1890-1941; Vice-Chairman 1909-37; Chairman of Finance Committee from its inception in 1905 to 1937. President WCA from its foundation in 1900 to 1920 and again from 1931 to 1933. Lady Chapman building named in her honour 1927. Donated many books to College Library and made Westfield her residuary legatee.

Daughter of Sir Edward Clive Bayley, KCSI. Married 1886 Major General Edward Francis Chapman (knighted 1906, died 1926). Served for many years on the Education Committee of Surrey County Council.

CHESNEY, KATHLEEN (1899-1976), MA, DPhil, DLitt, Oxon.

Principal of Westfield College 1951-1962. Honorary Fellow 1963.

Educated The Manor House, Brondesbury and Lady Margaret Hall, Oxford; Honour School of Modern Languages in French, Cl 1. Tutor in Modern Languages, St Hilda's College, Oxford, 1923, Fellow 1924, Vice-Principal 1941, Honorary Fellow 1951. University Lecturer in French, 1937-1951.

President WCA 1971-1974.

CLARK, MRS J ADAMS. See *Willoughby*.

DELF SMITH, ELLEN MARION (1883-1980), DSc London.

Daughter of TWH Delf, accountant. Educated James Allen's Girls' School, Dulwich and Girton College, Cambridge; Natural Sciences Tripos Pt 1, Cl 1, Pt II, Cl 1 (Botany).

Lecturer in Botany, Westfield College, 1906-14; DSc London (by thesis) 1912. Yarrow Research Fellow, Girton College, 1914-17. Research Assistant, Lister Institute, Chelsea, 1916-20. Head of Botany Department, Westfield College, 1918-1948, from 1921 Reader. Honorary Fellow 1955. President WCA 1950-55.

Visiting Research Fellow, Institute of Medical Research, Johannesburg, 1920-21. Served on Council of Scottish Seaweed Association. Active in South London Botanical Society, the Association of Women Science Teachers and the Linnean Society.

Married in 1928 Percy John Smith RDI, who died 1948.

DUDIN BROWN, ANN (1823-1917).

Founding benefactress of Westfield College. Member of Council from 1882 to 1917.

Only child of John Dudin Brown and Ann Round (both died 1855). John Dudin Brown (b 1795) was in business as a Thameside wharfinger and granary keeper but resided at Malvern House, Sydenham. Apprenticed to his maternal uncle, Henry Dudin, in 1809, he was admitted as a Freeman of the Company of Watermen and Lightermen in 1817 and elected Master 1844-5. The Company's asylum 'for poor, aged, decayed and maimed watermen, lightermen and their wives or widows' was built on land he gave at Penge (the buildings still stand, together with the obelisk erected in his memory, but the charity removed some years ago to Hastings) and it is known that he, with his wife and daughter, took a personal interest in the welfare of the inhabitants. He was also a prime mover in the building of the church of St John the Evangelist to serve the asylum and neighbouring population; his daughter's first known benefaction was for the provision of a belfry. Later Miss Dudin Brown contributed substantially to the building of two other churches in Penge, Holy Trinity (1872, foundation stone laid by Lord Shaftesbury) and Christ Church (1884); the advowsons of both were still vested in her in 1912. With Mrs Sarah Benedict Brown (*qv*), donated the land in Kidderpore Avenue, Hampstead, on which St Luke's Church and vicarage were built (1896).

Westfield possesses an ivory miniature of the portrait of John Dudin Brown commissioned from TP Knight in 1844 for the Watermen's Hall. In 1900 Miss Brown presented the College with a portrait of herself which now hangs in the Council Room.

For John Dudin Brown see H Humpherus, *History of the Origin and Progress of the Company of Water and*

Lightermen of the River Thames, iii (1887) and the unpublished thesis by PM Sampson, 'Social provision for the members of the Company of Watermen and Lightermen with special reference to the Almshouses at Penge', submitted to the Rachel MacMillan College in 1974 (copy in Bromley Public Library). For the churches in Penge, see DE Pullen, *Penge. A story of some of the people and surrounding district* (1975). For recollections of Miss Dudin Brown, see CL Maynard, *Ann Dudin Brown, Foundress of Westfield College* (1917).

FLEMING, JAMES BATTERSBY (1832-1908), MA, BD Cantab.

First Chairman of Westfield College Council, 1882-1894, and a member until shortly before his death.

Vicar of St Michael, Chester Square, London, from 1873 until his death; from 1879 Canon of York. Chaplain in ordinary to Queen Victoria and King Edward VII. Professor of preaching and elocution at the London College of Divinity (St John's Hall, Highbury). Honorary Secretary of the Religious Tract Society.

DNB

GEDGE, EVELYN COLPOYS (1888-1974), BA London, MA Cantab.

Secretary to Westfield College Council 1920-1948. Honorary Fellow 1949.

Daughter of the Rev EL Gedge. Educated Milton Mount College, Gravesend and Girton College, Cambridge; Classical Tripos 1910. London BA Hons Classics (External) 1909. Assistant Mistress St Paul's Girls' School 1910-14, then gave up full-time teaching to assist her father, afflicted with blindness. Part-time lecturer in Classics, Westfield College, 1914-33. Held office in the Classical Association 1924-47 and in the Virgil Society.

Licensed Diocesan Worker for London, attached to Holy Trinity Church, Sloane Square, and later to St Simon Zelotes. Co-founder and organiser of the 'Village Evangelists'.

GCR. Obituary (by RM Forster) in *Hermes* 1975.

GRAY, FRANCES RALPH (c 1863-1935), OBE, MA (TCD).

Lecturer Westfield College 1883-1894. Member of Council 1897-1929.

Daughter of James Gray of Roscrea, Co Tipperary and of Nottingham. Educated Plymouth High School

and Newnham College, Cambridge; Classical Tripos 1883. Associate of Newnham College 1910-25.

Headmistress of St Katherine's School, St Andrews, 1894-1903. First High Mistress of St Paul's Girls' School, 1903-1927. President of the Association of Headmistresses 1923-25. JP County of London 1920.

Instrumental in founding Westfield College Association, 1900; President 1928-31.

INSKIP, THOMAS WALKER HOBART (1867-1947), PC, CBE, KC, MA Cantab, LLD (Hon) Bristol, VISCOUNT CALDECOTE.

Chairman of Westfield College Council from January 1921 (member from 1919) to 1945. Honorary Fellow 1945.

Called to the Bar (Inner Temple) 1899. MP for Central Bristol 1918-29 and for Fareham 1931-39. Attorney-General 1928-9 and 1932-6. Minister for Co-ordination of Defence 1936-9. Secretary of State for Dominions 1939. Lord Chancellor 1939, 1940. Lord Chief Justice 1940-46. Knighted 1922; Viscount 1939.

His brother, John Hampden Inskip (KBE 1937) married in 1923 The Honorable Janet Maclay, student at Westfield 1916-19; for her father's gift of Selincourt Hall to Westfield see above chapter 4.

DNB.

KER, WILLIAM PATON (1855-1923), MA Oxon.

Member of Westfield College Council 1915-1923, from 1919 as representative (with Professor MJM Hill) of the University of London.

Fellow of All Souls' College, Oxford, 1879-1923. Quain Professor of English Language and Literature, University College, London, 1889-1922, and Director of Department of Scandinavian Studies 1917-23. Through his kindly interest he helped to promote linguistic studies at Westfield and was greatly beloved by Westfield students (tributes in *Hermes*, 1924).

DNB.

LODGE, ELEANOR CONSTANCE (1869-1936), CBE, MA D Litt Oxon, Litt D (Hon) Liverpool.

Principal of Westfield College 1921-1931. Honorary Fellow 1933.

Educated at private schools and Lady Margaret Hall, Oxford; Final Honours School, Modern History. Student 1895-6 at the Ecole des Hautes Etudes and Ecole des Chartes, Paris.

History Tutor, Lady Margaret Hall, 1899-1921, Vice-Principal from 1906. Voluntary work in France 1918 with Oxford Women's Canteens for French soldiers.

Member of a number of educational and learned bodies; Vice-President, Royal Historical Society. Member of Hampstead Borough Council.

President WCA 1934-36. Westfield was the ultimate beneficiary of the Eleanor Lodge Trust, set up after her death.

DNB

MALAN, CHARLES HAMILTON (1837-1881).

For his part in the pre-history of Westfield see above. Chapter 1.

Son of Soloman Caesar Malan, of French Protestant descent, who came to England from Geneva in 1833, took orders in the Church of England and won recognition as an oriental linguist and biblical scholar.

Educated Sandhurst. Army service in the Crimea, Canada, China and Capetown; attained rank of major. Sold his commission in 1872 and then devoted himself to missionary work in Africa (Trans-Kei region) and in London, especially among destitute children; in 1875 appointed trustee of Barnardo's East End Juvenile Mission (G Wagner, *Barnardo*, 1979, p 119).

For family history and early life see the biography of Malan senior by AN Malan, published 1897, which traces the descent and migrations of the Malan family in its European and South African branches. For details of his own career see entry in F Boase, *Modern English Biography 1851-1900* (1892-1921) and his volume of reminiscences, *A soldier's experience of God's love* ... (1874).

MATTHEWS, PAMELA WINIFRED, (née SAUNDERS O'MAHONEY) (1914-), BSC Econ, London.

Principal of Westfield College 1962-1965 (resigned).

Educated St Paul's Girls' School and London School of Economics; BSc Econ, Cl 1. Royal Institution of International Affairs 1938-9; Foreign Office 1939-40 and 1943-5; *The Economist*, 1940-3; Reuters 1945-61; National Institute for Social Work Training 1961-2. Independent member Advertising Standards Authority 1964-5.

Married 1938 HPS Matthews (Peter Matthews, died 1958).

MAYNARD, CONSTANCE LOUISA (1849-1935), MA Cantab.

Mistress of Westfield College from its foundation in 1882 to 1913 and Honorary Secretary 1882-1884. Honorary Fellow 1933.

Daughter of Henry Maynard and Louisa Hillyard, who was of Huguenot descent. Henry Maynard, partner in Maynard Bros, an export firm with outlets in South Africa, conducted his family business from an office in London but resided with his family at Hawkhurst in Kent.

Educated at home and at Belstead School, Suffolk. In 1872 entered The College, Hitchin and in the following year moved with it to Cambridge where it became Girton College; Moral Sciences Tripos 1875. Representative of former students on Girton Executive Committee 1881-86.

Assistant Mistress, Cheltenham Ladies' College, 1876-7 and St Leonards School, St Andrews, 1877-80. Part-time student, Slade School of Art, 1880-82.

Member of the governing council of The Church Schools' Society 1897-c 1905.

Her niece, Gabrielle Moilliet, was a student at Westfield 1899-1901; she left without taking a degree.

PHILLPOTTS, BERTHA SURTEES (1877-1932), DBE, MA Cantab, Litt D (TCD), DAME BERTHA NEWALL.

Principal of Westfield College 1919-1921. Member of Council 1922-32.

Educated at home (her father, JS Phillpotts, was Headmaster of Bedford Grammar School) and Girton College, Cambridge; Medieval and Modern Languages Tripos Cl 1. From 1902 to 1916 engaged in advanced study and research into early Scandinavian culture, partly in Cambridge and Oxford (Research Fellow, Somerville College, 1913), partly in Iceland and Denmark. Private Secretary to the British Minister in Stockholm, 1916-19. OBE 1919. Mistress of Girton College, Cambridge, 1922-25. University Lecturer and Director of Scandinavian Studies, University of Cambridge, 1926-32.

Member of Board of Education Consultative Committee 1919-21. Member of Statutory Commission, University of Cambridge, 1923-27 and of Statutory Commission, University of London, 1926-28. DBE 1929.

Married 1931 Professor HF Newall, FRS.

DNB. GCR

RICHARDSON, ANNE WAKEFIELD (1859-1942), BA London.

Classical Lecturer, Westfield College, 1887-1925, designated Senior Resident Lecturer c 1903 and from c 1915 Vice-Principal. Acting Principal from August 1917 to May 1919. Honorary Fellow 1933.

Daughter of John Grubb Richardson of Moyallen, Co Down, proprietor of Bessbrook Spinning Company, Co Armagh. Educated at home; at Newnham College, Cambridge, 1881-3; at Westfield College, January 1884-86. BA Hons Classics, Cl 1.

Active in many Quaker, Temperance and Missionary Societies.

President WCA 1921-27.

Two of her sisters became students at Westfield, Ethel J Richardson in 1889 and Mary K Richardson (Mrs Bell) in 1894; neither took a degree. Another sister, Jean Richardson, married Miss Maynard's younger brother, George Pitt Holland Maynard.

SELINCOURT, AGNES DE (1872-1917).

Principal of Westfield College 1913-1917 (died in office).

Daughter of Charles Alexander de Selincourt, merchant, of Balham. Educated Notting Hill High School, GPDSC, and Girton College, Cambridge; Medieval and Modern Languages Tripos Cl 1. Assistant Mistress Sheffield High School, GPDSC, 1894-5. Studied oriental languages at Somerville College, Oxford, 1895-6. Founded Missionary Settlement for University Women, Bombay, 1896. First Principal of the Lady Muir Memorial College, Allahabad, 1901-09. Organising Secretary, Student Christian Movement (with special responsibility for Student Volunteer Missionary Union) 1910-13.

Her brother, Ernest de Selincourt, Professor of English at Birmingham University 1908-35, was a member of Westfield College Council 1918-37.

GCR

SKEEL, CAROLINE ANNE JAMES (1872-1951), MA Cantab, D Lit London.

Founder of Westfield's school of History and the first Westfield teacher to be advanced to a Chair.

Educated South Hampstead High School and Notting Hill High School, both GPDSC, and Girton College, Cambridge; Classical Tripos Pt 1, Cl 1, Historical Tripos Cl 1. Undertook research which led to award of D Lit by thesis in 1904 as registered student of the London School of Economics. Honorary Yarrow Research Fellow, Girton College, 1914-17.

First appointed to Westfield as a Visiting Lecturer in 1895 to teach Classics and History; from 1899 to 1907 Resident Lecturer in History and Librarian. Head of History Department 1911-29. Reader 1919, Professor 1925; resigned for health reasons 1929. In 1931 donated a large part of her book collection to the College Library. Two successive Libraries at West-

field have been named in her honour. The Caroline Skeel Prize for History was established in 1930 from funds collected by her friends.

Active in the affairs of the Royal Historical Society (Fellow 1914), the Historical Association and the Economic History Society, of which she was a founder.

Her parents, William Skeel and Anne James, who were first cousins, left their native Pembrokeshire to settle in Hampstead, where Caroline was born and brought up. The family fortunes were established by her father (died 1899), who was in business as an export merchant, and substantially added to by her only brother, William Henry Skeel, who died in 1925 leaving as his heirs Caroline and her two elder sisters, Maria Elisabeth Skeel and Emily Jane Skeel. All three favoured Westfield with benefactions as well as giving generously to a great many other public and private causes.

GCR. Skeel Papers, Westfield College Archives.

STOCKS, MARY DANVERS (née BRINTON) (1891-1975), BSc Econ, London, LL D (Hon) Manchester, Litt D (Hon) Liverpool, BARONESS STOCKS OF THE ROYAL BOROUGH OF KENSINGTON AND CHELSEA.

Principal of Westfield College 1939-1951. Honorary Fellow 1952.

Daughter of RD Brinton, MD, of Kensington. Educated St Paul's Girls' School and London School of Economics; BSc Econ. Cl 1. Assistant Lecturer LSE 1916-19 (latterly part-time) and (1918) at King's College for Women, Department of Household and Social Science (afterwards Queen Elizabeth College). Extension Lecturer and Extra-Mural Tutor, University of Manchester, 1924-37. JP Manchester City 1930-36. General Secretary, London Council of Social Service, 1938-9.

Member of many government and other committees; for some of these see Chapter 6 above. Well-known in later life as a broadcaster.

Life Peeress 1966.

Married 1913 John L Stocks, MA Oxon, who died 1937.

TEMPLE, WILLIAM (1881-1940, MA Oxon, DD (Hon) Cambridge, Manchester, Durham and Dublin, D Litt (Hon) Sheffield, LL D (Hon) Leeds and Princton, DCL (Hon) Oxford, ARCHBISHOP OF CANT— ERBURY.

Member of Westfield College Council 1914-Dec 1920, from Feb 1916 as Chairman. Honorary Fellow 1933.

Fellow of Queen's College Oxford, 1904-10; Headmaster of Repton School 1910-14. Rector of St James, Piccadilly, 1914-18, Canon of Westminster 1919-21. Bishop of Manchester 1921-29; Archbishop of York 1929-42; Archbishop of Canterbury 1942-44.

DNB.

THWAITES, BRYAN (1923-), MA Cantab, PhD London.

Principal of Westfield College 1966-1983.

Educated at Dulwich College and Winchester College; Clare College, Cambridge. Scientific Officer National Physical Laboratory 1944-47; Lecturer Imperial College 1947-51; Assistant Master Winchester College 1951-59. Professor of Theoretical Mechanics 1959-66, and Honorary Professor 1983- , Southampton University.

Director of the School Mathematics Project, 1961-75 and Chairman of the Trustees, 1967- . President of the Institute of Mathematics and its Applications 1966-7 and member of its Council 1964- .

Chairman, Council of the Church of England Colleges of Education, 1969-71, and of the Church of England Higher Education Committee, 1974-76. Chairman of the Governing Body of Heythrop College 1978-82. Chairman of the Goldsmiths' College Delegacy 1975-80.

JP Winchester City 1966. Chairman of the Northwick Park Hospital Management Committee 1970-74, of Brent and Harrow Area Health Authority 1973-82, and of the Wessex Regional Health Authority 1982- .

Co-Chairman of EDUCATION 2000, 1982- .

TRISTRAM, KATHERINE ALICE (1858-1948), BA London.

First Resident Lecturer, Westfield College, 1882-1888. Honorary Fellow 1937.

Daughter of the Rev HB Tristram, Canon of Durham. Educated Cheltenham Ladies College; read for degree while teaching at Westfield. Teacher and missionary in Japan 1888-1927, from 1890 as Principal of Osaka Girls' School; after retirement worked in tuberculosis sanatorium, Tokyo. Awarded Ranju Hosto Medal by the Emperor of Japan 1931.

Her sister, Annie Tristram, was one of the five students admitted to Westfield in October 1882; she left without taking a degree.

WILLOUGHBY, CAROLINE ANNIE JOSEPHINE (1863-1945), MA Cantab.

Resident Lecturer in Science, Westfield College, 1885-1894.

Educated Plymouth High School and Newnham College, Cambridge; Natural Sciences Tripos Pt 1, Cl 1. London Society of Apothecaries Assistant's Examination 1896.

Married 1895 William Adams Clark, MD; assisted him in his medical practice in Penge.

APPENDIX II

Principals, Chairmen of Council, Treasurers
& Honorary Fellows of Westfield College

Principals

1882	Miss CL Maynard
1913	Miss A de Sélincourt
1917	Miss AW Richardson (Acting Principal)
1919	Miss BS Phillpotts, OBE, MA
1921	Miss EC Lodge, MA, D Litt
1931	Miss D Chapman, MA
1939	Mrs MD Stocks, BSc Econ
1951	Miss K Chesney, MA, D Litt
1962	Mrs PW Matthews, BSc Econ
1965	Professor M McKisack, MA (Acting Principal)
1966	Professor Bryan Thwaites, MA, PhD
1984	Professor JE Varey, MA. PhD

Chairmen of Council

1882	The Rev J B Fleming, MA, BD
1894	The Rev WH Barlow, MA, DD
1908	The Rt Hon Lord Alverstone
1916	The Rev W Temple, MA
1921	Sir TWH Inskip (later Lord Caldecote), CBE, MA
1946	The Hon Sylvia Fletcher-Moulton, OBE, MA
1953	The Rt Rev GA Ellison, MA
1967	Mr RE Ellison, CMG
1968	Mr Peter Parker, MVO, MA
1977	Sir Harry W Melville, KCB, D Sc, FRS
1983	Sir Norman Lindop, MSc, FRSC

Treasurers

1882	Mrs SB Brown
1884	Mr JH Master
1906	Mr R Story
1917	Mr AL Sturge
1939	The Hon Sylvia Fletcher-Moulton, MA
1948	Mr SA Boyd, MS, FRCS, JP
1962	Mrs M Sedgwick, MA
1969	Mr RE Ellison, CMG
1976	Miss GM Lewis, MBE, BA

Honorary Fellows (past and present)

1933	*The Right Hon and Most Rev William Temple, DD, D Litt*
1933	*Miss CL Maynard, MA*
1933	*Miss EC Lodge, MA, D Litt*
1933	*Miss Anne W Richardson, BA*
1933	*Professor Ernest de Sélincourt, LL D, D Litt, FBA*
1933	*Miss Eleanor McDougall, MA, Litt D*
1933	*Miss Katherine Tristram, BA*
1939	*Professor Norman Baynes, FBA*
1939	*Arthur Lloyd Sturge*
1945	*Sir Ernest Barker, LL D, Litt D, D Litt, FBA*
1945	*Miss CE Parker, MA*
1945	*The Rt Hon Viscount Caldecote, CBE*
1947	*Professor Gilbert Murray, OM*
1948	*The Very Rev WR Matthews, CH, KCVO, DD, D Litt*
1949	*Miss EC Gedge, MA*
1952	*The Lady Stocks of Kensington and Chelsea, B Sc (Econ), LL D*
1955	The Hon Sylvia Fletcher-Moulton, OBE, MA
1955	*Mrs EM Delf Smith, D Sc, FLS*
1960	*Miss D Chapman, MA*
1963	*Miss K Chesney, MA, D Phil, D Litt*
1963	Miss RM Forster, BA
1968	The Rt Rev & Rt Hon Dr GA Ellison, MA, DD
1968	The Lady Brooke of Ystradfelte, DBE
1971	Mrs Romney Sedgwick, OBE, MA, JP
1976	Dame Mary Green, DBE, BA
1976	Professor BMI White, MA, D Litt, FRSI, FR Hist S, FSA
1978	*Sir William Gorrell Barnes, KCMG, CB*
1978	RE Ellison, CMG
1978	Professor RMT Hill, MA, B Litt, FR Hist S, FSA, FRSA
1978	Miss DM Moore, BA, FLA
1978	Sir Peter Parker, MVO
1979	Miss M Beare, MA, Ph D
1981	JR Stewart, CBE
1982	Mrs Lena M Townsend, CBE
1982	Mr ER Nixon, CBE
1983	Sir Harry Melville, KCB, FRS
1983	The Rt Hon Lord Cottesloe, GBE, TD, DL

APPENDIX III

Tables showing distribution of
Westfield Honours graduates by subjects, 1920-1983

In both tables the first column shows the total number of Honours graduates for that decade. The following columns give the number of Honours graduates *expressed as a percentage* of the total number of Honours graduates for that decade.

Table A: 1920-1959

Decade	Total of Hons grads	Classics	English	French	German	Spanish	History	Botany	Maths
1920-29	305	10	26	16	–	–	28	13	7
1930-39	406	9	24	17	–	–	27	11	12
1940-49	502	8	19	20	9	–	23	9	12
1950-59	711	10	22	24	6	1*	22	–	15

*No graduates until 1957

Table B: 1960-1982. Arts Faculty

Decade	Total of Hons grads	Classics	English	French	German	Spanish	Two Languages	History	Hist of Art & another subject	Drama & another subject	Misc.[4]
1960-69	1245	6	14	14	8	6	–	12	–	–	
1970-79	2130	2	13	9	4	6	5	10	4	–	
1980-82	873	1	12	7	2	2	6	9	5	4	

Table B: 1960-1982. Science Faculty[1]

Decade	Total of Hons grads	Biological sciences	Environmental sciences	Chemistry	Physics	Maths	Computer science[2]	Combined sciences[3]	Misc.[4]
1960-69	1245	15	–	5	5	12	–	4	
1970-79	2130	20	3	4	5	8	1	6	
1980-82	873	17	8	2	3	5	6	8	

1 There were no Science graduates (save in Mathematics) before 1964. From 1964-1968 Botany and Zoology graduates were classified separately but are here conflated under Biological Sciences, as was the case in 1969; graduates in Marine, Freshwater Biology are included in this category.
2 There were no single Hons graduates in Computer Science before 1977.
3 'Combined Sciences' comprises (i) Hons graduates in General Science 1964-1968, and (ii) from 1969 Hons graduates in Combined Sciences or in two Sciences, eg Biochemistry and Chemistry, Mathematics and Physics, Mathematics and Computer Science, etc.
4 Includes graduates with 'Cross Faculty' degrees, in French-and-History and in Classical studies with another subject.

APPENDIX IV

Note on the history of 'Old House',
the original Kidderpore Hall

Kidderpore Hall was built for Mr John Teil, who in 1840 purchased from the heirs of Thomas Platt (died 1828) the twenty acres of land which became known as the Kidderpore Estate. The Hall was completed at latest by 1843, the year in which it is first mentioned in the Rate Books.*

In the title deeds John Teil is described initially as 'of Addison Road, Kensington', but he is later (1853) referred to as 'of Kidderpore near Calcutta in the East Indies, merchant'. The nature of his business is indicated by an entry in *The New Calcutta Directory* for 1861 which describes the firm of 'Teil (John) and Co.' of Kidderpore as 'leather manufacturers and army accoutrement makers', naming as sole partner one 'Thomas Teil'. This agrees with information in the title deeds that John Teil died in 1854 — presumably he left 'Thomas Teil' to carry on the Calcutta business singlehanded.

At the time of John Teil's death his Hampstead estate was mortgaged to several creditors, who under his will became his heirs and assigns. Copies of a notice of sale preserved in the College Archives imply that the entire estate, including the 'elegant well-built modern mansion called Kidderpore Hall' was offered for sale by auction in July 1855. Advertised as 'first class building land', the property was nevertheless sold in December 1856 to a private purchaser, Mr Charles Cannon, who preserved the estate intact and resided in the house with his wife and daughters until his death in June 1876. Charles Cannon, described in the title deeds as a 'Dyer' of '6 Davis Street', was thus the second owner-occupier of the house and not, as stated by some authorities, its original proprietor.

John Cannon's death in 1876 was followed by a protracted family law suit over the terms of his will. To meet the costs of the action, the plaintiffs were ordered in 1889 to sell by auction the freehold mansion and accompanying land. The successful bidder was the well-known marine engineer and ship-builder Alfred Fernandez Yarrow, under whose ownership the Kidderpore Estate was divided into plots to be sold for high class residential development on lines similar to that of Fitzjohn's Avenue, in which Yarrow

The Old House from the Rose Garden (from Hermes, 1930).

*Felicity Macqueen, 'The story of Kidderpore Hall', *Newsletter of the Camden History Society* (June 1976).

himself resided. The plot of two and a half acres on which the mansion stood was purchased in 1890 by Westfield College Council; further lots on the south-east side were subsequently purchased by Mrs Sarah Benedict Brown and donated by her to the College, which was thus enabled to extend its boundary to the Croftway.

A description of Kidderpore Hall and its situation is to be found in W Keene's *Beauties of Middlesex* (1850), which is the only source to give the name of the architect, 'T Howard'. At the time of Keene's visit, Kidderpore Hall commanded an extensive prospect 'over Willesdon and its beautiful scenery to the west' and beyond to 'the Surrey hills, Windsor, the hills of Buckinghamshire and parts of Herefordshire'. From the front steps (described by Keene as 'a long flight') there would have been an unimpeded view across the parts of the estate referred to in the title deeds as 'the Lower Pasture, the Hillfield and the Rickfield' to the hamlet of West End, with only the passage of horse-drawn traffic along the Turnpike (Finchley) Road to intervene. When the College took possession of Kidderpore Hall in April 1981 the development of the rest of the estate was already in progress. Plans published in *The Building News* for July 1891 show that the first roads to be built up were Heath Drive (then called West Hampstead Avenue) and the lower part of Kidderpore Avenue. The new occupants of

Architect's drawing (1890) showing a view from the south of the additions made to Kidderpore Hall on the College's removal from Maresfield Gardens in 1891. Falconer Macdonald was the son of the writer George Macdonald.

Kidderpore Hall therefore found themselves in surroundings which were still semi-rural but which were provided with the amenities of suburbia — made-up roads, main drainage, and the pillar box conveniently placed just outside the College shortly after its arrival (referred to Westfield College Council Minutes, June 1891).

So well did the mansion lend itself to College use that no structural changes were needed, apart from the construction of a passage linking the 'old' building with the newly-built Dining Hall and residential wing. Since this connecting corridor was placed at the rear, when viewed from the main frontage the house retained the form of a freestanding building, although the gap between it and the adjacent Dining Hall was admittedly small (as can be seen in older photographs). Subsequent alterations have affected only the parts of the mansion on the side nearest the newer work, with the result that the most important architectural features of John Teil's residence still match Keene's description of 1850: 'large porticoes of the Ionic order on the main and garden fronts' and the westward facing 'very large bow front with handsome circular porticoes of the same order'. The difference in style between the original mansion and its late Victorian adjuncts can hardly have been disguised by the coating of 'good beef red' chosen by Miss Maynard with the aim, it seems, of matching the brickwork of Falconer Macdonald's additions.

The layout of the principal rooms has undergone little alteration under College occupation, although the use of particular areas has changed over the years. Thus the original drawing room, now the Council Room, served at one time as the Junior Common Room and subsequently as the Senior Common Room, attaining its present apotheosis only within the last decade. The allocation of rooms in 'Old House' as lodgings for the Principal goes back to the time of Miss Maynard, whose apartments were on the ground floor. Her successor, Miss de Sélincourt, preferred as her base the large bow-fronted room upstairs (used until 1904 as the library and afterwards as a lecture room) and this precedent was followed by all later Principals. The tradition of a resident Principal was strongly supported by Dr Thwaites who, by occupying with his family the two upper floors of the mansion, in part restored 'Kidderpore Hall' to its originally domestic character.

INDEX

The original Library in 1895, on the first floor of the Old House (Kidderpore Hall).